Machine Learning for Imbalanced Data

Tackle imbalanced datasets using machine learning and deep learning techniques

Kumar Abhishek

Dr. Mounir Abdelaziz

BIRMINGHAM—MUMBAI

Machine Learning for Imbalanced Data

Group Product Manager: Niranjan Naikwadi

Publishing Product Manager: Sanjana Gupta

Book Project Manager: Kirti Pisat

Senior Editor: Rohit Singh

Technical Editor: Rahul Limbachiya

Copy Editor: Safis Editing

Proofreader: Safis Editing

Indexer: Pratik Shirodkar

Production Designer: Nilesh Mohite

DevRel Marketing Coordinator: Vinishka Kalra

First published: November 2023

Production reference: 2221123

Published by Packt Publishing Ltd.

Grosvenor House

11 St Paul's Square

Birmingham

B3 1RB, UK.

ISBN 978-1-80107-083-6

www.packtpub.com

Contributors

About the authors

Kumar Abhishek is a seasoned senior machine learning engineer at Expedia Group, US, specializing in risk analysis and fraud detection. With over a decade of machine learning and software engineering experience, Kumar has worked for companies such as Microsoft, Amazon, and a Bay Area start-up. Kumar holds a master's degree in computer science from the University of Florida, Gainesville.

To my incredible wife who has been my rock and constant source of inspiration, our adorable son who fills our lives with joy, my wonderful parents for their unwavering support, and my close friends. Immense thanks to Christian, who has been a pivotal mentor and guide, for his meticulous reviews. My deepest gratitude to my co-author, Mounir, and contributor, Anshul; their dedication and solid contributions were essential in shaping this book. Lastly, I extend my sincere appreciation to Abhiram and the Packt team for their unwavering support.

Dr. Mounir Abdelaziz is a deep learning researcher specializing in computer vision applications. He holds a Ph.D. in computer science and technology from Central South University, China. During his Ph.D. journey, he developed innovative algorithms to address practical computer vision challenges. He has also authored numerous research articles in the field of few-shot learning for image classification.

I would like to thank my family, especially my parents, for their support and encouragement. I also want to thank all the fantastic people I collaborated with, including my co-author, Packt editors, and reviewers. Without their help, writing this book wouldn't have been possible.

Other contributor

Anshul Yadav is a software developer and trainer with a keen interest in machine learning, web development, and theoretical computer science. He likes to solve technical problems: the slinkier, the better. He has a B.Tech. degree in computer science and engineering from IIT Kanpur. Anshul loves to share the joy of learning with his audience.

About the reviewers

Christian Monson has nine years of industry experience working as a machine learning scientist specializing in **Natural Language Processing** (**NLP**) and speech recognition. For five of those years, he worked at Amazon improving the Alexa personal assistant. During the 2000s, he was a graduate student at Carnegie Mellon University and a postdoc at Oregon Health and Science University working on NLP. Christian completed his bachelor's degree in computer science, with minors in math and physics, at Brigham Young University in 2000. In his free time, Christian creates video games and plays with his kids. Currently, he is a full-time tutor and mentor in machine learning. You can find Christian at www.aitalks.art or watch his videos at youtube.com/@_aitalks.

Abhiram Jagarlapudi is a principal software engineer with 10 years of experience in cloud computing and **Artificial Intelligence** (**AI**). At Amazon Web Services and Oracle Cloud, Abhiram was part of launching several public cloud services, later specializing in cloud AI services. He was part of a small team that built the software delivery infrastructure of Oracle Cloud, which started in 2016 and has since grown into a multi-billion-dollar business. He also designed and developed AI services for the Oracle Cloud and is passionate about applying that experience to improve and accelerate the delivery of machine learning.

Table of Contents

3

Undersampling Methods 63

4

Ensemble Methods 89

7

Data-Level Deep Learning Methods   175

8

Algorithm-Level Deep Learning Techniques   213

9

Hybrid Deep Learning Methods   245

10

Model Calibration   271

Appendix

Machine Learning Pipeline in Production   299

Assessments   303

Index   313

Other Books You May Enjoy   322

Preface

Hello and welcome! **Machine Learning** (**ML**) enables computers to learn from data using algorithms to make informed decisions, automate tasks, and extract valuable insights. One particular aspect that often garners attention is imbalanced data, where certain classes may have considerably fewer samples than others.

This book provides an in-depth guide to understanding and navigating the intricacies of skewed data. You will gain insights into best practices for managing imbalanced datasets in ML contexts.

While imbalanced data can present challenges, it's important to understand that the techniques to address this imbalance are not universally applicable. Their relevance and necessity depend on various factors such as the domain, the data distribution, the performance metrics you're optimizing, and the business objectives. Before adopting any techniques, it's essential to establish a baseline. Even if you don't currently face issues with imbalanced data, it can be beneficial to be aware of the challenges and solutions discussed in this book. Familiarizing yourself with these techniques will provide you with a comprehensive toolkit, preparing you for scenarios that you may not yet know you'll encounter. If you do find that model performance is lacking, especially for underrepresented (minority) classes, the insights and strategies covered in the book can be instrumental in guiding effective improvements.

As the domains of ML and artificial intelligence continue to grow, there will be an increasing demand for professionals who can adeptly handle various data challenges, including imbalance. This book aims to equip you with the knowledge and tools to be one of those sought-after experts.

Who this book is for

This comprehensive book is thoughtfully tailored to meet the needs of a variety of professionals, including the following:

- **ML researchers, ML scientists, ML engineers, and students**: Professionals and learners in the fields of ML and deep learning who seek to gain valuable insights and practical knowledge for tackling the challenges posed by data imbalance

- **Data scientists and analysts**: Experienced data experts eager to expand their knowledge of handling skewed data with practical, real-world solutions

- **Software engineers**: Software engineers who want to effectively integrate ML and deep learning solutions into their applications when dealing with imbalanced data

- **Practical insight seekers**: Professionals and enthusiasts from various backgrounds who want to use hands-on, industry-relevant approaches for efficiently dealing with data imbalance in ML and deep learning, enabling them to excel in their respective roles

What this book covers

Chapter 1, Introduction to Data Imbalance in Machine Learning, serves as an exploration of data imbalance within the context of ML. This chapter elucidates the nature of imbalanced data, distinguishing it from other dataset types. It also provides a comprehensive introduction to the essential components of ML and model performance metrics most relevant for cases when there is a data imbalance. The chapter looks into the issues and concerns involved in dealing with imbalanced data, explaining when it can occur and why it can sometimes be a challenge. More importantly, we will go over when not to worry about data imbalance at all or when it may not be worth worrying about. Furthermore, it introduces the `imbalanced-learn` library, offering invaluable insights and general guidelines to navigate the intricacies of dealing with imbalanced datasets effectively.

Chapter 2, Oversampling Methods, introduces the concept of oversampling, outlining when to employ it and when not to, and various techniques to augment imbalanced datasets. It guides you through the practical application of these techniques using the `imbalanced-learn` library and compares their performance across classical ML models. Practical advice on the effectiveness of these techniques in real-world scenarios concludes the chapter.

Chapter 3, Undersampling Methods, presents the concept of undersampling as an effective approach for data balancing when standard oversampling isn't an option. This chapter covers strategies to effectively remove examples from imbalanced data, different ways of addressing noisy observations, and procedures for handling easily categorized instances. We will also discuss when to avoid undersampling of the majority class.

Chapter 4, Ensemble Methods, explores the application of ensemble techniques, including bagging and boosting, to enhance the performance of ML models. Moreover, it tackles the challenge of imbalanced datasets, where traditional ensemble methods may be ineffective, by combining the ensemble methods with the techniques introduced in previous chapters.

Chapter 5, Cost-Sensitive Learning, explores some alternatives to sampling techniques, including oversampling and undersampling. This chapter highlights the significance of cost-sensitive learning as an effective strategy to overcome the problem of imbalanced datasets. We also discuss **threshold-tuning techniques**, which can be very relevant in the context of data imbalance.

Chapter 6, Data Imbalance in Deep Learning, presents the core concepts of deep learning and walks through the issues posed by imbalanced datasets. You will investigate typical types of imbalanced data challenges in various deep learning applications and develop an understanding of their impact.

Chapter 7, Data-Level Deep Learning Methods, marks a transition from classical ML to deep learning, exploring the adaptation of familiar data-level sampling techniques and unveiling opportunities for enhancing these methods in the context of deep learning models. It dives into combining deep learning with oversampling and undersampling techniques, covering dynamic sampling and data augmentation for images and text. It emphasizes the fundamental differences between deep learning and classical ML, particularly the nature of the data they handle, whereas deep learning deals with unstructured data such as images, text, audio, and video. The chapter also explores techniques to address class imbalance in computer vision and their applicability to **Natural Language Processing (NLP)** problems.

Chapter 8, Algorithm-Level Deep Learning Techniques, expands on the concepts from *Chapter 5, Cost-Sensitive Learning*, and applies them to deep learning models. We adapt deep learning models through loss function modifications using the PyTorch deep learning framework, ultimately enhancing model performance and enabling more effective predictions.

Chapter 9, Hybrid Deep Learning Methods, explores innovative techniques that bridge the gap between data-level and algorithm-level methods from the previous two chapters. This chapter introduces the concept of graph ML and employs a real-world Facebook social network dataset to provide valuable insights and practical applications for addressing data imbalance in deep learning. We will also introduce the concept of hard mining loss and build upon it to explore a specialized technique called **minority class incremental rectification**, which combines hard mining with cross-entropy loss.

Chapter 10, Model Calibration, takes a different angle of addressing data imbalance. Rather than focusing on data preprocessing or model building, this chapter highlights the post-processing of prediction scores obtained from trained models. Such post-processing can be valuable for both real-time predictions and offline model evaluation. The chapter offers insights into measuring the calibration of a model and explains why this aspect can be indispensable when dealing with imbalanced data. This is particularly important since data balancing techniques can often lead to model miscalibration.

Appendix, Machine Learning Pipeline in Production, offers a foundational guide to constructing ML pipelines in production environments that encounter imbalanced data. This appendix provides a brief roadmap, going over the sequence and stage at which techniques for addressing data imbalance should be integrated.

📌 Usage of techniques – In production tips

Throughout this book, you will come across "In production" tip boxes like the following one, highlighting real-world applications of the techniques discussed:

> 🚀 **Class reweighting in production at OpenAI**
>
> OpenAI was trying to solve the problem of bias in training data of the image generation model DALL-E 2 [1]. DALL-E 2 is trained on a massive dataset of images from the internet, which can contain biases. For example, the dataset may contain more images of men than women or more images of people from certain racial or ethnic groups than others.

These snippets offer insights into how well-known companies grappled with data imbalance and what strategies they adopted to effectively navigate these challenges. For instance, the tip on OpenAI's approach with DALL-E 2 sheds light on the intricate balance between filtering training data and inadvertently amplifying biases. Such examples underscore the importance of being both strategic and cautious when dealing with imbalanced data. To delve deeper into the specifics and understand the nitty-gritty of these implementations, you are encouraged to follow the company blog or paper links provided. These insights can provide a clearer understanding of how to adapt and apply techniques in varied real-world scenarios effectively.

To get the most out of this book

This book assumes some foundational knowledge of ML, deep learning, and Python programming. Some basic working knowledge of `scikit-learn` and `PyTorch` can be helpful, although they can be learned on the go.

Software/hardware covered in the book	Operating system requirements
Google Colab	Windows, macOS, or Linux

For the software requirements, you have two options to execute the code provided in this book. You can choose to either run the code within Google Colab online at `https://colab.research.google.com/` or download the code to your local computer and execute it there. Google Colab provides a hassle-free option as it comes with all the necessary libraries pre-installed, so you don't need to install anything on your local machine. All you need is a web browser to access Google Colab and a Google account. If you prefer to work locally, ensure that you have Python (3.6 or higher) installed, as well as the specified libraries such as PyTorch, torchvision, NumPy, and scikit-learn. A list of required libraries can be found in the GitHub repository of the book. These libraries are compatible with Windows, macOS, and Linux operating systems. A modern GPU can speed up the code execution for the deep learning chapters that appear later in the book; however, it's not mandatory.

If you are using the digital version of this book, we advise you to type the code yourself or access the code from the book's GitHub repository (a link is available in the next section). Doing so will help you avoid any potential errors related to the copying and pasting of code.

Regarding references, we use numbered references such as "[6]," where you can go to the *References* section at the end of that chapter and download the corresponding reference (paper/blog/article) either using the link (if mentioned) or searching for that reference on Google Scholar (`https://scholar.google.com/`).

At the conclusion of each chapter, you will find a set of questions designed to test your comprehension of the material covered. We strongly encourage you to engage with these questions to reinforce your learning. Solutions or answers to selected questions can be found in Assessments towards the end of this book.

Download the example code files

You can download the example code files for this book from GitHub at `https://github.com/PacktPublishing/Machine-Learning-for-Imbalanced-Data`. If there's an update to the code, it will be updated in the GitHub repository.

We also have other code bundles from our rich catalog of books and videos available at `https://github.com/PacktPublishing/`. Check them out!

Conventions used

There are a number of text conventions used throughout this book.

`Code in text`: Indicates code words in text, database table names, folder names, filenames, file extensions, pathnames, dummy URLs, user input, and Twitter handles. Here is an example: "Since it's possible to provide a base estimator to `BaggingClassifier`, let's use `DecisionTreeClassifier` with the maximum depth of the trees being 6."

A block of code is set as follows:

```
from collections import Counter

X, y = make_data(sep=2)
print(y.value_counts())
sns.scatterplot(data=X, x="feature_1", y="feature_2")
plt.title('Separation: {}'.format(separation))
plt.show()
```

Bold: Indicates a new term, an important word, or words that you see onscreen. For instance, words in menus or dialog boxes appear in **bold**. Here is an example: "**True Negative Rate** (**TNR**): TNR measures the proportion of actual negatives that are correctly identified as such."

> **Tips or important notes**
> Appear like this.

Get in touch

Feedback from our readers is always welcome.

General feedback: If you have questions about any aspect of this book, email us at `customercare@packtpub.com` and mention the book title in the subject of your message.

Errata: Although we have taken every care to ensure the accuracy of our content, mistakes do happen. If you have found a mistake in this book, we would be grateful if you would report this to us. Please visit `www.packtpub.com/support/errata` and fill in the form.

Piracy: If you come across any illegal copies of our works in any form on the internet, we would be grateful if you would provide us with the location address or website name. Please contact us at copyright@packt.com with a link to the material.

If you are interested in becoming an author: If there is a topic that you have expertise in and you are interested in either writing or contributing to a book, please visit authors.packtpub.com.

Share Your Thoughts

Once you've read *Machine Learning for Imbalanced Data*, we'd love to hear your thoughts! Scan the QR code below to go straight to the Amazon review page for this book and share your feedback.

https://packt.link/r/1-801-07083-0

Your review is important to us and the tech community and will help us make sure we're delivering excellent quality content.

Download a free PDF copy of this book

Thanks for purchasing this book!

Do you like to read on the go but are unable to carry your print books everywhere?

Is your eBook purchase not compatible with the device of your choice?

Don't worry, now with every Packt book you get a DRM-free PDF version of that book at no cost.

Read anywhere, any place, on any device. Search, copy, and paste code from your favorite technical books directly into your application.

The perks don't stop there, you can get exclusive access to discounts, newsletters, and great free content in your inbox daily

Follow these simple steps to get the benefits:

1. Scan the QR code or visit the link below

https://packt.link/free-ebook/9781801070836

2. Submit your proof of purchase

3. That's it! We'll send your free PDF and other benefits to your email directly

1

Introduction to Data Imbalance in Machine Learning

Machine learning algorithms have helped solve real-world problems as diverse as disease prediction and online shopping. However, many problems we would like to address with machine learning involve imbalanced datasets. In this chapter, we will discuss and define imbalanced datasets, explaining how they differ from other types of datasets. The ubiquity of imbalanced data will be demonstrated with examples of common problems and scenarios. We will also go through the basics of machine learning and cover the essentials, such as loss functions, regularization, and feature engineering. We will also learn about common evaluation metrics, particularly those that can be very helpful for imbalanced datasets. We will then introduce the `imbalanced-learn` library.

In particular, we will learn about the following topics:

- Introduction to imbalanced datasets
- Machine learning 101
- Types of datasets and splits
- Common evaluation metrics
- Challenges and considerations when dealing with imbalanced data
- When can we have an imbalance in datasets?
- Why can imbalanced data be a challenge?
- When to not worry about data imbalance
- Introduction to the `imbalanced-learn` library
- General rules to follow

Technical requirements

In this chapter, we will utilize common libraries such as `numpy` and `scikit-learn` and introduce the `imbalanced-learn` library. The code and notebooks for this chapter are available on GitHub at `https://github.com/PacktPublishing/Machine-Learning-for-Imbalanced-Data/tree/main/chapter01`. You can fire up the GitHub notebook using Google Colab by clicking on the **Open in Colab** icon at the top of this chapter's notebook or by launching it from `https://colab.research.google.com` using the GitHub URL of the notebook.

Introduction to imbalanced datasets

Machine learning algorithms learn from collections of examples that we call **datasets**. These datasets contain multiple data samples or points, which we may refer to as examples, samples, or instances interchangeably throughout this book.

A dataset can be said to have a balanced distribution when all the target classes have a similar number of examples, as shown in *Figure 1.1*:

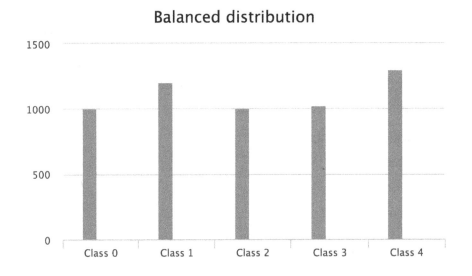

Figure 1.1 – Balanced distribution with an almost equal number of examples for each class

Imbalanced datasets or skewed datasets are those that have some target classes (also called labels) that outnumber the rest of the classes (*Figure 1.2*). Though this generally applies to classification problems (for example, fraud detection) in machine learning, they inevitably occur in regression problems (for example, house price prediction) too:

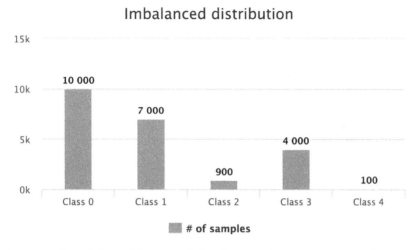

Figure 1.2 – An imbalanced dataset with five classes and a varying number of samples

We label the class with more instances as the "majority" or "negative" class and the one with fewer instances as the "minority" or "positive" class. Most of the time, our main interest lies in the minority class, which is why we often refer to the minority class as the "positive" class and to the majority class as the "negative" class:

Figure 1.3 – A visual guide to common terminology used in imbalanced classification

This can be scaled to more than two classes, and such classification problems are called multi-class classification. In the first half of this book, we will focus our attention only on binary class classification to keep the material easier to grasp. It's relatively easy to extend the concepts to multi-class classification.

Let's look at a few examples of imbalanced datasets:

- **Fraud detection** is where fraudulent transactions need to be detected out of several transactions. This problem is often encountered and widely used in finance, healthcare, and e-commerce industries.

- **Network intrusion detection** using machine learning involves analyzing large volumes of network traffic data to detect and prevent instances of unauthorized access and misuse of computer systems.

- **Cancer detection**. Cancer is not rare, but we still may want to use machine learning to analyze medical data to identify potential cases of cancer earlier and improve treatment outcomes.

In this book, we would like to focus on the class imbalance problem in general and look at various solutions where we see that class imbalance is affecting the performance of our model. A typical problem is that models perform quite poorly on the minority classes for which the model has seen a very low number of examples during model training.

Machine learning 101

Let's do a quick overview of machine learning and its related fields:

- **Artificial intelligence** is the superset of all intelligence-related problems. Classical machine learning encompasses problems that can be solved by training traditional classical models (such as decision trees or logistic regression) and predicting the target values. They typically work on tabular data, require extensive feature engineering (manual development of features), and are less effective on text and image data. Deep learning tends to do far better on image, text, speech, and video data, wherein, typically, no manual feature engineering is needed, and various layers in the neural network automatically do feature engineering for us.

- In **supervised learning**, we have both inputs and outputs (labels) in the dataset, and the model learns to predict the output during the training. Each input can be represented as a list of features. The output or labels can be a finite set of classes (classification), a real number (regression), or something more complex. A classic example of supervised learning in classification is the Iris flowers classification. In this case, the dataset includes features such as petal length, petal width, sepal length, and sepal width, and the labels are the species of the Iris flowers (setosa, versicolor, or virginica). A model can be trained on this dataset and then be used to classify new, unseen Iris flowers as one of these species.

- In **unsupervised learning**, models either don't have access to the labels or don't use the labels and then try to make some predictions – for example, clustering the examples in the dataset into different groups.

- In **reinforcement learning**, the model tries to learn by making mistakes and optimizing a goal or profit variable. An example would be training a model to play chess and adjusting its strategy based on feedback received through rewards and penalties.

In supervised learning (which is the focus of this book), there are two main types of problems: classification and regression. Classification problems involve categorizing data into predefined classes or labels, such as "fraud" or "non-fraud" and "spam" or "non-spam." On the other hand, regression problems aim to predict a continuous variable, such as the price of a house.

While data imbalance can also affect regression problems, this book will concentrate solely on classification problems. This focus is due to several factors, such as the limited scope of this book and the well-established techniques available for classification. In some cases, you might even be able to reframe a regression problem as a classification problem, making the methods discussed in this book still relevant.

When it comes to various kinds of models that are popular for classification problems, we have quite a few categories of classical supervised machine learning models:

- **Logistic regression**: This is a supervised machine learning algorithm that's used for binary classification problems. It predicts the probability of a binary target variable based on a set of predictor variables (features) by fitting a logistic function to the data, which outputs a value between 0 and 1.

- **Support Vector Machines** (**SVMs**): These are supervised machine learning algorithms that are mainly used for classification and can be extended to regression problems. SVMs classify data by finding the optimal hyperplane that maximally separates the different classes in the input data, thus making it a powerful tool for binary and multiclass classification tasks.

- **K-Nearest Neighbors** (**KNN**): This is a supervised machine learning algorithm that's used for classification and regression analysis. It predicts the target variable based on the k-nearest neighbors in the training dataset. The value of k determines the number of neighbors to consider when making a prediction, and it can be tuned to optimize the model's performance.

- **Tree models**: These are a type of supervised machine learning algorithm that's used for classification and regression analysis. They recursively split the data into smaller subsets based on the most important features to create a decision tree that predicts the target variable based on the input features.

- **Ensemble models**: These combine multiple individual models to improve predictive accuracy and reduce overfitting (explained later in this chapter). Ensemble techniques include bagging (for example, random forest), boosting (for example, XGBoost), and stacking. They are commonly used for classification as well as regression analysis.

- **Neural networks**: These models are inspired by the human brain, consist of multiple layers with numerous neurons in each, and are capable of learning complex functions. We will discuss these in more detail in *Chapter 6, Data Imbalance in Deep Learning.*

Figure 1.4 displays the decision boundaries of various classifiers we have reviewed so far. It shows that logistic regression has a linear decision boundary, while tree-based models such as decision trees, random forests, and XGBoost work by dividing examples into axis-parallel rectangles to form their decision boundary. SVM, on the other hand, transforms the data to a different space so that it can plot its non-linear decision boundary. Neural networks have a non-linear decision boundary:

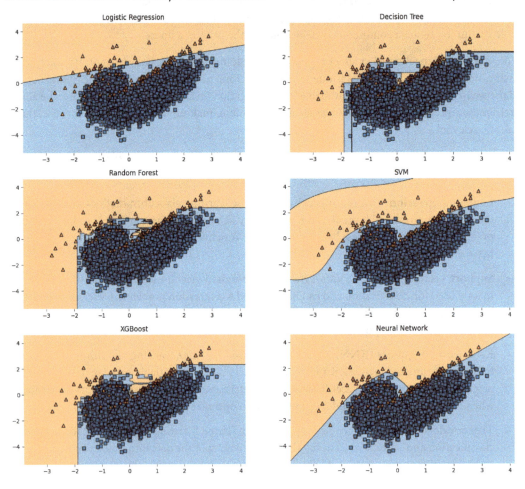

Figure 1.4 – The decision boundaries of popular machine learning algorithms on an imbalanced dataset

Next, we'll delve into the principles underlying the process of model training.

What happens during model training?

In the training phase of a machine learning model, we provide a dataset consisting of examples, each with input features and a corresponding label, to the model. Let X represent the list of features used for training, and y be the list of labels in the training dataset. The goal of the model is to learn a function, f, such that $f(X) \approx y$.

The model has adjustable parameters, denoted as θ, which are fine-tuned during the training process. The error function, commonly referred to as the **loss function**, is defined as $L(f(X;\theta), y)$. This error function needs to be minimized by a learning algorithm, which finds the optimal setting of these parameters, θ.

In classification problems, our typical loss functions are cross-entropy loss (also called the log loss):

$$CrossEntropyLoss\left(p\right) = \begin{cases} -log(p) & if\, y = 1 \\ -log(1-p) & otherwise \end{cases}$$

Here, p is the predicted probability from the model when $y = 1$.

When the model's prediction closely agrees with the target label, the loss function will approach zero. However, when the prediction deviates significantly from the target, the loss can become arbitrarily large, indicating a poor model fit.

As training progresses, the training loss keeps going down (*Figure 1.5*):

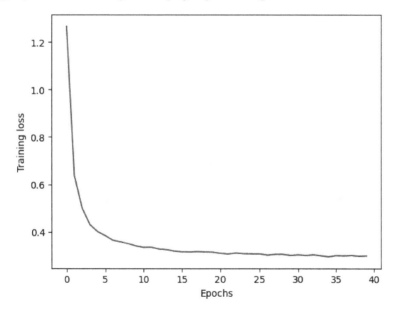

Figure 1.5 – Rate of change of the loss function as training progresses

This brings us to the concept of the fit of a model:

- A model is said to **underfit** if it is too simple and can't capture the data's complexity. It performs poorly on both training and new data.

- A model is of **right fit** if it accurately captures data patterns without learning noise. It performs well on both training and new data.

- An **overfit** model is too complex and learns noise along with data patterns. It performs well on training data but poorly on new data (*Figure 1.6*):

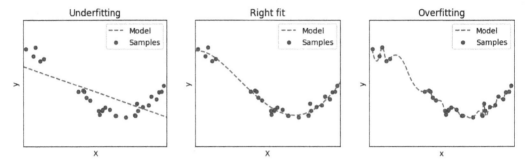

Figure 1.6 – Underfit, right fit, and overfit models for classification task

Next, let's briefly try to learn about two important concepts in machine learning:

- **Regularization** is a set of techniques that are used to prevent the overfitting of a model to the training data. One type of regularization (namely L1 or L2) adds a penalty term to the loss function, which encourages the model to have smaller weights and reduces its complexity. This helps prevent the model from fitting too closely to the training data and generalizes better to unseen data.

- **Feature engineering** is the process of selecting and transforming the input features of a model to improve its performance. Feature engineering involves selecting the most relevant features for the problem, transforming them to make them more informative, and creating new features from the existing ones. Good feature engineering can make a huge difference in the performance of a model and can often be more important than the choice of algorithm or hyperparameters.

Types of dataset and splits

Typically, we train our model on the training set and test the model on an independent unseen dataset called the test set. We do this to do a fair evaluation of the model. If we don't do this and train the model on the full dataset and evaluate the model on the same dataset, we don't know how good the model would do on unseen data, plus the model will likely be overfitted.

We may encounter three kinds of datasets in machine learning:

- **Training set**: A dataset on which the model is trained.

- **Validation set**: A dataset used for tuning the hyperparameters of the model. A validation set is often referred to as a development set.

- **Evaluation set or test set**: A dataset used for evaluating the performance of the model.

When working with small example datasets, it's common to allocate 80% of the data for the training set, 10% for the validation set, and 10% for the test set. However, the specific ratio between training and test sets is not as important as ensuring that the test set is large enough to provide statistically meaningful evaluation results. In the context of big data, a split of 98%, 1%, and 1% for training, validation, and test sets, respectively, could be appropriate.

Often, people don't have a dedicated validation set for hyperparameter tuning and refer to the test set as an evaluation set. This can happen when the hyperparameter tuning is not performed as a part of the regular training cycle and is a one-off activity.

Cross-validation

Cross-validation can be a confusing term to guess its meaning. Breaking it down: cross + validation, so it's some sort of validation on an extended (cross) something. *Something* here is the test set for us.

Let's see what cross-validation is:

- Cross-validation is a technique that's used to estimate how accurately a model will perform in practice

- It is typically used to detect overfitting – that is, failing to generalize patterns in data, particularly when the amount of data may be limited

Let's look at the different types of cross-validation:

- **Holdout**: In the holdout method, we randomly assign data points to two sets, usually called the training set and the test set, respectively. We then train (build a model) on the *training set* and test (evaluate its performance) on the *test set*.

- **k-fold**: This works as follows:

  - We randomly shuffle the data.

  - We divide all the data into k parts, also known as folds. We train the model on k-1 folds and evaluate it on the remaining fold. We record the performance of this model using our chosen model evaluation metric, then discard this model.

  - We repeat this process k times, each time holding out a different subset for testing. We take an average of the evaluation metric values (for example, accuracy) from all the previous models. This average represents the overall performance measure of the model.

k-fold cross-validation is mainly used when you have limited data points, say 100 points. Using 5 or 10 folds is the most common when doing cross-validation.

Let's look at the common evaluation metrics in machine learning, with a special focus on the ones relevant to problems with imbalanced data.

Common evaluation metrics

Several machine learning and deep learning metrics are used for evaluating the performance of classification models.

Let's look at some of the helpful metrics that can help evaluate the performance of our model on the test set.

Confusion matrix

Given a model that tries to classify an example as belonging to the positive or negative class, there are four possibilities:

- **True Positive (TP)**: This occurs when the model correctly predicts a sample as part of the positive class, which is its actual classification

- **False Negative (FN)**: This happens when the model incorrectly classifies a sample from the positive class as belonging to the negative class

- **True Negative (TN)**: This refers to instances where the model correctly identifies a sample as part of the negative class, which is its actual classification

- **False Positive (FP)**: This occurs when the model incorrectly predicts a sample from the negative class as belonging to the positive class

Table 1.1 shows in what ways the model can get "confused" when making predictions, aptly called the **confusion matrix**. The confusion matrix forms the basis of many common metrics in machine learning:

	Predicted Positive	**Predicted Negative**
Actually Positive	True Positive (TP)	False Negative (FN)
Actually Negative	False Positive (FP)	True Negative (TN)

Table 1.1 – Confusion matrix

Let's look at some of the most common metrics in machine learning:

- **True Positive Rate** (**TPR**) measures the proportion of actual positive examples correctly classified by the model:

$$TPR = \frac{\text{Positives classified correctly}}{\text{Total positives}} = \frac{TP}{TP + FN}$$

- **False Positive Rate** (**FPR**) measures the proportion of actual negative examples that are incorrectly identified as positives by the model:

$$FPR = \frac{\text{Negatives classified incorrectly}}{\text{Total negatives}} = \frac{FP}{FP + TN}$$

- **Accuracy**: Accuracy is the fraction of correct predictions made out of all the predictions that the model makes. This is mathematically equal to $\frac{TP + TN}{(TP + TN + FP + FN)}$. This functionality is available in the `sklearn` library as `sklearn.metrics.accuracy_score`.

- **Precision**: Precision, as an evaluation metric, measures the proportion of true positives over the number of items that the model predicts as belonging to the positive class, which is equal to the sum of the true positives and false positives. A high precision score indicates that the model has a low rate of false positives, meaning that when it predicts a positive result, it is usually correct. You can find this functionality in the `sklearn` library under the name `sklearn.metrics.precision_score`. Precision $= \frac{TP}{TP + FP}$.

- **Recall (or sensitivity, or true positive rate)**: Recall measures the proportion of true positives over the number of items that belong to the positive class. The number of items that belong to the positive class is equal to the sum of true positives and false negatives. A high recall score indicates that the model has a low rate of false negatives, meaning that it correctly identifies most of the positive instances. It is especially important to measure recall when the cost of mislabeling a positive example as negative (false negatives) is high.

  Recall measures the model's ability to correctly detect all the positive instances. Recall can be considered to be the accuracy of the positive class in binary classification. You can find this functionality in the `sklearn` library under the name `sklearn.metrics.recall_score`. Recall $= \frac{TP}{TP + FN}$.

Table 1.2 summarizes the differences between precision and recall:

	Precision	**Recall**
Definition	Precision is a measure of trustworthiness	Recall is a measure of completeness
Question to ask	When the model says something is positive, how often is it right?	Out of all the positive instances, how many did the model correctly identify?
Example (using an email filter)	Precision measures how many of the emails the model flags as spam are actually spam, as a percentage of all the flagged emails	Recall measures how many of the actual spam emails the model catches, as a percentage of all the spam emails in the dataset
Formula	$\text{Precision} = \frac{\text{TP}}{\text{TP} + \text{FP}}$	$\text{Recall} = \frac{\text{TP}}{\text{TP} + \text{FN}}$

Table 1.2 – Precision versus recall

Why can accuracy be a bad metric for imbalanced datasets?

Let's assume we have an imbalanced dataset with 1,000 examples, with 100 labels belonging to class 1 (the minority class) and 900 belonging to class 0 (the majority class).

Let's say we have a model that always predicts 0 for all examples. The model's accuracy for the minority class is $\frac{900 + 0}{(900 + 0 + 100 + 0)} = 90\%$.

Figure 1.7 – A comic showing accuracy may not always be the right metric

This brings us to the **precision-recall trade-off** in machine learning. Usually, precision and recall are inversely correlated – that is, when recall increases, precision most often decreases. Why? Note that recall = $\frac{TP}{TP+FN}$ and for recall to increase, FN should decrease. This means the model needs to classify more items as positive. However, if the model classifies more items as positive, some of these will likely be incorrect classifications, leading to an increase in the number of **false positives** (**FPs**). As the number of FPs increases, precision, defined as $\frac{TP}{TP+FP}$, will decrease. With similar logic, you can argue that when recall decreases, precision often increases.

Next, let's try to understand some of the precision and recall-based metrics that can help measure the performance of models trained on imbalanced data:

- **F1 score**: The F1 score (also called F-measure) is the harmonic mean of precision and recall. It combines precision and recall into a single metric. The F1 score varies between 0 and 1 and is most useful when we want to give equal priority to precision and recall (more on this later). This is available in the `sklearn` library as `sklearn.metrics.f1_score`.

- **F-beta score or F-measure**: The F-beta score is a generalization of the F1 score. It is a weighted harmonic mean of precision and recall, where the beta parameter controls the relative importance of precision and recall.

  The formula for the F-beta (F_β) score is as follows:

  $$F_\beta = \frac{(1 + \beta^2) \times (precision \times recall)}{(\beta^2 \times precision) + recall}$$

  Here, beta (β) is a positive parameter that determines the weight given to precision in the calculation of the score. When beta (β) is set to 1, the F1 score is obtained, which is the harmonic mean of precision and recall. The F-beta score is a useful metric for imbalanced datasets, where one class may be more important than the other. By adjusting the beta parameter, we can control the relative importance of precision and recall for a particular class. For example, if we want to prioritize precision over recall for the minority class, we can set beta < 1. To see why that's the case, set $\beta = 0$ in the F_β formula, which implies $F_\beta = precision$.

  Conversely, if we want to prioritize recall over precision for the minority class, we can set beta > 1 (we can set $\beta = \infty$ in the F_β formula to see it reduce to recall).

  In practice, the choice of beta parameter depends on the specific problem and the desired trade-off between precision and recall. In general, higher values of beta result in more emphasis on recall, while lower values of beta result in more emphasis on precision. This is available in the `sklearn` library as `sklearn.metrics.fbeta_score`.

- **Balanced accuracy score**: The balanced accuracy score is defined as the average of the recall obtained in each class. This metric is commonly used in both binary and multiclass classification scenarios to address imbalanced datasets. This is available in the `sklearn` library as `sklearn.metrics.balanced_accuracy_score`.

- **Specificity (SPE)**: Specificity is a measure of the model's ability to correctly identify the negative samples. In binary classification, it is calculated as the ratio of true negative predictions to the total number of negative samples. High specificity indicates that the model is good at identifying the negative class, while low specificity indicates that the model is biased toward the positive class.

- **Support**: Support refers to the number of samples in each class. Support is one of the values returned by the `sklearn.metrics.precision_recall_fscore_support` and `imblearn.metrics.classification_report_imbalanced` APIs.

- **Geometric mean**: The geometric mean is a measure of the overall performance of the model on imbalanced datasets. In `imbalanced-learn`, `geometric_mean_score()` is defined by the geometric mean of "accuracy on positive class examples" (recall or sensitivity or TPR) and "accuracy on negative class examples" (specificity or TNR). So, even if one class is heavily outnumbered by the other class, the metric will still be representative of the model's overall performance.

- **Index Balanced Accuracy (IBA)**: The IBA [1] is a measure of the overall accuracy of the model on imbalanced datasets. It takes into account both the sensitivity and specificity of the model and is calculated as the mean of the sensitivity and specificity, weighted by the imbalance ratio of each class. The IBA metric is useful for evaluating the overall performance of the model on imbalanced datasets and can be used to compare the performance of different models. IBA is one of the several values returned by `imblearn.metrics.classification_report_imbalanced`.

Table 1.3 shows the associated metrics and their formulas as an extension of the confusion matrix:

	Predicted Positive	**Predicted Negative**	
Actually Positive	True positive (TP)	False negative (FN)	$Recall = Sensitivity = True\ positive$ rate $(TPR) = \frac{TP}{TP+FN}$
Actually Negative	False positive (FP)	True negative (TN)	$Specificity = \frac{TN}{TN + FP}$
	Precision = TP/(TP+FP)		$Accuracy = \frac{TP + TN}{TP + TN + FP + FN}$
	FPR = FP/(FP+TN)		$F1 - score = \frac{2 * Precision * Recall}{Precision + Recall}$

Table 1.3 – Confusion matrix with various metrics and their definitions

ROC

Receiver Operating Characteristics, commonly known as **ROC** curves, are plots that display the TPR on the *y*-axis against the **FPR** on the *x*-axis for various threshold values:

- The ROC curve essentially represents the proportion of correctly predicted positive instances on the *y*-axis, contrasted with the proportion of incorrectly predicted negative instances on the *x*-axis.

- In classification tasks, a threshold is a cut-off value that's used to determine the class of an example. For instance, if a model classifies an example as "positive," a threshold of 0.5 might be set to decide whether the instance should be labeled as belonging to the "positive" or "negative" class. The ROC curve can be used to identify the optimal threshold for a model. This topic will be discussed in detail in *Chapter 5, Cost-Sensitive Learning*.

- To create the ROC curve, we calculate the TPR and FPR for many various threshold values of the model's predicted probabilities. For each threshold, the corresponding TPR value is plotted on the *y*-axis, and the FPR value is plotted on the *x*-axis, creating a single point. By connecting these points, we generate the ROC curve (*Figure 1.8*):

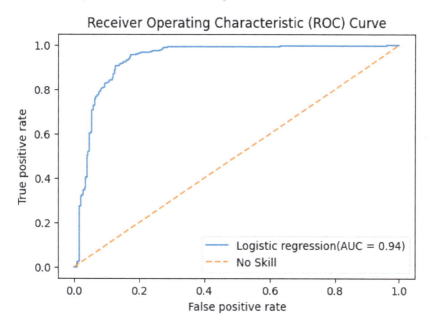

Figure 1.8 – The ROC curve as a plot of TPR versus FPR (the dotted line shows a model with no skill)

Some properties of the ROC curve are as follows:

- The **Area Under Curve** (**AUC**) of a ROC curve (also called **AUC-ROC**) serves a specific purpose: it provides a single numerical value that represents the model's performance across all possible classification thresholds:

  - AUC-ROC represents the degree of separability of the classes. This means that the higher the AUC-ROC, the more the model can distinguish between the classes and predict a positive class example as positive and a negative class example as negative. A poor model with an AUC near 0 essentially predicts a positive class as a negative class and vice versa.

  - The AUC-ROC of a random classifier is 0.5 and is the diagonal joining the points (0,0) and (1,0) on the ROC curve.

  - The AUC-ROC has a probabilistic interpretation: an AUC of 0.9 indicates a 90% likelihood that the model will assign a higher score to a randomly chosen positive class example than to a negative class example. That is, AUC-ROC can be depicted as follows:

$$P(score(x+) > score(x-))$$

  Here, $x+$ denotes the positive (minority) class, and $x-$ denotes the negative (majority) class.

  - In the context of evaluating model performance, it's crucial to use a test set that reflects the distribution of the data the model will encounter in real-world scenarios. This is particularly relevant when considering metrics such as the ROC curve, which remains consistent regardless of changes in class imbalance within the test data. Whether we have 1:1, 1:10, or 1:100 as the minority_class: majority_class distribution in the test set, the ROC curve remains the same [2]. The reason for this is that both of these rates are independent of the class distribution in the test data because they are calculated only based on the correctly and incorrectly classified instances of each class, not the total number of instances of each class. This is not to be confused with the change in imbalance in the training data, which can adversely impact the model's performance and would be reflected in the ROC curve.

Now, let's look at some of the problems in using ROC for imbalanced datasets:

- ROC does not distinguish between the various classes – that is, it does not emphasize one class more over the other. This can be a problem for imbalanced datasets where, often, the minority class is more important to detect than the majority class. Because of this, it may not reflect the minority class well. For example, we may want better recall over precision.

- While ROC curves can be useful for comparing the performance of models across a full range of FPRs, they may not be as relevant for specific applications that require a very low FPR, such as fraud detection in financial transactions or banking applications. The reason the FPR needs to be very low is that such applications usually require limited manual intervention. The number of transactions that can be manually checked may be as low as 1% or even 0.1% of all the data, which means the FPR can't be higher than 0.001. In these cases, anything to the right of an FPR equal to 0.001 on the ROC curve becomes irrelevant [3]. To further understand this point, let's consider an example:

- Let's say that for a test set, we have a total of 10,000 examples and only 100 examples of the positive class, making up 1% of the examples. So, any FPR higher than 1% - that is, 0.01 – is going to raise too many alerts to be handled manually by investigators.

- The performance on the far left-hand side of the ROC curve becomes crucial in most real-world problems, which are often dominated by a large number of negative instances. As a result, most of the ROC curve becomes irrelevant for applications that need to maintain a very low FPR.

Precision-Recall curve

Similar to ROC curves, **Precision-Recall** (**PR**) curves plot a pair of metrics for different threshold values. But unlike ROC curves, which plot TPR and FPR, PR curves plot precision and recall. To demonstrate the difference between the two curves, let's say we compare the performance of two models – Model 1 and Model 2 – on a particular handcrafted imbalanced dataset:

- In *Figure 1.9 (a)*, the ROC curves for both models appear to be close to the top-left corner (point (0, 1)), which might lead you to conclude that both models are performing well. However, this can be misleading, especially in the context of imbalanced datasets.

- When we turn our attention to the PR curves in *Figure 1.9 (b)*, a different story unfolds. Model 2 comes closer to the ideal top-right corner (point (1, 1)) of the plot, indicating that its performance is much better than Model 1 when precision and recall are considered.

- The PR curve reveals that Model 2 has an advantage over Model 1.

This discrepancy between the ROC and PR curves also underscores the importance of using multiple metrics for model evaluation, particularly when dealing with imbalanced data:

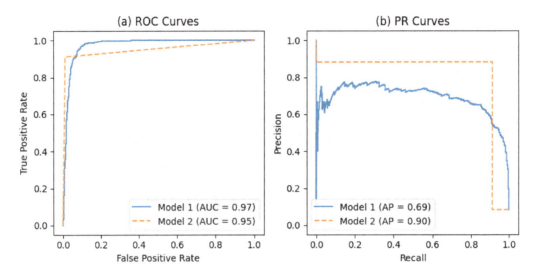

Figure 1.9 – The PR curve can show obvious differences between models compared to the ROC curve

Let's try to understand these observations in detail. While the ROC curve shows very little difference between the performance of the two models, the PR curve shows a much bigger gap. The reason for this is that the ROC curve uses FPR, which is FP/(FP+TN). Usually, TN is really high for an imbalanced dataset, and hence even if FP changes by a decent amount, FPR's overall value is overshadowed by TN. Hence, ROC doesn't change by a whole lot.

The conclusion of which classifier is superior can change with the distribution of classes in the test set. In the case of skewed datasets, the PR curve can more clearly show that the model did not work well compared to the ROC curve, as shown in the preceding figure.

The **average precision** is a single number that's used to summarize a PR curve, and the corresponding API in `sklearn` is `sklearn.metrics.average_precision_score`.

Relation between the ROC curve and PR curve

The primary distinction between the ROC curve and the PR curve lies in the fact that while ROC assesses how well the model can "calculate" both positive and negative classes, PR solely focuses on the positive class. Therefore, when dealing with a balanced dataset scenario and you are concerned with both the positive and negative classes, ROC AUC works exceptionally well. In contrast, when dealing with an imbalanced situation, PR AUC is more suitable. However, it's important to keep in mind that PR AUC only evaluates the model's ability to "calculate" the positive class. *Because PR curves are more sensitive to the positive (minority) class, we will be using PR curves throughout the first half of this book.*

We can reimagine the PR curve with precision on the *x*-axis and TPR, also known as recall, on the *y*-axis. The key difference between the two curves is that while the ROC curve uses FPR, the PR curve uses precision.

As discussed earlier, FPR tends to be very low when dealing with imbalanced datasets. This aspect of having low FPR values is crucial in certain applications such as fraud detection, where the capacity for manual investigations is inherently limited. Consequently, this perspective can alter the perceived performance of classifiers. As shown in *Figure 1.9*, it's also possible that the performances of the two models seem reversed when compared using average precision (0.69 versus 0.90) instead of AUC-ROC (0.97 and 0.95).

Let's summarize this:

- The AUC-ROC is the area under the curve plotted with TPR on the *y*-axis and FPR on the *x*-axis.

- The AUC-PR is the area under the curve plotted with precision on the *y*-axis and recall on the *x*-axis.

As TPR equals recall, the two plots only differ in what recall is compared to – either precision or FPR. Additionally, the plots are rotated by 90 degrees relative to each other:

	AUC-ROC	**AUC-PR**
General formula	AUC(TPR, FPR)	AUC(Precision, Recall)
Expanded formula	$\text{AUC}\left(\frac{\text{TP}}{\text{TP}+\text{FN}}, \frac{\text{FP}}{\text{FP}+\text{TN}}\right)$	$\text{AUC}\left(\frac{\text{TP}}{\text{TP}+\text{FP}}, \frac{\text{TP}}{\text{TP}+\text{FN}}\right)$
Equivalence	AUC(Recall, FPR)	AUC(Precision, Recall)

Table 1.4 – Comparing the ROC and PR curves

In the next few sections, we'll explore the circumstances that lead to imbalances in datasets, the challenges these imbalances can pose, and the situations where data imbalance might not be a concern.

Challenges and considerations when dealing with imbalanced data

In certain instances, directly using data for machine learning without worrying about data imbalance can yield usable results suitable for a given business scenario. Yet, there are situations where a more dedicated effort is needed to manage the effects of imbalanced data.

Broad statements claiming that you must always or never adjust for imbalanced classes tend to be misleading. The truth is that the need to address class imbalance is contingent on the specific characteristics of the data, the problem at hand, and the definition of an acceptable solution. Therefore, the approach to dealing with class imbalance should be tailored according to these factors.

When can we have an imbalance in datasets?

In this section, we'll explore various situations and causes leading to an imbalance in datasets, such as rare event occurrences or skewed data collection processes:

- **Inherent in the problem**: Sometimes, the task we need to solve involves detecting outliers in datasets – for example, patients with a certain disease or fraud cases in a set of transactions. In such cases, the dataset is inherently imbalanced because the target events are rare to begin with.

- **High cost of data collection while bootstrapping a machine learning solution**: The cost of collecting data might be too high for certain classes. For example, collecting data on COVID-19 patients incurs high costs due to the need for specialized medical tests, protective equipment, and the ethical and logistical challenges of obtaining informed consent in a high-stress healthcare environment.

- **Noisy labels for certain classes**: This may happen when a lot of noise is introduced into the labels of the dataset for certain classes during data collection.

- **Labeling errors**: Errors in labeling can also contribute to data imbalance. For example, if some samples are mistakenly labeled as negative when they are positive, this can result in an imbalance in the dataset. Additionally, if a class is already inherently rare, human annotators might be biased and overlook the few examples of that rare class that do exist.

- **Sampling bias**: Data collection methods can sometimes introduce bias in the dataset. For example, if a survey is conducted in a specific geographical area or among a specific group of people, the resulting dataset may not be representative of the entire population.

- **Data cleaning**: During the data cleaning or filtering process, some classes or samples may be removed due to incomplete or missing data. This can result in an imbalance in the remaining dataset.

Why can imbalanced data be a challenge?

Let's delve into the difficulties posed by imbalanced data on model predictions and their impact on model performance:

- **Failure of metrics such as accuracy**: As we discussed previously, conventional metrics such as accuracy can be misleading in the context of imbalanced data (a 99% imbalanced dataset would still achieve 99% accuracy). Threshold-invariant metrics such as the PR curve or ROC curve attempt to expose the performance of the model over a wide range of thresholds. The real challenge lies in the disproportionate influence of the "true negative" cell in the confusion matrix. Metrics that focus less on "true negatives," such as precision, recall, or F1 score, are more appropriate for evaluating model performance. It's important to note that these metrics have a hidden hyperparameter – the classification threshold – that should not be ignored but optimized for real-world applications (refer to *Chapter 5, Cost-Sensitive Learning*, to learn more about threshold tuning).

- **Imbalanced data can be a challenge for a model's loss function**: This may happen because the loss function is typically designed to minimize the errors between the predicted outputs and the true labels of the training data. When the data is imbalanced, there are more instances of one class than another, and the model may become biased toward the majority class. We will discuss solutions to this issue in more detail in *Chapter 5, Cost-Sensitive Learning*, and *Chapter 8, Algorithm-Level Deep Learning Techniques*.

- **Different misclassification costs for different classes**: Often, it may be more expensive to misclassify positive examples than to misclassify negative examples. We may have false positives that are more expensive than false negatives. For example, usually, the cost of misclassifying a patient with cancer as healthy (false negative) will be much higher than misclassifying a healthy patient as having cancer (false positive). Why? Because it's much cheaper to go through some extra tests to revalidate the test results in the second case instead of detecting it much later in the first case. This is called the cost of misclassification, which could be different for the majority and minority classes, making things complicated for imbalanced datasets. We will discuss more about this in *Chapter 5, Cost-Sensitive Learning*.

- **Constraints on computational resources**: In sectors such as finance, healthcare, and retail, handling big data is a common challenge. Training on these large datasets is not only time-consuming but also costly due to the computational power needed. In such scenarios, downsampling or undersampling the majority class becomes essential, as will be discussed in *Chapter 3, Undersampling Methods*. Additionally, acquiring more samples for the minority class can further increase dataset size and computational costs. Memory limitations may also restrict the amount of data that can be processed.

- **Not enough variation in the minority class examples to sufficiently represent its distribution**: Often, an absolute number of samples of the minority class is not as big of a problem as the **variation** in the samples of the minority class. The dataset might look large, but there might not be many variations or varieties in the samples that adequately represent the distribution of minority classes. This can lead to the model not being able to learn the classification boundary properly, which would lead to poor performance of the model (*Figure 1.10*). This can often happen in computer vision problems, such as object detection, where we may have very few samples of certain classes. In such cases, data augmentation techniques (discussed in *Chapter 7, Data-Level Deep Learning Methods*) can help significantly:

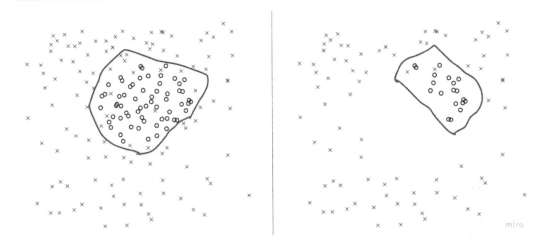

Figure 1.10 – Change in decision boundary with a different distribution of minority class examples – the crosses denote the majority class, and the circles denote the minority class

- **Poor performance of uncalibrated models**: Imbalanced data can be a challenge for uncalibrated models. Uncalibrated models are models that do not output well-calibrated probabilities, which means that the predicted probabilities may not reflect the true likelihood of the predicted classes:

  - When dealing with imbalanced data, uncalibrated models can be particularly susceptible to producing biased predictions toward the majority class as they may not be able to effectively differentiate between the minority and majority classes. This can lead to poor performance in the minority class, where the model may produce overly confident predictions or predictions that are too conservative.

  - For example, an uncalibrated model that is trained on imbalanced data may incorrectly classify instances that belong to the minority class as majority class examples, often with high confidence. This is because the model may not have learned to adjust its predictions based on the imbalance in the data and may not have a good understanding of the minority class examples.

  - To address this challenge, it is important to use well-calibrated models [4] that can output probabilities that reflect the true likelihood of the predicted classes. This can be achieved through techniques such as Platt scaling or isotonic regression, which can calibrate the predicted probabilities of an uncalibrated model to produce more accurate and reliable probabilities. Model calibration will be discussed in detail in *Chapter 10, Model Calibration*.

- **Poor performance of models because of non-adjusted thresholds**: It's important to use intelligent thresholding when making predictions using models trained on imbalanced datasets. Simply predicting 1 when the model probability is over 0.5 may not always be the best approach. Instead, we should consider other thresholds that may be more effective. This can be achieved by examining the PR curve of the model rather than relying solely on its success rate with a default probability threshold of 0.5. Threshold adjustment can be quite important, even for models trained on naturally or artificially balanced datasets. We will discuss threshold adjustment in detail in *Chapter 5, Cost-Sensitive Learning*.

Next, let's try to see when we shouldn't do anything about data imbalance.

When to not worry about data imbalance

Class imbalance may not always negatively impact performance, and using imbalance-specific methods can sometimes worsen results [5]. Therefore, it's crucial to accurately assess whether a task is genuinely affected by class imbalance before applying any specialized techniques. One such strategy can be as simple as setting up a baseline model without worrying about class imbalance and observing the model's performance on various classes using various performance metrics.

Let's explore scenarios where data imbalance may not be a concern and no corrective measures may be needed:

- **When the imbalance is small**: If the imbalance in the dataset is relatively small, with the ratio of the minority class to the majority class being only slightly skewed (say 4:5 or 2:3), the impact on the model's performance may be minimal. In such cases, the model may still perform reasonably well without requiring any special techniques to handle the imbalance.

- **When the goal is to predict the majority class**: In some cases, the focus may be on predicting the majority class accurately, and the minority class may not be of particular interest. For example, in online ad placement, the focus can be on targeting users (majority class) likely to click on ads to maximize click-through rates and immediate revenue, while less attention is given to users (minority class) who may find ads annoying.

- **When the cost of misclassification is nearly equal for both classes**: In some applications, the cost of misclassifying a positive class example is not high (that is, false negative). An example is classifying emails as spam or non-spam. It's totally fine to miss a spam email once in a while and misclassify it as non-spam. In such cases, the impact of misclassification on the performance metrics may be negligible, and the imbalance may not be a concern.

- **When the dataset is sufficiently large**: Even if the ratio of minority to majority class samples is very low, such as 1:100, and if the dataset is sufficiently large, with a large number of samples in both the minority and majority classes, the impact of data imbalance on the model's performance may be reduced. With a larger dataset, the model may be able to learn the patterns in the minority class more effectively. However, it would still be advisable to compare the baseline model's performance with the performance of models that take the data imbalance into account. For example, compare a baseline model to models with threshold adjustment, oversampling, and undersampling (*Chapter 2, Oversampling Methods*, and *Chapter 3, Undersampling Methods*), and algorithm-based techniques such as cost-sensitive learning (*Chapter 5, Cost-Sensitive Learning*).

In the next section, we will become familiar with a library that can be very useful when dealing with imbalanced data. We will train a model on an imbalanced toy dataset and look at some metrics to evaluate the performance of the trained model.

Introduction to the imbalanced-learn library

imbalanced-learn (imported as imblearn) is a Python package that offers several techniques to deal with data imbalance. In the first half of this book, we will rely heavily on this library. Let's install the imbalanced-learn library:

```
pip3 install imbalanced-learn==0.11.0
```

We can use imbalanced-learn to create a synthetic dataset for our analysis:

```
from sklearn.datasets import make_classification
import pandas as pd
import matplotlib.pyplot as plt
import seaborn as sns

def make_data(sep):
    X, y = make_classification(n_samples=50000,
        n_features=2, n_redundant=0,
        n_clusters_per_class=1, weights=[0.995],
        class_sep=sep, random_state=1)

    X = pd.DataFrame(X, columns=['feature_1', 'feature_2'])
    y = pd.Series(y)
    return X, y
```

Let's analyze the generated dataset:

```
from collections import Counter

X, y = make_data(sep=2)
print(y.value_counts())
sns.scatterplot(data=X, x="feature_1", y="feature_2", hue=y)
plt.title('Separation: {}'.format(separation))
plt.show()
```

Here's the output:

```
0       49498
1         502
```

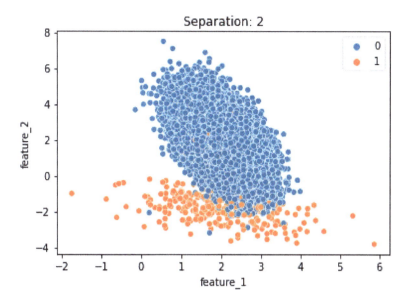

Figure 1.11 – 2 class dataset with two features

Let's split this dataset into training and test sets:

```
From sklearn.model_selection import train_test_split

X_train, X_test, y_train, y_test = train_test_split(X, y, stratify = \
    y, test_size=0.2, random_state=42)
print('train data: ', Counter(y_train))
print('test data: ', Counter(y_test))
```

Here's the output:

```
train data:  Counter({0: 39598, 1: 402})
test data:  Counter({0: 9900, 1: 100})
```

Note the usage of stratify in the train_test_split API of sklearn. Specifying stratify=y ensures we maintain the same ratio of majority and minority classes in both the training set and the test set. Let's understand stratification in more detail.

Stratified sampling is a way to split the dataset into various subgroups (called "strata") based on certain characteristics they share. It can be highly valuable when dealing with imbalanced datasets because it ensures that the train and test datasets have the same proportions of class labels as the original dataset.

In an imbalanced dataset, the minority class constitutes a small fraction of the total data. If we perform a simple random split without any stratification, there's a risk that the minority class may not be adequately represented in the training set or could be entirely left out from the test set, which may lead to poor performance and unreliable evaluation metrics.

With stratified sampling, the proportion of each class in the overall dataset is preserved in both training and test sets, ensuring representative sampling and a better chance for the model to learn from the minority class. This leads to a more robust model and a more reliable evaluation of the model's performance.

> **The scikit-learn APIs for stratification**
>
> The `scikit-learn` APIs, such as `RepeatedStratifiedKFold` and `StratifiedKFold`, employ the concept of stratification to evaluate model performance through cross-validation, especially when working with imbalanced datasets.

Now, let's train a logistic regression model on training data:

```
from sklearn.linear_model import LogisticRegression

lr = LogisticRegression(random_state=0, max_iter=2000)
lr.fit(X_train, y_train)
y_pred = lr.predict(X_test)
```

Let's get the report metrics from the `sklearn` library:

```
from sklearn.metrics import classification_report

print(classification_report(y_test, y_pred))
```

This outputs the following:

```
              precision    recall  f1-score   support
0                  0.99      1.00      1.00      9900
1                  0.94      0.17      0.29       100

accuracy                              0.99     10000
macro avg          0.97      0.58      0.64     10000
weighted avg       0.99      0.99      0.99     10000
```

Let's get the report metrics from `imblearn`:

```
from imblearn.metrics import classification_report_imbalanced

print(classification_report_imbalanced(y_test, y_pred))
```

This outputs a lot more columns:

```
                pre     rec     spe     f1      geo     iba     sup

        0       0.99    1.00    0.17    1.00    0.41    0.18    9900
        1       0.94    0.17    1.00    0.29    0.41    0.16     100

avg / total     0.99    0.99    0.18    0.99    0.41    0.18   10000
```

Figure 1.12 – Output of the classification report from imbalanced-learn

Do you notice the extra metrics here compared to the API of `sklearn`? We got three additional metrics: `spe` for specificity, `geo` for geometric mean, and `iba` for index balanced accuracy.

The `imblearn.metrics` module has several such functions that can be helpful for imbalanced datasets. Apart from `classification_report_imbalanced()`, it offers APIs such as `sensitivity_specificity_support()`, `geometric_mean_score()`, `sensitivity_score()`, and `specificity_score()`.

General rules to follow

Usually, the first step in any machine learning pipeline should be to split the data into train/test/validation sets. We should avoid applying any techniques to handle the imbalance until after the data has been split. We should begin by splitting the data into training, testing, and validation sets and then proceed with any necessary adjustments to the training data. Applying techniques such as oversampling (see *Chapter 2, Oversampling Methods*) before splitting the data can result in data leakage, overfitting, and over-optimism [6].

We should ensure that the validation data closely resembles the test data. Both validation data and test data should represent real-world scenarios on which the model will be used for prediction. Avoid applying any sampling techniques or modifications to the validation set. The only requirement is to include a sufficient number of samples from all classes.

Let's switch to discussing a bit about using unsupervised learning algorithms. **Anomaly detection** or **outlier detection** is a class of problems that can be used for dealing with imbalanced data problems. Anomalies or outliers are data points that deviate significantly from the rest of the data. These anomalies often correspond to the minority class in an imbalanced dataset, making unsupervised methods potentially useful.

The term that's often used for these kinds of problems is **one-class classification**. This technique is particularly beneficial when the positive (minority) cases are sparse or when gathering them before the training is not feasible. The model is trained exclusively on what is considered the "normal" or majority class. It then classifies new instances as "normal" or "anomalous," effectively identifying what could be the minority class. This can be especially useful for binary imbalanced classification problems, where the majority class is deemed "normal," and the minority class is considered an anomaly.

However, it does have a drawback: outliers or positive cases during training are discarded [7], which could lead to the potential loss of valuable information.

In summary, while unsupervised methods such as one-class classification offer an alternative for managing class imbalance, our discussion in this book will remain centered on supervised learning algorithms. Nevertheless, we recommend that you explore and experiment with such solutions when you find them appropriate.

Summary

Let's summarize what we've learned so far. Imbalanced data is a common problem in machine learning, where there are significantly more instances of one class than another. Imbalanced datasets can arise from various situations, including rare event occurrences, high data collection costs, noisy labels, labeling errors, sampling bias, and data cleaning. This can be a challenge for machine learning models as they may be biased toward the majority class.

Several techniques can be used to deal with imbalanced data, such as oversampling, undersampling, and cost-sensitive learning. The best technique to use depends on the specific problem and the data.

In some cases, data imbalance may not be a concern. When the dataset is sufficiently large, the impact of data imbalance on the model's performance may be reduced. However, it is still advisable to compare the baseline model's performance with the performance of models that have been built using techniques that address data imbalance, such as threshold adjustment, data-based techniques (oversampling and undersampling), and algorithm-based techniques.

Traditional performance metrics such as accuracy can fail in imbalanced datasets. Some more useful metrics for imbalanced datasets are the ROC curve, the PR curve, precision, recall, and F1 score. While ROC curves are suitable for balanced datasets, PR curves are more suitable for imbalanced datasets when one class is more important than the other.

The `imbalanced-learn` library is a Python package that offers several techniques to deal with data imbalance.

There are some general rules to follow, such as splitting the data into train/test/validation sets before applying any techniques to handle the imbalance in the data, ensuring that the validation data closely resembles the test data and that test data represents the data on which the model will make final predictions, and avoiding applying any sampling techniques or modifications to the validation set and test set.

One-class classification or anomaly detection is another technique that can be used for dealing with unsupervised imbalanced data problems. In this book, we will focus our discussion on supervised learning algorithms only.

In the next chapter, we will look at one of the common ways to handle the data imbalance problem in datasets by applying oversampling techniques.

Questions

1. How does the choice of loss function when training a model affect the performance of the model on imbalanced datasets?

2. Can you explain why the PR curve is more informative than the ROC curve when dealing with highly skewed datasets?

3. What are some of the potential issues with using accuracy as a metric for model performance on imbalanced datasets?

4. How does the concept of "class imbalance" affect the process of feature engineering in machine learning?

5. In the context of imbalanced datasets, how does the choice of "k" in k-fold cross-validation affect the performance of the model? How would you fix the issue?

6. How does the distribution of classes in the test data affect the PR curve, and why? What about the ROC curve?

7. What are the implications of having a high AUC-ROC but a low AUC-PR in the context of an imbalanced dataset?

8. How does the concept of "sampling bias" contribute to the challenge of imbalanced datasets in machine learning?

9. How does the concept of "labeling errors" contribute to the challenge of imbalanced datasets in machine learning?

10. What are some of the real-world scenarios where dealing with imbalanced datasets is inherently part of the problem?

11. **Matthews Correlation Coefficient** (**MCC**) is a metric that takes all the cells of the confusion matrix into account and is given by the following formula:

$$\frac{TP \cdot TN - FP \cdot FN}{\sqrt{(TP + FP) \cdot (TP + FN) \cdot (TN + FP) \cdot (TN + FN)}}$$

A. What can be the minimum and maximum values of the metric?

B. Because it takes TN into account, its value may not change much when we are comparing different models, but it can tell us if the predictions for various classes are going well. Let's illustrate this through an artificial example where we take a dummy model that always predicts 1 for an imbalanced test set made of 100 examples, with 90 of class 1 and 10 of class 0. Compute the various terms in the MCC formula and the value of MCC. Also, compute the values of accuracy, precision, recall, and F1 score.

C. What can you conclude about the model from the MCC value that you just computed in the previous question?

D. Create an imbalanced dataset using imblearn's `fetch_dataset` API and then compute the values of MCC, accuracy, precision, recall, and F1 score. See if the MCC value can be a useful metric for this dataset.

References

1. V. García, R. A. Mollineda, and J. S. Sánchez, *Index of Balanced Accuracy: A Performance Measure for Skewed Class Distributions*, in Pattern Recognition and Image Analysis, vol. 5524, H. Araujo, A. M. Mendonça, A. J. Pinho, and M. I. Torres, Eds. Berlin, Heidelberg: Springer Berlin Heidelberg, 2009, pp. 441–448. Accessed: Mar. 18, 2023. [Online]. Available at `http://link.springer.com/10.1007/978-3-642-02172-5_57`.

2. T. Fawcett, *An introduction to ROC analysis*, Pattern Recognition Letters, vol. 27, no. 8, pp. 861–874, Jun. 2006, doi: 10.1016/j.patrec.2005.10.010.

3. Y.-A. Le Borgne, W. Siblini, B. Lebichot, and G. Bontempi, *Reproducible Machine Learning for Credit Card Fraud Detection - Practical Handbook*. Université Libre de Bruxelles, 2022. [Online]. Available at `https://github.com/Fraud-Detection-Handbook/fraud-detection-handbook`.

4. W. Siblini, J. Fréry, L. He-Guelton, F. Oblé, and Y.-Q. Wang, *Master your Metrics with Calibration*, vol. 12080, 2020, pp. 457–469. doi: 10.1007/978-3-030-44584-3_36.

5. Xu-Ying Liu, Jianxin Wu, and Zhi-Hua Zhou, *Exploratory Undersampling for Class-Imbalance Learning*, IEEE Trans. Syst., Man, Cybern. B, vol. 39, no. 2, pp. 539–550, Apr. 2009, doi: 10.1109/TSMCB.2008.2007853.

6.   M. S. Santos, J. P. Soares, P. H. Abreu, H. Araujo, and J. Santos, *Cross-Validation for Imbalanced Datasets: Avoiding Overoptimistic and Overfitting Approaches [Research Frontier]*, IEEE Comput. Intell. Mag., vol. 13, no. 4, pp. 59–76, Nov. 2018, doi: 10.1109/MCI.2018.2866730.

7.   A. Fernández, S. García, M. Galar, R. Prati, B. Krawczyk, and F. Herrera, *Learning from Imbalanced Data Sets*. Springer International Publishing, 2018

2

Oversampling Methods

In machine learning, we often don't have enough samples of the minority class. One solution might be to gather more samples of such a class. For example, in the problem of detecting whether a patient has cancer or not, if we don't have enough samples of the cancer class, we can wait for some time to gather more samples. However, such a strategy is not always feasible or sensible and can be time-consuming. In such cases, we can augment our data by using various techniques. One such technique is oversampling.

In this chapter, we will introduce the concept of oversampling, discuss when to use it, and the various techniques to perform it. We will also demonstrate how to utilize these techniques through the `imbalanced-learn` library APIs and compare their performance using some classical machine learning models. Finally, we will conclude with some practical advice on which techniques tend to work best under specific real-world conditions.

In this chapter, we will cover the following topics:

- Random oversampling
- SMOTE
- SMOTE variants
- ADASYN
- Model performance comparison of various oversampling methods
- Guidance for using various oversampling techniques
- Oversampling in multi-class classification

Technical requirements

In this chapter, we will utilize common libraries such as numpy, scikit-learn, and imbalanced-learn. The code and notebooks for this chapter are available on GitHub at https://github.com/PacktPublishing/Machine-Learning-for-Imbalanced-Data/tree/master/chapter02. You can just fire up the GitHub notebook using Google Colab by clicking on the **Open in Colab** icon at the top of this chapter's notebook or by launching it from https://colab.research.google.com using the GitHub URL of the notebook.

What is oversampling?

Sampling involves selecting a subset of observations from a larger set of observations. In this chapter, we'll initially focus on binary classification problems with two classes: the positive class and the negative class. The minority class has significantly fewer instances than the majority class. Later in this chapter, we will explore multi-class classification problems. Toward the end of this chapter, we will look into oversampling for multi-class classification problems.

Oversampling is a data balancing technique that generates more samples of the minority class. However, this can be easily scaled to work for any number of classes where there are multiple classes with an imbalance. *Figure 2.1* shows how samples of minority and majority classes are imbalanced (**a**) initially and balanced (**b**) after applying an oversampling technique:

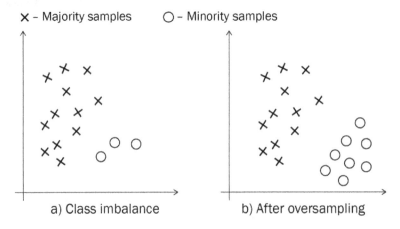

Figure 2.1 – An increase in the number of minority class samples after oversampling

Why is oversampling needed, you ask? It is required so that we give the model enough samples of the minority class to learn from it. If we offer too few instances of the minority class, the model may choose to ignore these minority class examples and focus solely on the majority class examples. This, in turn, would lead to the model not being able to learn the decision boundary well.

Let's generate a two-class imbalanced dataset with a 1:99 ratio using the `sklearn` library's `make_classification` API, which creates a normally distributed set of points for each class. This will generate an imbalanced dataset of two classes: one being the minority class with label 1 and the other being the majority class with label 0. We will apply various oversampling techniques throughout this chapter to balance this dataset:

```
from collections import Counter
from sklearn.datasets import make_classification
X, y = make_classification(n_samples=10000, n_features=2,\
    n_redundant=0, n_classes=2, flip_y=0, n_clusters_per_class=2,\
    class_sep=0.79, weights=[0.99], random_state=81)
```

This code generates 100 examples of class 1 and 9,900 examples of class 0 with an imbalance ratio of 1:99. By plotting the dataset, we can see how the examples are distributed:

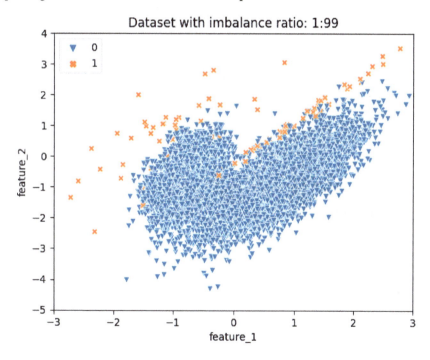

Figure 2.2 – The dataset with an imbalance ratio of 1:99

In this section, we understood the need for oversampling. We also generated a synthetic imbalanced binary classification dataset to demonstrate the application of various oversampling techniques.

Random oversampling

The simplest strategy to balance the imbalance in a dataset is to randomly choose samples of the minority class and repeat or duplicate them. This is also called **random oversampling with replacement**.

To increase the number of minority class observations, we can replicate the minority class data observations enough times to balance the two classes. Does this sound too trivial? Yes, but it works. By increasing the number of minority class samples, random oversampling reduces the bias toward the majority class. This helps the model learn the patterns and characteristics of the minority class more effectively.

We will use random oversampling from the `imbalanced-learn` library. The `fit_resample` API from the `RandomOverSampler` class resamples the original dataset and balances it. The `sampling_strategy` parameter is used to specify the new ratio of various classes. For example, we could say `sampling_strategy=1.0` to have an equal number of the two classes.

There are various ways to specify `sampling_strategy`, such as a float value, string value, or `dict` – for example, {0: 50, 1: 50}:

```
from imblearn.over_sampling import RandomOverSampler
ros = RandomOverSampler(sampling_strategy=1.0, random_state=42)
X_res, y_res = ros.fit_resample(X, y)
print('Resampled dataset shape %s' % Counter(y_res))
```

Here is the output:

```
Resampled dataset shape Counter({0: 9900, 1: 9900})
```

So, we went from a ratio of 1:99 to 1:1, which is what we expected with `sampling_strategy=1.0`.

Let's plot the oversampled dataset:

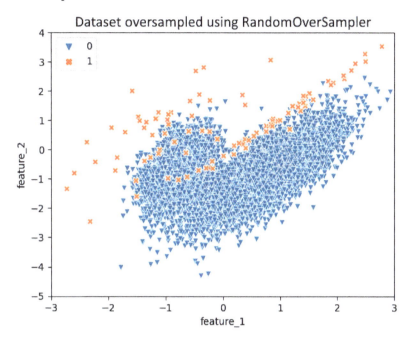

Figure 2.3 – Dataset oversampled using RandomOverSampler
(label 1 examples appear unchanged due to overlap)

After applying random oversampling, the examples with label 1 overlap each other, creating the impression that nothing has changed. Repeating the same data point over and over can cause the model to memorize the specific data points and not be able to generalize to new, unseen examples. The `shrinkage` parameter in `RandomOverSampler` lets us perturb or shift each point by a small amount.

The value of the `shrinkage` parameter has to be greater than or equal to 0 and can be `float` or `dict`. If a `float` data type is used, the same shrinkage factor will be used for all classes. If a `dict` data type is used, the shrinkage factor will be specific for each class.

In *Figure 2.4*, we can observe the impact of random oversampling with `shrinkage=0.2`:

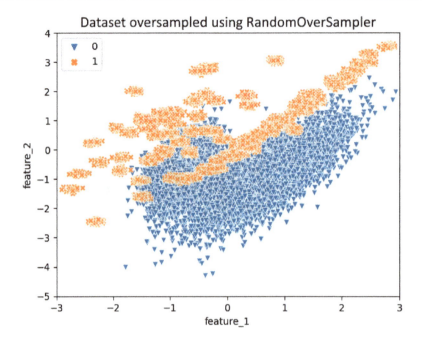

Figure 2.4 – Result of applying random oversampling with shrinkage=0.2

Toward the end of this chapter, we will compare the performance of random oversampling with various other oversampling techniques across multiple models and datasets. This will provide insights into their effectiveness in real-world applications.

> 🚀 **Random oversampling in production at Grab**
>
> Grab, a ride-hailing and food delivery service in Southeast Asia, developed an image collection platform [1] for storing and retrieving imagery and map data. A key feature of this platform was its ability to automatically detect and blur **Personally Identifiable Information** (**PII**), such as faces and license plates, in street-level images. This was essential for maintaining user privacy. The dataset that was used for this purpose had a significant imbalance, with far more negative samples (images without PII) than positive ones (images with PII). Manual annotation was not feasible, so they turned to machine learning to solve this problem.
>
> To address the data imbalance, Grab employed the random oversampling technique to increase the number of positive samples, thereby enhancing the performance of their machine learning model.

Problems with random oversampling

Random oversampling can often lead to overfitting of the model since the generated synthetic observations get repeated, and the model sees the same observations again and again. Shrinkage tries to handle that in some sense, but it may be challenging to come up with an apt value of shrinkage, and shrinkage doesn't care if the generated synthetic samples overlap with the majority class samples, which can lead to other problems.

In the previous section, we learned about the most basic and practical technique for applying oversampling to balance a dataset and reduce bias toward the majority class. Many times, random oversampling itself might give us such a high boost to our model's performance that we may not even need to apply more advanced techniques. In production settings, it would also be beneficial to keep things plain and simple until we are ready to introduce more complexity in the pipeline. As they say, "premature optimization is the root of all evil," so we start with something simple, so long as it does improve our model's performance.

In the subsequent sections, we will explore some alternative techniques, such as SMOTE and ADASYN, which adopt a different approach to oversampling and alleviate some of the problems associated with the random oversampling technique.

SMOTE

The main problem with random oversampling is that it duplicates the observations from the minority class. This can often cause overfitting. **Synthetic Minority Oversampling Technique (SMOTE)** [2] solves this problem of duplication by using a technique called **interpolation**.

Interpolation involves creating new data points in the range of known data points. Think of interpolation as being similar to the process of reproduction in biology. In reproduction, two individuals come together to produce a new individual with traits of both of them. Similarly, in interpolation, we pick two observations from the dataset and create a new observation by choosing a random point on the line joining the two selected points.

We oversample the minority class by interpolating synthetic examples. That prevents the duplication of minority samples while generating new synthetic observations similar to the known points. *Figure 2.5* depicts how SMOTE works:

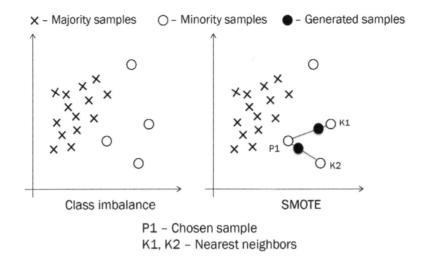

Figure 2.5 – Working of SMOTE

Here, we can see the following:

- The majority and minority class samples are plotted (left)
- The synthetic samples are generated by taking a random point on the line joining a minority sample to two nearest neighbor majority class samples (right)

SMOTE was originally designed for continuous inputs. To keep the explanations simple, we'll start with continuous inputs and discuss other kinds of inputs later.

First, we will examine the functioning of SMOTE and explore any potential disadvantages associated with this technique.

How SMOTE works

The SMOTE algorithm works as follows:

1. It considers only the samples from the minority class.
2. It trains KNN on the minority samples. A typical value of k is 5.
3. For each minority sample, a line is drawn between the point and each of its KNN examples.
4. For each such line segment, a point on the segment is randomly picked to create a new synthetic example.

Let's use SMOTE using APIs from the `imbalanced-learn` library:

```
from imblearn.over_sampling import SMOTE
sm = SMOTE(random_state=0)
X_res, y_res = sm.fit_resample(X, y)
print('Resampled dataset shape %s' % Counter(y_res))
```

Here is the output:

```
Resampled dataset shape Counter({0: 9900, 1: 9900})
```

The oversampled dataset looks like this:

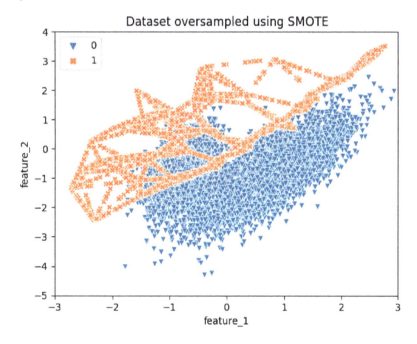

Figure 2.6 – Oversampling using SMOTE

> 🚀 Oversampling techniques in production at Microsoft
>
> In a real-world application at Microsoft [3], machine learning was employed to forecast **Live Site Incidents (LSIs)** for early detection and escalation of incidents for engineering teams. Every day, a high volume of incidents was being generated, most of which started as low-severity issues. Due to limited resources, it was impractical for engineering teams to investigate all incidents, leading to potential delays in mitigating critical issues until they had a significant customer impact.
>
> To address this, Microsoft employed machine learning to forecast which LSIs could escalate into severe problems, aiming for proactive identification and early resolution. The challenge was the data imbalance in the training set: out of approximately 40,000 incidents, fewer than 2% escalated to high severity. Microsoft used two different oversampling techniques— bagged classification (covered in *Chapter 4, Ensemble Methods*), and SMOTE, which were the most effective in improving the model's performance. They used a two-step pipeline for balancing classes: first, oversampling with **SMOTE** and then undersampling with **RandomUnderSampler** (covered in *Chapter 3, Undersampling Methods*). The pipeline automatically selected the optimal sampling ratios for both steps, and SMOTE performed better when combined with undersampling. The resulting end-to-end automated model was designed to be generic, making it applicable across different teams within or outside Microsoft, provided historical incidents were available for learning. The LSI insight tool used this model, which was adopted by various engineering teams.

Next, we will look at the limitations of using SMOTE.

Problems with SMOTE

SMOTE has its pitfalls – for example, it can add noise to an already noisy dataset. It can also lead to class overlap issues as follows:

- SMOTE generates minority class samples without considering the majority class distribution, which may increase the overlap between the classes. In *Figure 2.7*, we're plotting the binary classification imbalanced dataset before and after applying SMOTE. We can see a lot of overlap between the two classes after applying SMOTE:

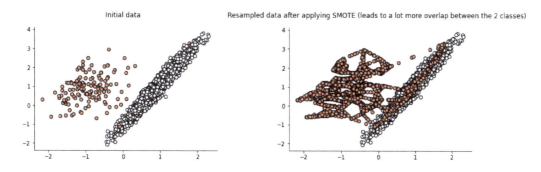

Figure 2.7 – Binary classification dataset before (left) and after (right) applying
SMOTE (see the overlap between two classes on the right)

- The other case may be that you have a huge amount of data, and running SMOTE may increase the runtime of your pipeline.

Problem 1 can be solved by using the SMOTE variant Borderline-SMOTE (discussed in the next section).

In this section, we learned about SMOTE, which uses the nearest neighbor technique to generate synthetic samples of the minority class. Sometimes, SMOTE may perform better than random oversampling since it exploits the proximity to other minority class samples to generate new samples.

SMOTE variants

Now, let's look at some of the SMOTE variants, such as Borderline-SMOTE, SMOTE-NC, and SMOTEN. These variants apply the SMOTE algorithm to samples of a certain kind and may not always be applicable.

Borderline-SMOTE

Borderline-SMOTE [4] is a variation of SMOTE that generates synthetic samples from the minority class samples that are near the classification boundary, which divides the majority class from the minority class.

Why consider samples on the classification boundary?

The idea is that the examples near the classification boundary are more prone to misclassification than those far away from the decision boundary. Producing more such minority samples along the boundary would help the model learn better about the minority class. Intuitively, it is also true that the points away from the classification boundary likely won't make the model a better classifier.

Here's a step-by-step algorithm for Borderline-SMOTE:

1. We run a KNN algorithm over the whole dataset.

2. Then, we divide the minority class points into three categories:

    - *Noise* points are minority class examples that have all the neighbors from the majority class. These points are buried among majority-class neighbors. They are likely outliers and can safely be ignored as "noise."

    - *Safe* points have more minority-class neighbors than majority-class neighbors. Such observations don't contain much information and can be safely ignored.

    - *Danger* points have more majority-class neighbors than minority-class neighbors. This implies that such observations are on or close to the boundary between the two classes.

3. Then, we train a KNN model only on the minority class examples.

4. Finally, we apply the SMOTE algorithm to the `Danger` points. Note that the neighbors of these `Danger` points may or may not be marked as `Danger`.

As shown in *Figure 2.8*, Borderline-SMOTE focuses on the danger class points for synthetic data generation:

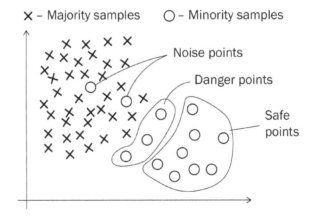

Figure 2.8 – The Borderline-SMOTE algorithm uses only danger points to generate synthetic samples. Danger points have more majority-class neighbors than minority-class ones

Figure 2.9 shows how Borderline-SMOTE focuses on the minority class samples that are near the classification boundary, which separates the majority and minority classes:

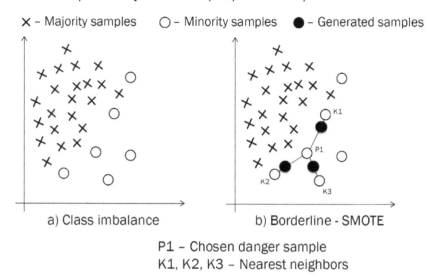

a) Class imbalance   b) Borderline - SMOTE

P1 – Chosen danger sample
K1, K2, K3 – Nearest neighbors

Figure 2.9 – Illustrating Borderline-SMOTE

Here, we can see the following:

a) Plots of majority and minority class samples

b) Synthetic samples generated using neighbors near the classification boundary

Let's see how we can use Borderline-SMOTE from the `imbalanced-learn` library to perform oversampling of the data:

```
print("Before: ", sorted(Counter(y).items()))
from imblearn.over_sampling import BorderlineSMOTE
X_resampled, y_resampled = BorderlineSMOTE().fit_resample(X, y)
print("After: ", sorted(Counter(y_resampled).items()))
```

Here is the output:

```
Before: [(0, 9900), (1, 100)]
After:  [(0, 9900), (1, 9900)]
```

Can you guess the problem with focusing solely on data points on the decision boundary of the two classes?

Since this technique focuses so heavily on a very small number of points on the boundary, the points inside the minority class clusters are not sampled at all:

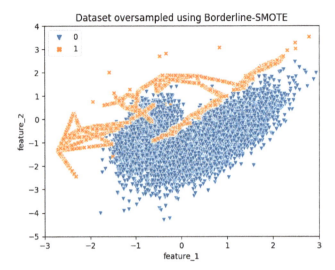

Figure 2.10 – The Borderline-SMOTE algorithm utilizing danger points, with more
majority- than minority-class neighbors, to generate synthetic samples

In this section, we learned about Borderline-SMOTE, which generates synthetic minority class samples by focusing on the samples that are close to the classification boundary of the majority and minority classes, which, in turn, may help in improving the discrimination power of the model.

🚀 **Oversampling techniques in production at Amazon**

In a real-world application, Amazon used machine learning to optimize packaging types for products, aiming to reduce waste while ensuring product safety [5]. In their training dataset, which featured millions of product and package combinations, Amazon faced a significant class imbalance, with as few as 1% of the examples representing unsuitable product-package pairings (minority class).

To tackle this imbalance, Amazon used various oversampling techniques:

- Borderline-SMOTE oversampling, which resulted in a 4%-7% increase in PR-AUC but increased the training time by 25%-35%.

- A hybrid of random oversampling and random undersampling, where they randomly oversampled the minority class and undersampled the majority class. It led to a 6%-10% improvement in PR-AUC and increased the training time by up to 25%.

The best-performing technique was two-phase learning with random undersampling (discussed in *Chapter 7, Data-Level Deep Learning Methods*), which improved PR-AUC by 18%-24% with no increase in training time.

They mentioned that the effectiveness of a technique in dealing with dataset imbalance is both domain- and dataset-specific. This real-world example underscores the effectiveness of oversampling techniques in tackling class imbalance issues.

Next, we will learn about another oversampling technique, called ADASYN, that oversamples examples near boundaries and in other low-density regions without completely ignoring data points that do not lie on the boundary.

ADASYN

While SMOTE doesn't distinguish between the density distribution of minority class samples, **Adaptive Synthetic Sampling (ADASYN)** [6] focuses on harder-to-classify minority class samples since they are in a low-density area. ADASYN uses a weighted distribution of the minority class based on the difficulty of classifying the observations. This way, more synthetic data is generated from harder samples:

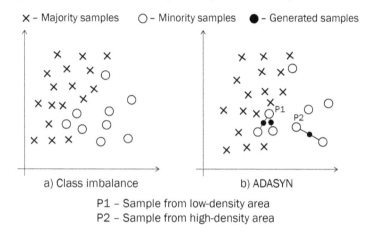

a) Class imbalance   b) ADASYN

P1 – Sample from low-density area
P2 – Sample from high-density area

Figure 2.11 – Illustration of how ADASYN works

Here, we can see the following:

- a) The majority and minority class samples are plotted
- b) Synthetic samples are generated depending on the hardness factor (explained later)

While SMOTE uses all samples from the minority class for oversampling uniformly, in ADASYN, the observations that are harder to classify are used more often.

Another difference between the two techniques is that, unlike SMOTE, ADASYN also uses the majority class observations while training KNN. It then decides the hardness of samples based on how many majority observations are its neighbors.

Working of ADASYN

ADASYN follows a simple algorithm. Here is the step-by-step working of ADASYN:

1.   First, it trains a KNN on the entire dataset.

2. For each observation of the minority class, we find the hardness factor. This factor tells us how difficult it is to classify that data point. The hardness factor, denoted by r, is the ratio of the number of majority class neighbors with the total number of neighbors. Here, $r = \frac{M}{K}$, where M is the count of majority class neighbors and K is the total number of nearest neighbors.

3. For each minority observation, we generate synthetic samples proportional to the hardness factor by drawing a line between the minority observation and its neighbors (neighbors could be from the majority class or minority class). The harder it is to classify a data point, the more synthetic samples will be created for it.

Let's see how we can use the ADASYN API from the `imbalanced-learn` library to perform oversampling of the data:

```
from imblearn.over_sampling import ADASYN
X_resampled, y_resampled = ADASYN().fit_resample(X, y)
print(sorted(Counter(y_resampled).items()))
```

Here is the output:

```
[(0, 9900), (1, 9900)]
```

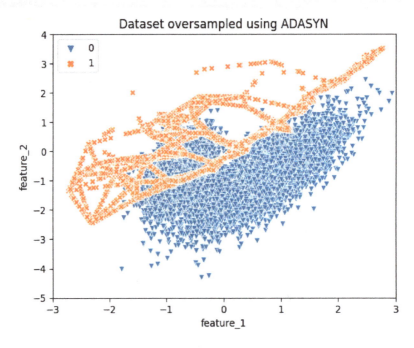

Figure 2.12 – ADASYN prioritizes harder samples and incorporates
majority class examples in KNN to assess sample hardness

Figure 2.13 – A memory aid summarizing various oversampling techniques

In this section, we learned about ADASYN. Next, let's see how we can deal with cases when our data contains categorical features.

Categorical features and SMOTE variants (SMOTE-NC and SMOTEN)

What if your data contains categorical features? A categorical feature can take one of a limited or fixed number of possible values, and it's a parallel to enumerations (enums) in computer science. These could be nominal categorical features that lack a natural order (for example, hair color, ethnicity, and so on) or ordinal categorical features that have an inherent order (for example, low, medium, and high):

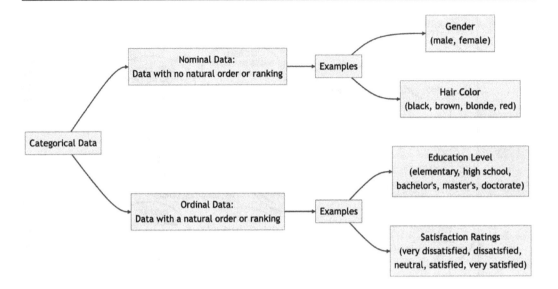

Figure 2.14 – Categorical data and its types with examples

- For ordinal features, we can just encode them via sklearn's `OrdinalEncoder`, which assigns the categories to the values 0, 1, 2, and so on.

- For nominal features, none of the SMOTE variants we have learned so far will work. However, `RandomOverSampler` can handle nominal features too:

```
from imblearn.over_sampling import RandomOverSampler
X_cat_mix = np.array([["abc", 1], ["def", 2],\
    ["ghi", 3]], dtype=object)

y_cat_mix = np.array([0, 0, 1])

print('X_cat_mix:', X_cat_mix, '\n y_cat_mix: ', y_cat_mix)

X_resampled, y_resampled = RandomOverSampler().fit_resample(\
    X_cat_mix, y_cat_mix)

print('X_resampled:', X_resampled, '\n y_resampled: ',\
    y_resampled)
```

Here is the output:

```
X_cat_mix: [['abc' 1]
 ['def' 2]
 ['ghi' 3]]
 y_cat_mix:  [0 0 1]
```

```
X_resampled: [['abc' 1]
 ['def' 2]
 ['ghi' 3]
 ['ghi' 3]]
 y_resampled:   [0 0 1 1]
```

However, SMOTE, by default, works only on continuous data and cannot be directly used on categorical data. *Why?* That's because SMOTE works by generating a random point on the line joining two different data points of the minority class (also called interpolation). If our data is categorical and has values of "yes" and "no," we would first need to transform such values into numbers. Even when we do so, say "yes" is mapped to 1 and "no" is mapped to 0, the interpolation via SMOTE may end up producing a new point of 0.3, which does not map to any real category.

Also, we cannot use the `shrinkage` parameter in `RandomOverSampler` with categorical data because this parameter is designed only for continuous values.

However, two variants of SMOTE can deal with categorical features:

- **Synthetic Minority Oversampling TEchnique-Nominal Continuous (SMOTE-NC)** [1] is used when we have both categorical (nominal – for example, T-shirt size, hair color, and so on) and numerical (continuous – for example, age, salary, and so on) features in the data. However, it's important to note that SMOTE-NC doesn't work with only categorical features; it requires some numerical features as well. The reason for this is the way the SMOTE-NC algorithm works. For the new synthetic minority sample, the continuous features are created using SMOTE's usual method. The nominal (categorical) feature takes the value most common among the KNNs.

  Let's use the SMOTENC API from `imbalanced-learn` to oversample our dataset. The first item in the dataset is categorical, and the second item is continuous:

  ```
  from imblearn.over_sampling import SMOTENC
  X_cat_mix = np.array([["small", 1],\
      ["medium", 2],\
      ["large", 3],\
      ["large", 4],\
      ["large", 5]], dtype=object)
  y_cat_mix = np.array([0, 0, 1, 0, 1])
  print('X_cat_mix:', X_cat_mix, '\n y_cat_mix: ', y_cat_mix)

  X_resampled, y_resampled = SMOTENC(
      categorical_features=[0], k_neighbors=1, random_state=1
  ).fit_resample(X_cat_mix, y_cat_mix)
  print('X_resampled:', X_resampled, '\ny_resampled: ', \
      y_resampled)
  ```

Here is the output:

```
X_cat_mix:  [['small' 1]
             ['medium' 2]
             ['large' 3]
             ['large' 4]
             ['large' 5]]
y_cat_mix:  [0 0 1 0 1]

X_resampled:  [['small' 1.0]
               ['medium' 2.0]
               ['large' 3.0]
               ['large' 4.0]
               ['large' 5.0]
               ['large' 3.005630378122263]]
y_resampled:   [0 0 1 0 1 1]
```

- **Synthetic Minority Oversampling Technique for Nominal (SMOTEN)** is used for nominal categorical data. SMOTEN performs the majority vote similar to SMOTE-NC for all the features. It considers all features as nominal categorical, and the feature value of new samples is decided by taking the most frequent category of the nearest neighbors. The distance metric that's used for calculating the nearest neighbors is called the **Value Distance Metric** (**VDM**). VDM computes the distance between two attribute values by considering the distribution of class labels associated with each value. It is based on the idea that two attribute values are more similar if they have similar distributions of class labels. This way, VDM can capture the underlying relationships between categorical attributes and their corresponding class labels.

Let's look at some example code that uses SMOTEN:

```python
from imblearn.over_sampling import SMOTEN
X_original = np.array([["abc"], \
                       ["def"], \
                       ["ghi"], \
                       ["ghi"], \
                       ["ghi"]], dtype=object)

y_original = np.array([0, 0, 1, 1, 1])

print('X_original:', X_original, '\ny_original: ', y_original)
X_resampled, y_resampled = \
    SMOTEN(k_neighbors=1).fit_resample(X_original, y_original)

print('X_resampled:', X_resampled, '\ny_resampled:', \
    y_resampled)
```

Here is the output:

```
X_original: [['abc']
             ['def']
             ['ghi']
             ['ghi']
             ['ghi']]
y_original:  [0 0 1 1 1]

X_resampled: [['abc']
              ['def']
              ['ghi']
              ['ghi']
              ['ghi']
              ['abc']]
y_resampled:  [0 0 1 1 1 0]
```

In *Table 2.1*, we can see SMOTE, SMOTEN, and SMOTENC, with a few examples for each technique to demonstrate the difference between them:

Type of SMOTE	Features Supported	Example Data
SMOTE	Only numerical	features: [2.3, 4.5, 1.2], label: 0
		features: [3.4, 2.2, 5.1], label: 1
SMOTEN	Categorical (nominal or ordinal)	features: ['green', 'square'], label: 0
		features: ['red', 'circle'], label: 1
SMOTENC	Numerical or categorical (nominal or ordinal)	features: [2.3, 'green', 'small', 'square'], label: 0
		features: [3.4, 'red', 'large', 'circle'], label: 1

Table 2.1 – SMOTE and some of its common variants with example data

In summary, we should use SMOTENC when we have a mix of categorical and continuous data types, while SMOTEN can only be used when all the columns are categorical. You might be curious about how the various oversampling methods compare with each other in terms of model performance. We'll explore this topic in the next section.

Model performance comparison of various oversampling methods

Let's examine how some popular models perform with the different oversampling techniques we've discussed. We'll use two datasets for this comparison: one synthetic and one real-world dataset. We'll evaluate the performance of four oversampling techniques, as well as no sampling, using logistic regression and random forest models.

You can find all the related code in this book's GitHub repository. In *Figure 2.15* and *Figure 2.16*, we can see the average precision score values for both models on the two datasets:

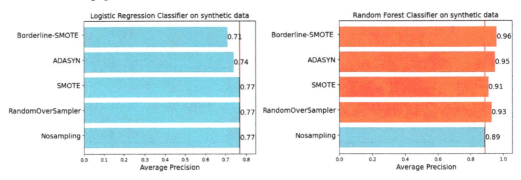

Figure 2.15 – Performance comparison of various oversampling techniques on a synthetic dataset

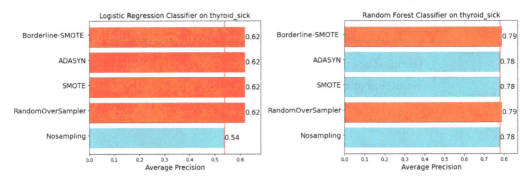

Figure 2.16 – Performance comparison of various oversampling techniques on the thyroid_sick dataset

Based on these plots, we can draw some useful conclusions:

- **Effectiveness of oversampling**: In general, using oversampling techniques seems to improve the average precision score compared to not using any sampling (NoSampling).

- **Algorithm sensitivity**: The effectiveness of oversampling techniques varies depending on the machine learning algorithm used. For example, random forest seems to benefit more from oversampling techniques than logistic regression, especially on synthetic data.

- **Data sensitivity**: The effectiveness also depends on the type of data. For instance, all oversampling techniques performed similarly on the `thyroid_sick` dataset but showed variations in the synthetic data.

- **Best performers**:

  - For logistic regression, all the oversampling techniques had a similar performance on the `thyroid_sick` data

  - For random forest, Borderline-SMOTE had the highest average precision score on synthetic data

- **Borderline-SMOTE special case**: Borderline-SMOTE performed exceptionally well with random forest on synthetic data but was on par with other techniques on the `thyroid_sick` data.

- **No clear winner**: There is no single oversampling technique that outperforms all others across all conditions. The choice of technique may depend on the specific algorithm and dataset being used.

Please note that the models used here are not tuned with the best hyperparameters.

Tuning the hyperparameters of random forest and logistic regression models may improve the models' performance further.

In general, there is no single technique that will always do better than the rest. We have multiple variables at play here, namely the "model" and the "data." Most of the time, the only way to know is to try out a bunch of these techniques and find the one that works the best for our model and data. You may find yourself curious about how to choose from the numerous oversampling options available.

Guidance for using various oversampling techniques

Now, let's review some guidelines on how to navigate through the various oversampling techniques we went over and how these techniques differ from each other:

1. Train a model without applying any sampling techniques. This will be our model with baseline performance. Any oversampling technique we apply is expected to give a boost to this performance.

2. Start with random oversampling and add some shrinkage too. We may have to play with some values of shrinkage to see if the model's performance improves.

3. When we have categorical features, we have a couple of options:

   I.   Convert all categorical features into numerical features first using one-hot encoding, label encoding, feature hashing, or other feature transformation techniques.

   II.   (Only for nominal categorical features) Use SMOTENC and SMOTEN directly on the data.

4. Apply various oversampling techniques – random oversampling, SMOTE, Borderline-SMOTE, and ADASYN – and measure the model's performance on metrics applicable to your problem, such as the average precision score, ROC-AUC, precision, recall, F1 score, and more.

5. Since oversampling alters the distribution of the training dataset, which is not the case for the test set or the real world, using oversampling can potentially generate biased predictions. After using oversampling, it can be essential to recalibrate our model's probability scores depending on the application. Recalibration of the model corrects any bias introduced by altering the class distribution, ensuring more reliable decision-making when deployed. Similarly, adjusting the classification threshold is key for accurate model interpretation, especially with imbalanced datasets. For more details on recalibration and threshold adjustment, please see *Chapter 10, Model Calibration*, and *Chapter 5, Cost-Sensitive Learning*, respectively.

When to avoid oversampling

In *Chapter 1, Introduction to Data Imbalance in Machine Learning*, we discussed scenarios where data imbalance may not be a concern. Those considerations should be revisited before you opt for oversampling techniques. Despite criticisms, the applicability of oversampling should be evaluated on a case-by-case basis. Here are some additional technical considerations to keep in mind when choosing to apply oversampling techniques:

- **Computational cost**: Oversampling increases the dataset's size, leading to higher computational demands in terms of processing time and hardware resources.

- **Data quality**: If the minority class data is noisy or has many outliers, oversampling can introduce more noise, reducing model reliability.

- **Classifier limitations**: In scenarios with system constraints, such as extremely low latency, or when dealing with legacy systems, the use of strong classifiers (complex and more accurate models) may not be feasible. In these cases, we may be limited to using weak classifiers. Weak classifiers are simpler and less accurate but require fewer computational resources and have lower runtime latency. In such situations, oversampling can be beneficial [7]. For strong classifiers, oversampling may offer diminishing returns, and optimizing the decision threshold could sometimes serve as a simpler, less resource-intensive alternative.

Consider these factors when deciding whether to use oversampling methods for imbalanced datasets.

Table 2.2 summarizes the key ideas, pros, and cons of various oversampling techniques. This can help you better evaluate which oversampling method to choose:

	SMOTE	Borderline-SMOTE	ADASYN	SMOTE-NC and SMOTEN
Key idea	Choose random points on the line joining the nearest neighbors of minority class examples.	Choose the minority samples on the boundary between the majority and minority classes. Perform SMOTE for such samples on the boundary.	Automatically decides the number of minority class samples to generate according to density distribution. More points are generated where the density distribution is low.	It performs a majority vote for the categorical features.
Pro	Usually reduces false negatives.	Creates synthetic samples that are not naïve copies of the known data.	It cares about the density distribution of different classes.	It works with categorical data.
Con	Overlapping classes may occur and can introduce more noise to data. This may not work well with high-dimensional data or multi-class classification problems.	It does not care about the distribution of minority class examples.	It focuses on areas where there is overlap between classes. It may focus too much on outliers, resulting in poor model performance.	The same as SMOTE.

Table 2.2 – Summarizing the various oversampling techniques that were discussed in this chapter

In this section, we looked at some general guidelines to apply the various oversampling techniques we learned about in this chapter and the pros and cons of using them. Next, we will look at how to extend the various oversampling methods to multi-class classification problems.

Oversampling in multi-class classification

In multi-class classification problems, we have more than two classes or labels to be predicted, and hence more than one class may be imbalanced. This adds some more complexity to the problem. However, we can apply the same techniques to multi-class classification problems as well. The `imbalanced-learn` library provides the option to deal with multi-class classification in almost all the supported methods. We can choose from various sampling strategies using the `sampling_strategy` parameter. For multi-class classification, we can pass some fixed string values (called built-in strategies) to the `sampling_strategy` parameter in the SMOTE API. We can also pass a dictionary with the following:

- Keys as the class labels
- Values as the number of samples of that class

Here are the built-in strategies for `sampling_strategy` when using the parameter as a string:

- The `minority` strategy resamples only the minority class.

- The `not minority` strategy resamples all classes except the minority class. This may be helpful in the case of multi-class imbalance, where we have more than two classes and multiple classes are imbalanced, but we don't want to touch the minority class.

- The `not majority` strategy resamples all classes except the majority class.

- The `all` strategy resamples all classes.

- The `auto` strategy is the same as the `not majority` strategy.

The following code shows the usage of SMOTE for multi-class classification using various sampling strategies.

First, let's create a dataset containing 100 samples with three classes that have weights of 0.1, 0.4, and 0.5:

```
X, y = make_classification(n_classes=3, class_sep=2, \
    weights=[0.1, 0.4, 0.5], n_clusters_per_class=1, \
    n_samples=100, random_state=10)
print('Original dataset shape %s' % Counter(y))
```

Here is the output:

```
Original dataset shape Counter({2: 50, 1: 40, 0: 10})
```

As expected, our dataset contains the three classes in the ratio 10:40:50 for classes 0, 1, and 2, respectively.

Now, let's apply SMOTE with the "*minority*" sampling strategy. This will oversample the class with the least number of samples:

```
over_sampler = SMOTE(sampling_strategy='minority')
X_res, y_res = over_sampler.fit_resample(X, y)
print('Resampled dataset shape using minority strategy: %s'% \
    Counter(y_res))
```

Here is the output:

```
Resampled dataset shape using minority strategy: Counter({0: 50, 2:
50, 1: 40})
```

Since class 0 previously had the least number of samples, the "*minority*" sampling strategy only oversampled class 0, making the number of samples equal to the number of samples in the majority class.

In the following code, we're using a dictionary for oversampling. Here, for each class label (0, 1, or 2) as key in the `sampling_strategy` dictionary, we have the number of desired samples for each targeted class as value:

```
print('Original dataset shape %s' % Counter(y))
over_sampler = SMOTE(sampling_strategy={
                        0 : 40,
                        1 : 40,
                        2 : 50})
X_res, y_res = over_sampler.fit_resample(X, y)
print('Resampled dataset shape using dict strategy: %s\n'% \
    Counter(y_res))
```

Here is the output:

```
Original dataset shape Counter({2: 50, 1: 40, 0: 10})

Resampled dataset shape using dict strategy:
        Counter({2: 50, 0: 40, 1: 40})
```

> **Tip**
> Please note that when using `dict` within `sampling_strategy`, the number of desired samples for each class should be greater than or equal to the original number of samples. Otherwise, the `fit_resample` API will throw an exception.

In this section, we saw how to extend oversampling strategies to handle cases when we have imbalanced datasets with more than two classes. Most of the time, the "auto" `sampling_strategy` would be good enough and would balance all the classes.

Summary

In this chapter, we went through various oversampling techniques for dealing with imbalanced datasets and applied them using Python's `imbalanced-learn` library (also called `imblearn`). We also saw the internal workings of some of the techniques by implementing them from scratch. While random oversampling generates new minority class samples by duplicating them, SMOTE-based techniques work by choosing random samples in the direction of nearest neighbors of the minority class samples. Though oversampling can potentially overfit the model on your data, it usually has more pros than cons, depending on the data and model.

We applied them to some of the synthesized and publicly available datasets and benchmarked their performance and effectiveness. We saw how different oversampling techniques may lead to model performance on a varying scale, so it becomes crucial to try a few different oversampling techniques to decide on the one that's most optimal for our data.

If you feel intrigued by the prospect of discovering oversampling approaches relevant to deep learning models, we invite you to check out *Chapter 7, Data-Level Deep Learning Methods*, where we'll discuss data-level techniques within the realm of deep learning.

In the next chapter, we will go over various undersampling techniques.

Exercises

1. Explore the two variants of SMOTE, namely KMeans-SMOTE and SVM-SMOTE, from the `imbalanced-learn` library, not discussed in this chapter. Compare their performance with vanilla SMOTE, Borderline-SMOTE, and ADASYN using the logistic regression and random forest models.

2. For a classification problem with two classes, let's say the minority class to majority class ratio is 1:20. How should we balance this dataset? Should we apply the balancing technique at test or evaluation time? Please provide a reason for your answer.

3. Let's say we are trying to build a model that can estimate whether a person can be granted a bank loan or not. Out of the 5,000 observations we have, only 500 people got the loan approved. To balance the dataset, we duplicate the approved people data and then split it into train, test, and validation datasets. Are there any issues with using this approach?

4. Data normalization helps in dealing with data imbalance. Is this true? Why or why not?

5. Explore the various oversampling APIs available from the `imbalanced-learn` library here: `https://imbalanced-learn.org/stable/references/over_sampling.html`. Pay attention to the various parameters of each of the APIs.

References

1. *Protecting Personal Data in Grab's Imagery* (2021), `https://engineering.grab.com/protecting-personal-data-in-grabs-imagery`.

2. N. V. Chawla, K. W. Bowyer, L. O. Hall, and W. P. Kegelmeyer, *SMOTE: Synthetic Minority Over-sampling Technique*, jair, vol. 16, pp. 321–357, Jun. 2002, doi: `10.1613/jair.953`.

3. *Live Site Incident escalation forecast* (2023), `https://medium.com/data-science-at-microsoft/live-site-incident-escalation-forecast-566763a2178`.

4. H. Han, W.-Y. Wang, and B.-H. Mao, *Borderline-SMOTE: A New Over-Sampling Method in Imbalanced Data Sets Learning*, in Advances in Intelligent Computing, D.-S. Huang, X.-P. Zhang, and G.-B. Huang, Eds., in Lecture Notes in Computer Science, vol. 3644. Berlin, Heidelberg: Springer Berlin Heidelberg, 2005, pp. 878–887. doi: `10.1007/11538059_91`.

5. P. Meiyappan and M. Bales, *Position Paper: Reducing Amazon's packaging waste using multimodal deep learning*, (2021), article: `https://www.amazon.science/latest-news/deep-learning-machine-learning-computer-vision-applications-reducing-amazon-package-waste`, paper: `https://www.amazon.science/publications/position-paper-reducing-amazons-packaging-wasteusing-multimodal-deep-learning`.

6. Haibo He, Yang Bai, E. A. Garcia, and Shutao Li, *ADASYN: Adaptive synthetic sampling approach for imbalanced learning*, in 2008 IEEE International Joint Conference on Neural Networks (IEEE World Congress on Computational Intelligence), Hong Kong, China: IEEE, Jun. 2008, pp. 1322–1328. doi: `10.1109/IJCNN.2008.4633969`.

7. Y. Elor and H. Averbuch-Elor, *To SMOTE, or not to SMOTE?*, arXiv, May 11, 2022. Accessed: Feb. 19, 2023. [Online]. Available at `http://arxiv.org/abs/2201.08528`.

3
Undersampling Methods

Sometimes, you have so much data that adding more data by oversampling only makes things worse. Don't worry, as we have a strategy for those situations as well. It's called undersampling, or downsampling. In this chapter, you will learn about the concept of undersampling, including when to use it and the various techniques to perform it. You will also see how to use these techniques via the `imbalanced-learn` library APIs and compare their performance with some classical machine learning models.

In this chapter, we will cover the following topics:

- Introducing undersampling
- When to avoid undersampling in the majority class
- Removing examples uniformly
- Strategies for removing noisy observations
- Strategies for removing easy observations

By the end of this chapter, you'll have mastered various undersampling techniques for imbalanced datasets and will be able to confidently apply them with the `imbalanced-learn` library to build better machine learning models.

Technical requirements

This chapter will make use of common libraries such as `matplotlib`, `seaborn`, `pandas`, `numpy`, `scikit-learn`, and `imbalanced-learn`. The code and notebooks for this chapter can be found on GitHub at `https://github.com/PacktPublishing/Machine-Learning-for-Imbalanced-Data/tree/master/chapter03`. To run the notebook, there are two options: you can click the **Open in Colab** icon at the top of the chapter's notebook, or you can launch it directly from `https://colab.research.google.com` using the GitHub URL of the notebook.

Introducing undersampling

Two households, both alike in dignity,

In fair Verona, where we lay our scene,

From ancient grudge break to new mutiny,

Where civil blood makes civil hands unclean.

– Opening lines of *Romeo and Juliet*, by Shakespeare

Let's look at a scenario inspired by Shakespeare's play *Romeo and Juliet*. Imagine a town with two warring communities (viz., the Montagues and Capulets). They have been enemies for generations. The Montagues are in the minority and the Capulets are in the majority in the town. The Montagues are super rich and powerful. The Capulets are not that well off. This creates a complex situation in the town. There are regular riots in the town because of this rivalry. One day, the Montagues win the king's favor and conspire to eliminate some Capulets to bring their numbers down. The idea is that if fewer Capulets are in the town, the Montagues will no longer be in the minority. The king agrees to the plan as he hopes for peace after its execution. We will use this story in this chapter to illustrate various undersampling algorithms.

Sometimes, it is not sufficient to oversample the minority class. With oversampling, you can run into problems such as overfitting and longer training time. To solve these problems and to approach the issue of class imbalance differently, people have thought of the opposite of oversampling—that is, **undersampling**. This is also often referred to in the literature as **downsampling** or **negative downsampling** to denote that the negative class (that is, the majority class) is being undersampled.

Undersampling techniques reduce the number of samples in the majority class(es). This method has two obvious advantages over oversampling:

- **The data size remains in check**: Even if data imbalance is not a concern, dealing with massive datasets—ranging from terabytes to petabytes—often necessitates data reduction for practical training. The sheer volume can make training impractical both in terms of time and computational costs. Cloud providers such as Amazon Web Services, Microsoft Azure, and Google Cloud charge for compute units in addition to storage, making large-scale training expensive. Given that you're likely to use only a fraction of the available training data anyway, it's crucial to be strategic about which data to retain and which to discard. Undersampling becomes not just a method for balancing classes but also a cost-effective strategy for efficient training, potentially reducing training time from days to hours.

- **There is a smaller chance of overfitting**: By using undersampling techniques, the number of majority class instances can be reduced, allowing the model to focus more on the minority class instances. This, in turn, improves the model's ability to generalize across both classes. As a result, the model becomes less likely to overfit to the majority class and is better equipped to handle new, unseen data, thus reducing the likelihood of overfitting. We are going to discuss the various undersampling methods in this chapter.

Figure 3.1 shows the general idea behind undersampling graphically.

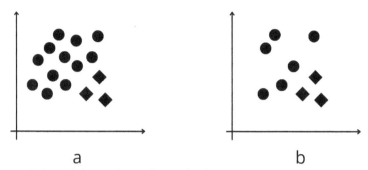

a) Imbalanced data with two classes, b) The same data after undersampling

Figure 3.1 – General idea behind undersampling showing (a) imbalanced
data with two classes and (b) data after undersampling

In *Figure 3.1(a)*, we show the original data containing many data points from the circle class. In *Figure 3.1(b)*, we show the resampled data after removing some data points from the circle class.

When to avoid undersampling the majority class

Undersampling is not a panacea and may not always work. It depends on the dataset and model under consideration:

- **Too little training data for all the classes**: If the dataset is already small, undersampling the majority class can lead to a significant loss of information. In such cases, it is advisable to try gathering more data or exploring other techniques, such as oversampling the minority class to balance the class distribution.

- **Majority class equally important or more important than minority class**: In specific scenarios, such as the spam filtering example mentioned in *Chapter 1, Introduction to Data Imbalance in Machine Learning*, it is crucial to maintain high accuracy in identifying the majority class instances. In such situations, undersampling the majority class might reduce the model's ability to accurately classify majority class instances, leading to a higher false positive rate. Instead, alternative methods, such as cost-sensitive learning or adjusting the decision threshold (both of these are discussed in *Chapter 5, Cost-Sensitive Learning*), can be considered.

- **When undersampling harms model performance or causes overfitting of the model**: Undersampling the majority class might decrease overall model performance, as it discards potentially valuable information. Some of the undersampling methods discard the examples near the decision boundary, which can also alter the decision boundary. Also, by reducing the size of the majority class, undersampling can cause underfitting, where the model becomes too simple to capture the underlying trends in the limited training data and performs poorly on new, unseen data. There is some risk of overfitting as well when using undersampling techniques if the model memorizes the reduced dataset. In such cases, exploring other techniques such as ensemble methods (*Chapter 4, Ensemble Methods*), hybrid methods that combine oversampling and undersampling (discussed toward the end of this chapter), or using different algorithms less prone to overfitting might be better.

🚀 **Undersampling techniques in production at Meta, Microsoft, and Uber**

The main challenge in tasks such as ad click prediction is handling massive and imbalanced datasets. For instance, a single day of Facebook ads can contain hundreds of millions of instances, with an average **ClickThrough Rate** (**CTR**) of just 0.1%. To address this, Meta employs two specialized techniques, as detailed in the paper *Practical Lessons from Predicting Clicks on Ads at Facebook* [1]. The first is uniform subsampling, which uniformly reduces the training data volume and has shown that using just 10% of the data results in only a 1% reduction in model performance. The second is negative downsampling, which specifically targets negative ("no-click") examples and uses an optimal downsampling rate of 0.025.

Similarly, Microsoft and Uber have very similar approaches to tackling these challenges. To estimate the CTR of sponsored ads on Bing search [2], Microsoft uses a 50% negative downsampling rate for non-click cases, effectively halving the training time while maintaining similar performance metrics. Uber Eats also employs negative downsampling to reduce the training data in order to train models that predict whether to send push notifications to customers about new restaurants [3]. In addition, they remove the least important features when building the final version of the model.

Let's look at one of the ways of classifying undersampling methods next.

Fixed versus cleaning undersampling

Undersampling methods can be divided into two categories based on how data points get removed from the majority class. These categories are fixed methods and cleaning methods.

In **fixed methods**, the number of examples in the majority class is reduced to a fixed number. Usually, we reduce the number of majority class samples to the size of the minority class. For example, if there are 100 million samples in the majority class and 10 million samples in the minority class, you will be left with only 10 million samples of both classes after applying the fixed method. Some such methods are random undersampling and instance hardness-based undersampling.

In **cleaning methods**, the number of samples of the majority class is reduced based on some pre-determined criteria, independent of the absolute number of examples. Once this criterion is met, the algorithm doesn't care about the size of the majority or minority class.

Table 3.1 summarizes the key differences between the two methods in a tabular format:

	Fixed undersampling methods	**Cleaning undersampling methods**
Key idea	Selects a specific number of majority class instances to remove	Identifies and removes noisy, redundant, or misclassified majority class instances aiming to improve decision boundaries between classes
Relationship between instances	Doesn't consider relationships between instances	Evaluates relationships between instances
Performance and ease of implementation	Faster and easier to implement	Sometimes, may have a better model performance and generalization than fixed undersampling methods
Examples	Random undersampling	Tomek links
	Instance hardness-based undersampling	Neighborhood cleaning rule

Table 3.1 – Fixed versus cleaning undersampling methods

Let's create an imbalanced dataset using the `make_classification` API from `sklearn`. We will apply various undersampling techniques throughout this chapter to balance this dataset:

```
from collections import Counter
from sklearn.datasets import make_classification
X, y = make_classification(n_samples=10000, n_features=2,
    n_redundant=0, n_classes=2, flip_y=0,
    n_clusters_per_class=2, class_sep=0.79,
    weights=[0.99], random_state=81)
```

Figure 3.2 shows what the dataset looks like on a 2D plot. For the complete notebook code, please refer to the GitHub repository of this chapter.

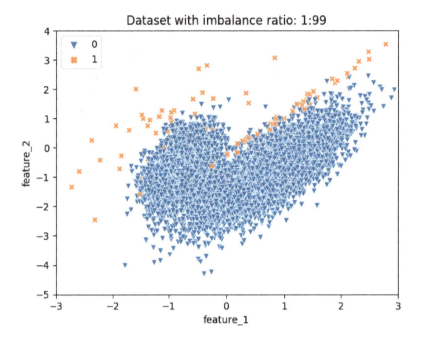

Figure 3.2 – Plotting a dataset with an imbalance ratio of 1:99

Model calibration and threshold adjustment

After applying undersampling techniques, you may want to recalibrate the model's probability scores. Why? As undersampling alters the original distribution of the classes, the model's confidence estimates are biased [4] and may no longer accurately reflect the true likelihood of each class in the real-world scenario. Failing to recalibrate can lead to misleading or suboptimal decision-making when the model is deployed. Therefore, recalibrating the model's probability scores ensures that the model not only classifies instances correctly but also estimates the probabilities in a manner that is consistent with the actual class distribution, enhancing its reliability. For a deeper understanding of this process, especially how to recalibrate model scores to account for the effects of downsampling, please refer to *Chapter 10, Model Calibration*.

In the context of imbalanced datasets, threshold adjustment techniques can be a critical complement to undersampling methods. Whether or not we end up applying any sampling techniques, adjusting the threshold to determine the correct class label can be crucial for correctly interpreting the model's performance. For a more in-depth understanding of various threshold adjustment techniques, you can refer to *Chapter 5, Cost-Sensitive Learning*.

Undersampling approaches

Let's look at a second way to categorize undersampling algorithms. There are a few ways the king can eliminate some Capulets:

- He can eliminate the Capulets uniformly from the whole town, thereby removing a few Capulets from all areas of the town

- Alternatively, the king can remove the Capulets who live near the houses of the Montagues

- Lastly, he can remove the Capulets who live far away from the houses of the Montagues

These are the three major approaches used in undersampling techniques. We either remove the majority samples uniformly, remove the majority samples near the minority samples, or remove the majority samples far from the minority samples. We can also combine the last two approaches by removing some nearby and some far away samples. The following diagram gives the classification of these methods:

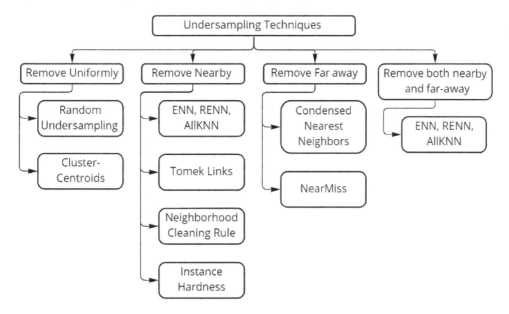

Figure 3.3 – Categorization of undersampling techniques

The following figure illustrates the difference between the two criteria. In *Figure 3.4(a)*, we show the original dataset. In *Figure 3.4(b)*, we show the same dataset after removing the examples close to the decision boundary. Notice how examples closer to the class boundary are removed.

Majority class examples far from the minority class may not effectively help models establish a decision boundary. Hence, such majority class examples away from the decision boundary can be removed. In *Figure 3.4(c)*, we show the dataset after removing examples far away from the boundary. The examples far from the decision boundary can be considered easy-to-classify examples.

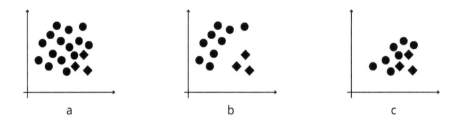

a) Imbalanced data with two classes, b) After removing noisy samples, c) After removing samples away from the boundary

Figure 3.4 – Difference between two general approaches to undersampling

Having discussed various ways to classify the various undersampling techniques, let's now look at them in more detail.

Removing examples uniformly

There are two major ways of removing the majority class examples uniformly from the data. The first way is to remove the examples randomly, and the other way involves using clustering techniques. Let's discuss both of these methods in detail.

Random UnderSampling

The first technique the king might think of is to pick Capulets randomly and remove them from the town. This is a naïve approach. It might work, and the king might be able to bring peace to the town. But the king might cause unforeseen damage by picking up some influential Capulets. However, it is an excellent place to start our discussion. This technique can be considered a close cousin of random oversampling. In **Random UnderSampling** (**RUS**), as the name suggests, we randomly extract observations from the majority class until the classes are balanced. This technique inevitably leads to data loss, might harm the underlying structure of the data, and thus performs poorly sometimes.

Figure 3.5 – Comic explaining the main idea behind the RUS method

The following is the code sample for using RUS:

```
from imblearn.under_sampling import RandomUnderSampler

rus = RandomUnderSampler(sampling_strategy=1.0, random_state=42)
X_res, y_res = rus.fit_resample(X, y)
```

The `sampling_strategy` value can be used to specify the desired ratio of minority and majority classes, the default being that they will be made equal in number. *Figure 3.6* shows the application of the `RandomUnderSampler` technique, where the right plot shows that most of the negative class samples got dropped:

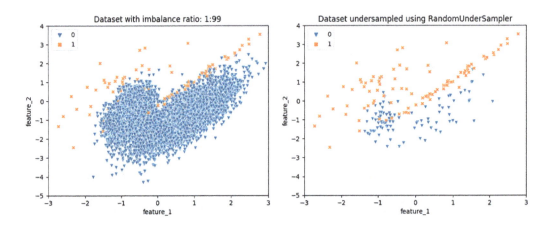

Figure 3.6 – Plotting datasets before and after undersampling using RandomUnderSampler

Next, we transition to a smarter technique that forms groups among majority class examples.

ClusterCentroids

The second technique the king might follow to carry out uniform undersampling is to divide the Capulet population into groups based on location. Then, keep one Capulet from each group and remove other Capulets from the group. This method of undersampling is called the **ClusterCentroids** method. If there are N items in the minority class, we create N clusters from the points of the majority class. For example, this can be done using the K-means algorithm. K-means is a clustering algorithm that groups nearby points into different clusters and assigns centroids to each group.

Figure 3.7 – Comic illustrating the main idea behind the ClusterCentroids method

In the ClusterCentroids technique, we first apply the K-means algorithm to all of the majority class data. Then, for each cluster, we keep the centroid and remove all other examples within that cluster. It's worth noting that the centroid might not even be a part of the original data, which is an important aspect of this method.

In *Figure 3.8*, we show the working of ClusterCentroids. In *Figure 3.8(a)*, we start with an imbalanced dataset. In *Figure 3.8(b)*, we calculate the centroids for the three clusters. These centroids are shown as stars in the diagram. Finally, we remove all majority class samples except the centroids from the dataset in *Figure 3.8(c)*.

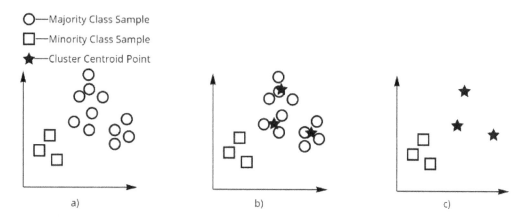

Figure 3.8 – Illustrating how the ClusterCentroids method works

Here is the code for using ClusterCentroids:

```
from imblearn.under_sampling import ClusterCentroids
cc = ClusterCentroids(random_state=42)
X_res, y_res = cc.fit_resample(X,y)
print('Resampled dataset shape %s' % Counter(y_res))
```

The following is the output:

```
Resampled dataset shape Counter({0: 100, 1: 100})
```

Figure 3.9 shows the application of the ClusterCentroids technique, where the right plot shows that most of the negative class samples got dropped.

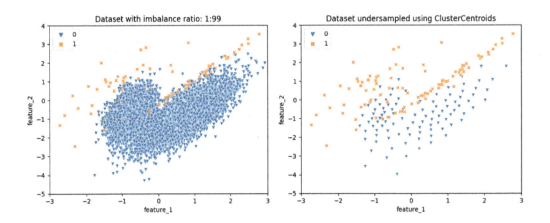

Figure 3.9 – Plotting datasets before and after undersampling using ClusterCentroids

One thing to note is that ClusterCentroids can be computationally expensive because it uses the K-means algorithm by default, which can be slow. We recommend exploring various parameters in the ClusterCentroids method, such as the estimator, which specifies the clustering method to be used. For example, K-means can be replaced with MiniBatchKMeans, a faster variant of the K-means clustering algorithm.

In the following section, we will attempt to eliminate the majority class examples in a more strategic manner.

Strategies for removing noisy observations

The king might decide to look at the friendships and locations of the citizens before removing anyone. The king might decide to remove the Capulets who are rich and live near the Montagues. This could bring peace to the city by separating the feuding clans. Let's look at some strategies to do that with our data.

ENN, RENN, and AllKNN

The king can remove the Capulets based on their neighbors. For example, if one or more of the three closest neighbors of a Capulet is a Montague, the king can remove the Capulet. This technique is called **Edited Nearest Neighbors** (**ENN**) [5]. ENN removes the examples near the decision boundary to increase the separation between classes. We fit a KNN to the whole dataset and remove the examples whose neighbors don't belong to the same class. The imbalanced-learn library gives us options to decide which classes we would like to resample and what kind of class arrangement the neighbors of the sample should have.

There are two different criteria that we can follow for excluding the samples:

- We can choose to exclude samples whose one or more neighbors are not from the same class as themselves

- We can decide to exclude samples whose majority of neighbors are not from the same class as themselves

In *Figure 3.10*, we show the working of the ENN algorithm. Here, we remove the majority samples that have one or more minority neighbors. In *Figure 3.10(a)*, we show the original dataset. In *Figure 3.10(b)*, we highlight the majority class samples that have one or more minority class nearest neighbors. The highlighted majority class samples are shown as solid boxes, and their neighbors are shown by creating curves around them.

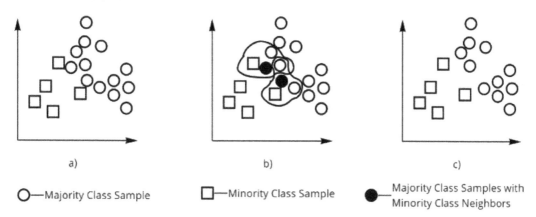

Figure 3.10 – Illustrating how the ENN method works

Here is the code for using ENN:

```
from imblearn.under_sampling import EditedNearestNeighbours
enn = EditedNearestNeighbours(
    sampling_strategy='auto', n_neighbors=200, kind_sel='all')
X_res, y_res = enn.fit_resample(X, y)
print('Resampled dataset shape %s' % Counter(y_res))
```

The following is the output:

```
Resampled dataset shape Counter({0: 7852, 1: 100})
```

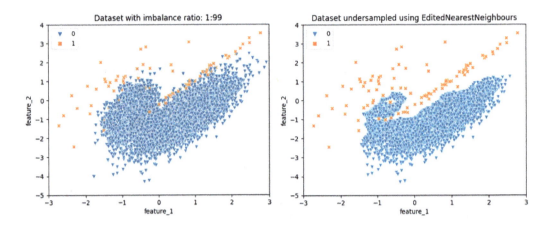

Figure 3.11 – Plotting datasets before and after undersampling using ENN

Here, n_neighbors is the size of the neighborhood to consider to compute the nearest neighbors.

There are two variants of ENN that we won't dive into, but you can explore them if you are interested: **RENN** (imblearn.under_sampling.RepeatedEditedNearestNeighbours) and **AllKNN** (imblearn.under_sampling.AllKNN). In RENN [6], we repeat the process followed in ENN until there are no more examples that can be removed or the maximum number of cycle counts has been reached. This algorithm also removes the noisy data. It is stronger in removing the boundary examples as the algorithm is repeated several times (*Figure 3.12*).

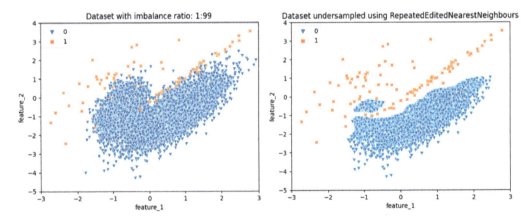

Figure 3.12 – Plotting datasets before and after undersampling using RENN

In the **AllKNN** method [6], we repeat **ENN** but with the number of neighbors going from 1 to K.

Tomek links

In 1976, Ivan Tomek proposed the idea of **Tomek links** [7]. Two examples are said to form Tomek links if they belong to two different classes, and there is no third point with a shorter distance to them than the distance between the two points. The intuition behind Tomek links is that "*if two points are from different classes, they should not be nearest to each other.*" These points are part of the noise, and we can eliminate the majority member or both points to reduce noise. This is as if the king decides to remove the Capulets whose best friends are Montagues.

We can use the `TomekLinks` API as follows:

```
from imblearn.under_sampling import TomekLinks
tklinks = TomekLinks(sampling_strategy='auto')
X_res, y_res = tklinks.fit_resample(X, y)
print('Resampled dataset shape %s' % Counter(y_res))
```

The following is the output:

```
Resampled dataset shape Counter({0: 9875, 1: 100})
```

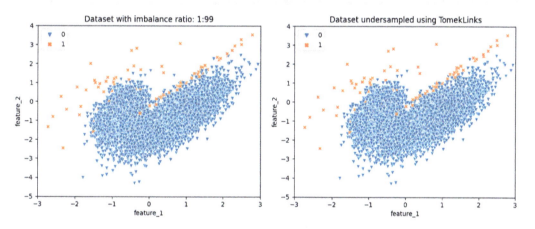

Figure 3.13 – Plotting datasets before and after undersampling using TomekLinks

Figure 3.14 shows the working of the Tomek links algorithm. In *Figure 3.14(a)*, we have the original dataset. In *Figure 3.14(b)*, we find and highlight the Tomek links. Notice that the points in these links are close to each other. In *Figure 3.14(c)*, we show the dataset after removing the majority class samples (depicted as circles) that belong to the Tomek links. Notice the two circles present in part *(b)* but missing in part *(c)*. Similarly, we show the dataset after removing all the points in Tomek links in part *(d)* of the diagram.

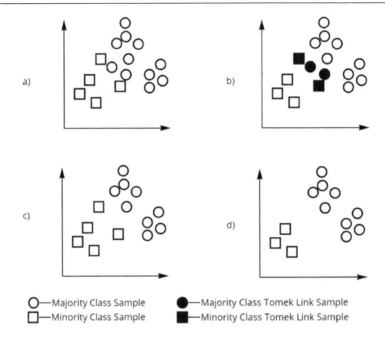

Figure 3.14 – Illustrating how the TomekLinks algorithm works

Tomek links is a resource-intensive method due to its requirement of calculating pairwise distances between all examples. As stated in *A Study of the Behavior of Several Methods for Balancing Machine Learning Training Data* [8], performing this process on a reduced dataset would be more computationally efficient when dealing with large amounts of data.

In the next method, we will try to remove majority class examples from the perspective of minority class examples. Can we remove the nearest neighbors of the minority class that belong to the majority class?

Neighborhood Cleaning Rule

Apart from removing the Capulets whose one or more nearest neighbors are Montagues, the king might decide to look at the nearest neighbors of Montagues and remove the Capulets who might come up as one of the nearest neighbors for a Montague. In the **Neighborhood Cleaning Rule (NCR)** [9], we apply an ENN algorithm, train a KNN on the remaining data, and then remove all the majority class samples that are the nearest neighbors of a minority sample.

Here is the code for using `NeighourhoodCleaningRule`:

```
from imblearn.under_sampling import NeighbourhoodCleaningRule
ncr = NeighbourhoodCleaningRule(
    sampling_strategy='auto', n_neighbors=200, threshold_cleaning=0.5)
X_res, y_res = ncr.fit_resample(X, y)
print('Resampled dataset shape %s' % Counter(y_res))
```

The following is the output:

```
Resampled dataset shape Counter({0: 6710, 1: 100})
```

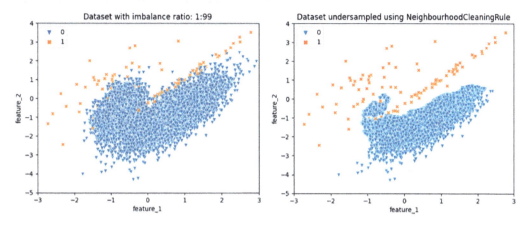

Figure 3.15 – Plotting datasets before and after undersampling using NCR

Instance hardness threshold

The king might ask a minister, "*Which Capulets have mixed well with Montagues?*" The minister, based on their knowledge of the town, will give a list of those Capulets. Then, the king will remove the Capulets whose names are on the list. This method of using another model to identify noisy samples is known as the **instance hardness threshold**. In this method, we train a classification model on the data, such as a decision tree, random forest, or linear SVM.

In addition to predicting the class of an instance, these classifiers can return their class probabilities. Class probabilities show the confidence the model has in classifying the instances. With the instance hardness threshold method [10], we remove the majority class samples that received low probability estimates (referred to as the "hard instances"). These instances are considered "hard to classify" due to class overlap, a principal contributor to instance hardness.

The `imbalanced-learn` library provides an API for utilizing `InstanceHardnessThreshold`, where we can specify the estimator used to estimate the hardness of the examples. In this case, we use `LogisticRegression` as the estimator:

```
from imblearn.under_sampling import InstanceHardnessThreshold
nm = InstanceHardnessThreshold(
    sampling_strategy='auto', estimator=LogisticRegression())
X_res, y_res = nm.fit_resample(X, y)
print('Resampled dataset shape %s' % Counter(y_res))
```

The following is the output:

```
Resampled dataset shape Counter({0: 100, 1: 100})
```

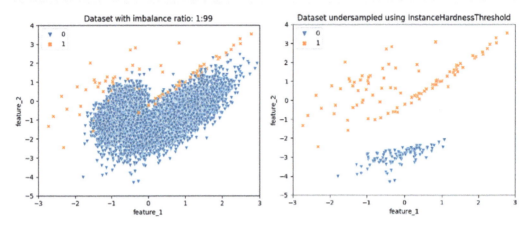

Figure 3.16 – Plotting datasets before and after undersampling using InstanceHardnessThreshold

Since classification models need to draw a decision boundary between the majority and minority classes, the majority class examples that are too far away from the minority class examples may not help the model decide this decision boundary. Considering this, we will look at methods in the next section that will remove such easy majority class examples.

Strategies for removing easy observations

The reverse of the strategy to remove the rich and famous Capulets is to remove the poor and weak Capulets. This section will discuss the techniques for **removing the majority samples far away from the minority samples**. Instead of removing the samples from the boundary between the two classes, we use them for training a model. This way, we can train a model to better discriminate between the classes. However, one downside is that these algorithms risk retaining noisy data points, which could then be used to train the model, potentially introducing noise into the predictive system.

Condensed Nearest Neighbors

Condensed Nearest Neighbors (CNNeighbors) [11] is an algorithm that works as follows:

1. We add all minority samples to a set and one randomly selected majority sample. Let's call this set C.

2. We train a KNN model with $k = 1$ on set C.

3. Now, we repeat the following four steps for each of the remaining majority samples:

I.   We consider one majority sample; let's call it e.

II.   We try to predict the class of e using KNN.

III. If the predicted class matches the original class, we remove the sample. The intuition is that there is little to learn from e as even a *1-NN* classifier can learn it.

IV.   Otherwise, we add the sample to our set C and train the *1-NN* on C again.

This method removes the easy-to-classify samples from the majority class.

The code to use `CondensedNearestNeighbour` is as follows:

```
from imblearn.under_sampling import CondensedNearestNeighbour
cnn = CondensedNearestNeighbour(random_state=42)
X_res, y_res = cnn.fit_resample(X, y)
print('Resampled dataset shape %s' % Counter(y_res))
```

The following is the output:

```
Resampled dataset shape Counter({0: 198, 1: 100})
```

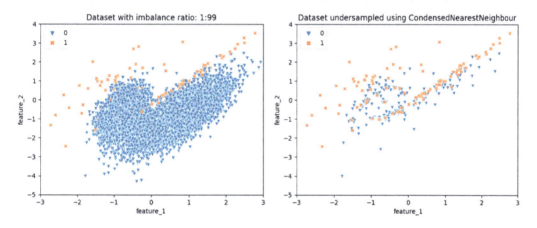

Figure 3.17 – Plotting datasets before and after undersampling using CNNeighbors

However, the CNNeighbors method can be computationally expensive, as it evaluates each majority class example using the KNN algorithm. This makes the CNNeighbors method unsuitable for big data applications.

One-sided selection

The king might decide to remove some rich and many poor Capulets. This way, only the middle-class Capulets will stay in the town. In one-sided selection [12], we do just that. This method is a combination of CNNeighbors and Tomek links. We first resample using a CNNeighbors. Then, we remove the Tomek links from the resampled data. It reduces both noisy and easy-to-identify samples.

Here is the code for `OneSidedSelection`. When we don't provide the `n_neighbors` parameter, the default value of 1 is taken:

```
from imblearn.under_sampling import OneSidedSelection
oss = OneSidedSelection(random_state=0, n_seeds_S=10)
X_res, y_res = oss.fit_resample(X, y)
print('Resampled dataset shape %s' % Counter(y_res))
```

The following is the output:

```
Resampled dataset shape Counter({0: 4276, 1: 100})
```

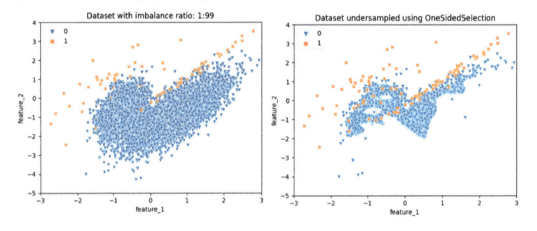

Figure 3.18 – Plotting datasets before and after undersampling using OneSidedSelection

Here, `n_seeds_S` is the number of minority class samples used as seeds in the method, and it can significantly impact the method's performance. It is advisable to tune this parameter.

Combining undersampling and oversampling

You might wonder whether we can combine undersampling techniques with oversampling techniques to produce even better results. The answer is yes. Oversampling methods increase the number of samples of the minority class but also usually increase the noise in the data. Some undersampling techniques can help us remove the noise, for example, ENN, Tomek links, NCR, and instance hardness. We can combine these methods with SMOTE to produce good results. The combination of SMOTE with

ENN [13] and Tomek links [14] has been well researched. Also, the `imbalanced-learn` library supports both of them: `SMOTEENN` and `SMOTETomek`.

Model performance comparison

Let's explore how some popular models perform using the various undersampling techniques we've discussed. We use two datasets for this comparison: one synthetic dataset and one real-world dataset called `thyroid_sick` from the `imbalanced-learn` library. We'll evaluate the performance of 11 different undersampling techniques against a baseline of no sampling, using both logistic regression and random forest models. *Figures 3.19* to *3.22* show the average precision values for models trained using these various methods.

You can find the notebook in the GitHub repository of the chapter.

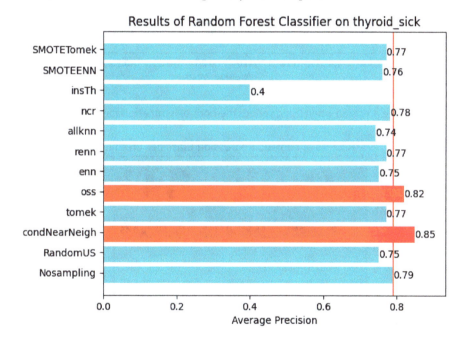

Figure 3.19 – Average precision when using various methods on
the thyroid_sick dataset using random forest

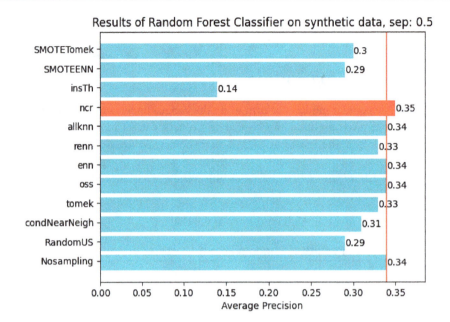

Figure 3.20 – Average precision when using various methods on synthetic data using random forest

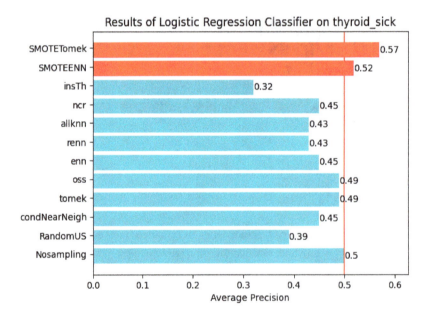

Figure 3.21 – Average precision when using various methods on
the thyroid_sick dataset using logistic regression

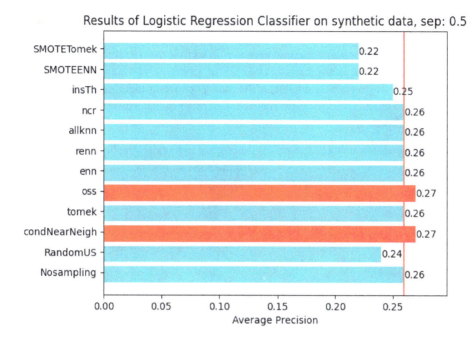

Figure 3.22 – Average precision when using various methods on synthetic data using logistic regression

Here are some more observations:

- The effectiveness of undersampling techniques can vary significantly depending on the dataset and its characteristics

- No single technique dominates across all datasets, emphasizing the need for empirical testing to choose the best method for your specific problem

So, which method will work best for your data? There is no easy answer to this question. The key here is to develop an intuition about the inner workings of these methods and have a pipeline that can help you test different techniques.

However, certain techniques can be time-consuming. In our testing on a dataset with a million examples, methods such as `CondensedNearestNeighbor`, `ClusterCentroids`, and `ALLKNN` took longer than others. If you're dealing with large amounts of data, planning to scale in the future, or are pressed for time, you may want to avoid these methods or tune their parameters. Techniques such as `RandomUnderSampler` and `InstanceHardnessThreshold` are more suitable for rapid iterative development.

That brings us to the end of this chapter.

Summary

In this chapter, we discussed undersampling, an approach to address the class imbalance in datasets by reducing the number of samples in the majority class. We reviewed the advantages of undersampling, such as keeping the data size in check and reducing the chances of overfitting. Undersampling methods can be categorized into fixed methods, which reduce the number of majority class samples to a fixed size, and cleaning methods, which reduce majority class samples based on predetermined criteria.

We went over various undersampling techniques, including random undersampling, instance hardness-based undersampling, ClusterCentroids, ENN, Tomek links, NCR, instance hardness, CNNeighbors, one-sided selection, and combinations of undersampling and oversampling techniques, such as SMOTEENN and SMOTETomek.

We concluded with a performance comparison of various undersampling techniques from the imbalanced-learn library on logistic regression and random forest models, using a few datasets, and benchmarked their performance and effectiveness.

Once you identify that your dataset is imbalanced and could potentially benefit from applying undersampling techniques, go ahead and experiment with the various methods discussed in this chapter. Evaluate their effectiveness using the appropriate metrics, such as PR-AUC, to find the most suitable approach for improving your model's performance.

In the next chapter, we will go over various ensemble-based techniques.

Exercises

1. Explore the various undersampling APIs available from the imbalanced-learn library at https://imbalanced-learn.org/stable/references/under_sampling.html.

2. Explore the NearMiss undersampling technique, available through the imblearn.under_sampling.NearMiss API. Which class of methods does it belong to? Apply the NearMiss method to the dataset that we used in the chapter.

3. Try all the undersampling methods discussed in this chapter on the us_crime dataset from UCI. You can find this dataset in the fetch_datasets API of the imbalanced-learn library. Find the undersampling method with the highest f1-score metric for LogisticRegression and XGBoost models.

4. Can you identify an undersampling method of your own? (Hint: think about combining the various approaches to undersampling in new ways.)

References

1. X. He et al., *"Practical Lessons from Predicting Clicks on Ads at Facebook,"* in Proceedings of the Eighth International Workshop on Data Mining for Online Advertising, New York NY USA: ACM, Aug. 2014, pp. 1–9. doi: `10.1145/2648584.2648589`.

2. X. Ling, W. Deng, C. Gu, H. Zhou, C. Li, and F. Sun, *"Model Ensemble for Click Prediction in Bing Search Ads,"* in Proceedings of the 26th International Conference on World Wide Web Companion - WWW '17 Companion, Perth, Australia: ACM Press, 2017, pp. 689–698. doi: `10.1145/3041021.3054192`.

3. *How Uber Optimizes the Timing of Push Notifications using ML and Linear Programming*: `https://www.uber.com/blog/how-uber-optimizes-push-notifications-using-ml/`.

4. A. D. Pozzolo, O. Caelen, R. A. Johnson, and G. Bontempi, *"Calibrating Probability with Undersampling for Unbalanced Classification,"* in 2015 IEEE Symposium Series on Computational Intelligence, Cape Town, South Africa: IEEE, Dec. 2015, pp. 159–166. doi: `10.1109/SSCI.2015.33`.

5. (Introducing the ENN method) D. L. Wilson, *"Asymptotic Properties of Nearest Neighbor Rules Using Edited Data,"* IEEE Trans. Syst., Man, Cybern., vol. SMC-2, no. 3, pp. 408–421, Jul. 1972, doi: `10.1109/TSMC.1972.4309137`.

6. (Introducing the RENN and AllKNN methods) *"An Experiment with the Edited Nearest-Neighbor Rule,"* IEEE Trans. Syst., Man, Cybern., vol. SMC-6, no. 6, pp. 448–452, Jun. 1976, doi: `10.1109/TSMC.1976.4309523`.

7. I. Tomek, *"Two Modifications of CNN,"* IEEE Trans. Syst., Man, Cybern., vol. SMC-6, no. 11, pp. 769–772, Nov. 1976, doi: `10.1109/TSMC.1976.4309452`.

8. G. E. A. P. A. Batista, R. C. Prati, and M. C. Monard, *"A study of the behavior of several methods for balancing machine learning training data,"* SIGKDD Explor. Newsl., vol. 6, no. 1, pp. 20–29, Jun. 2004, doi: `10.1145/1007730.1007735`.

9. (Introducing the neighborhood cleaning rule method) J. Laurikkala, *"Improving Identification of Difficult Small Classes by Balancing Class Distribution,"* in Artificial Intelligence in Medicine, S. Quaglini, P. Barahona, and S. Andreassen, Eds., in Lecture Notes in Computer Science, vol. 2101. Berlin, Heidelberg: Springer Berlin Heidelberg, 2001, pp. 63–66. doi: `10.1007/3-540-48229-6_9`.

10. (Introducing the instance hardness threshold technique) M. R. Smith, T. Martinez, and C. Giraud-Carrier, *"An instance level analysis of data complexity,"* Mach Learn, vol. 95, no. 2, pp. 225–256, May 2014, doi: `10.1007/s10994-013-5422-z`.

11. P. Hart, *"The condensed nearest neighbor rule (corresp.),"* IEEE transactions on information theory, vol. 14, no. 3, pp. 515–516, 1968, `https://citeseerx.ist.psu.edu/document?repid=rep1&type=pdf&doi=7c3771fd6829630cf450af853df728ecd8da4ab2`.

12. (Introducing the one-sided selection method) M. Kubat and S. Matwin, *"Addressing The Curse Of Imbalanced Training Sets: One-sided Selection"*.

13. (Application of SMOTEENN and SMOTETomek methods) Gustavo EAPA Batista, Ronaldo C Prati, and Maria Carolina Monard. *A study of the behavior of several methods for balancing machine learning training data.* ACM SIGKDD explorations newsletter, 6(1):20–29, 2004.

14. (Application of the SMOTETomek method) Gustavo EAPA Batista, Ana LC Bazzan, and Maria Carolina Monard. *Balancing training data for automated annotation of keywords: a case study.* In WOB, 10–18. 2003.

4
Ensemble Methods

Think of a top executive at a major company. They don't make decisions on their own. Throughout the day, they need to make numerous critical decisions. How do they make those choices? Not alone, but by consulting their advisors.

Let's say that an executive consults five different advisors from different departments, each proposing a slightly different solution based on their expertise, skills, and domain knowledge. To make the most effective decision, the executive combines the insights and opinions of all five advisors to create a hybrid solution that incorporates the best parts of each proposal. This scenario illustrates the concept of **ensemble methods**, where multiple weak classifiers are combined to create a stronger and more accurate classifier. By combining different approaches, ensemble methods can often achieve better performance than relying on a single classifier.

We can create a strong model through ensemble methods by combining the results from multiple weak classifiers. These weak classifiers, such as simplified decision trees, neural networks, or support vector machines, perform slightly better than random guessing. In contrast, a strong model, created by ensembling these weak classifiers, performs significantly better than random guessing. The weak classifiers can be fed different sources of information. There are two general approaches for building ensembles of models: bagging and boosting.

The problem with traditional ensemble methods is that they use classifiers that assume balanced data. Thus, they may not work very well with imbalanced datasets. So, we combine the popular machine learning ensembling methods with the techniques for dealing with imbalanced data that we studied in previous chapters. We are going to discuss those combinations in this chapter.

Here are the topics that will be covered in this chapter:

- Bagging techniques for imbalanced data
- Boosting techniques for imbalanced data
- Ensemble of ensembles
- Model performance comparison

In *Figure 4.1*, we have categorized the various ensembling techniques that we will cover in this chapter:

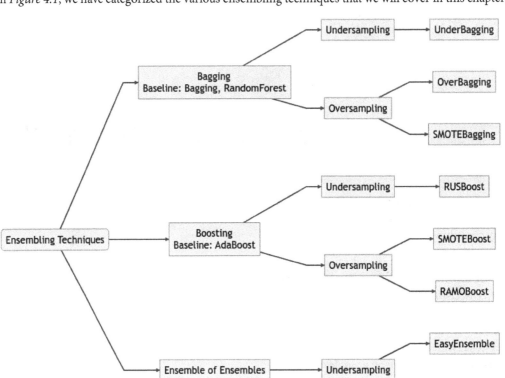

Figure 4.1 – Overview of ensembling techniques

By the end of this chapter, you will understand how to adapt ensemble models such as bagging and boosting to account for class imbalances in datasets.

Technical requirements

The Python notebooks for this chapter are available on GitHub at https://github.com/ PacktPublishing/Machine-Learning-for-Imbalanced-Data/tree/master/ chapter04. As usual, you can open the GitHub notebook using Google Colab by clicking on the **Open in Colab** icon at the top of this chapter's notebook or by launching it from https://colab. research.google.com using the GitHub URL of the notebook.

In this chapter, we will continue to use a synthetic dataset generated using the make_classification API, just as we did in the previous chapters. Toward the end of this chapter, we will test the methods we learned in this chapter on some real datasets. Our full dataset contains 90,000 examples with a 1:99 imbalance ratio. Here is what the training dataset looks like:

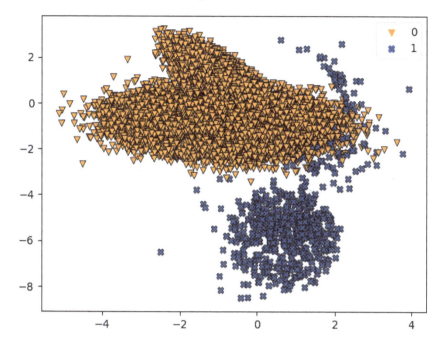

Figure 4.2 – Plot of a dataset with a 1:99 imbalance ratio

With our imbalanced dataset ready to use, let's look at the first ensembling method, called bagging.

Bagging techniques for imbalanced data

Imagine a business executive with thousands of confidential files regarding an important merger or acquisition. The analysts assigned to the case don't have enough time to review all the files. Each can randomly select some files from the set and start reviewing them. Later, they can combine their insights in a meeting to draw conclusions.

This scenario is a metaphor for a process in machine learning called bagging [1], which is short for **bootstrap aggregating**. In bagging, much like the analysts in the previous scenario, we create several subsets of the original dataset, train a weak learner on each subset, and then aggregate their predictions.

Why use weak learners instead of strong learners? The rationale applies to both bagging and boosting methods (discussed later in this chapter). There are several reasons:

- **Speed**: Weak learners are computationally efficient and inexpensive to execute.

- **Diversity**: Weak learners are more likely to make different types of errors, which is advantageous when combining their predictions. Using strong learners could result in them all making the same type of error, leading to less effective ensembles.

- **Overfitting**: As a corollary to the previous point, the diversity in errors helps reduce the risk of overfitting in the ensemble.

- **Interpretability**: While the ensemble as a whole may not be easily interpretable, its individual components – often simpler models – are easier to understand and interpret.

Now, back to bagging. The first step of the algorithm is called **bootstrapping**. In this step, we make several subsets or smaller groups of data by randomly picking items from the main data. The data is picked with the possibility of picking the same item more than once (this process is called "random sampling with replacement"), so these smaller groups may have some items in common. Then, we train our classifiers on each of these smaller groups.

The second step is called **aggregating**. The test sample is passed to each classifier at the time of prediction. After this, we take the average or majority prediction as the real answer.

As shown in *Figure 4.3*, the dataset is first sampled with replacement into three subsets. Then, separate classifiers are trained on each of the subsets. Finally, the results of the classifiers are combined at the time of prediction:

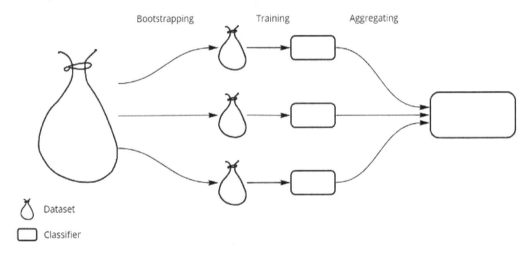

Figure 4.3 – Demonstrating how bagging works

Figure 4.4 summarizes the bagging algorithm in a pseudocode format:

Algorithm 1 Bagging Classifier Algorithm

1: **Input:** Given some training data and some classifiers
2: **Output:** An aggregated classifier
3: **for** each classifier **do**
4:     **Sample:** Perform sampling with replacement to create a subset of training data
5:     **Train:** Train current classifier on the subset from previous step
6: **end for**
7: **Combine Classifiers:** Create an aggregated classifier by taking votes from all the classifiers

---

Figure 4.4 – Bagging pseudocode

We'll train a bagging classifier model from `sklearn` on the dataset we created previously. Since it's possible to provide a base estimator to BaggingClassifier, we'll use DecisionTreeClassifier with the maximum depth of the trees being 6:

```
from sklearn.ensemble import BaggingClassifier
from sklearn.metrics import PrecisionRecallDisplay
clf = BaggingClassifier(\
    estimator=DecisionTreeClassifier(max_depth=6), random_state=0
).fit(X_train, y_train)
```

Let's plot the decision boundary:

```
plot_decision_boundary(X_train, y_train, clf, 'BaggingClassifier')
plt.show()
```

You may refer to the definition of plot_decision_boundary() in the corresponding notebook on GitHub. We use the DecisionBoundaryDisplay API from the sklearn.inspection module to plot the decision boundary.

Figure 4.5 shows the learned decision boundary on the training data:

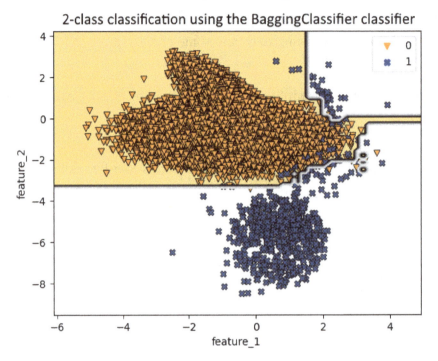

Figure 4.5 – The decision boundary of BaggingClassifier on the training data

Let's also note the baseline metric of average precision when using this model on our test set:

```
PrecisionRecallDisplay.from_estimator(
    clf, X_test, y_test, ax = plt.gca(),name = "BaggingClassifier")
```

Figure 4.6 shows the resulting PR curve:

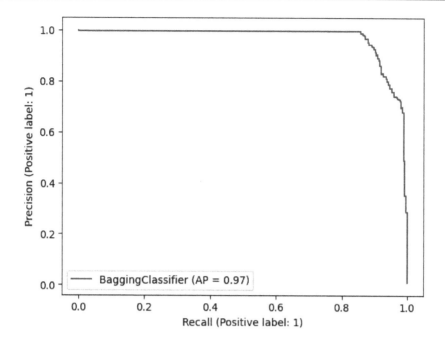

Figure 4.6 – Precision-recall curve of BaggingClassifier on the test data

Here are some other metrics:

```
Average Precision Score: 0.969
AUC-ROC Score: 0.999
F2-score: 0.891
Precision: 0.967
Recall: 0.874
```

In this chapter, we will also consider the **F2 score** (Fbeta-score with beta=2.0), which proportionally combines precision and recall, giving more weight to recall and less weight to precision.

So, what problems may we face when using BaggingClassifier on an imbalanced dataset? An obvious thing could be that when bootstrapping, some subsets on which base classifiers get trained may have very few minority class examples or none at all. This would mean that each of the individual base classifiers is going to perform poorly on the minority class, and combining their performance would still be poor.

We can combine undersampling techniques with bagging (one such method is UnderBagging) or oversampling techniques with bagging (one such method is OverBagging) to get better results. We will discuss such techniques next.

UnderBagging

The UnderBagging [2] technique uses random undersampling at the time of bootstrapping (or selection of subsets). We choose the whole set of the minority class examples for each classifier and bootstrap with replacement as many examples from the majority class as there are minority class examples. The aggregation step remains the same as in bagging. We can choose any classifier, say a decision tree, for training.

There are variants of UnderBagging where resampling with replacement of the minority class can also be applied to obtain more diverse ensembles.

The flowchart in *Figure 4.7* represents the main steps in the UnderBagging algorithm with three subsets of data. It involves creating multiple subsets of data, performing random undersampling for the majority class in each subset, training classifiers on each subset, and finally combining the predictions of the classifiers:

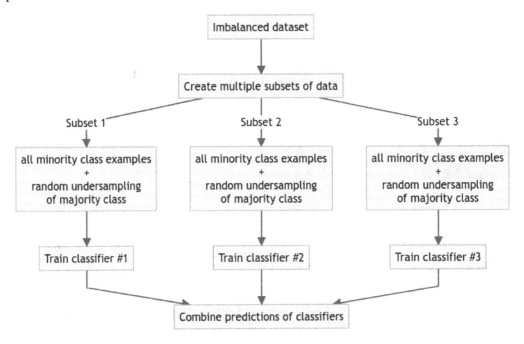

Figure 4.7 – Demonstrating how the UnderBagging algorithm works

The imbalanced-learn library provides an implementation for BalancedBaggingClassifier. By default, this classifier uses a decision tree as the base classifier and RandomUnderSampler as the sampler via the sampler parameter. *Figure 4.8* shows the decision boundary of the trained UnderBagging model:

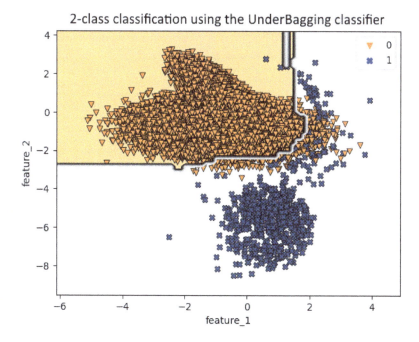

Figure 4.8 – The decision boundary of the UnderBagging classifier on the training data

🚀 **Bagging classifier in production at Microsoft**

In a real-world application at Microsoft [3], the team faced a significant challenge in forecasting Live Site Incident escalations (previously mentioned in *Chapter 2, Oversampling Methods*). The dataset was highly imbalanced, making it difficult for standard classifiers to perform well. To tackle this issue, Microsoft employed ensemble methods, specifically `BalancedBaggingClassifier` from the `imbalanced-learn` library. They used UnderBagging, where each bootstrap sample is randomly undersampled to get a balanced class distribution. As we have just discussed, UnderBagging uses all minority class samples and a random selection of majority class samples to train the model.

Bagged classification delivered the best results during their evaluation and also proved to be more consistent after they tracked it over a few months. They were able to significantly improve their forecasting accuracy for incident escalations.

OverBagging

Instead of random undersampling of the majority class samples, the minority class is oversampled (with replacement) at the time of bootstrapping. This method is called OverBagging [2]. As a variant, both minority and majority class examples can be resampled with replacements to achieve an equal number of majority and minority class examples.

The flowchart in *Figure 4.9* represents the main steps in the OverBagging algorithm with three subsets of data. It involves creating multiple subsets of data, performing random oversampling for the minority class in each subset, training classifiers on each subset, and finally combining the predictions of the classifiers:

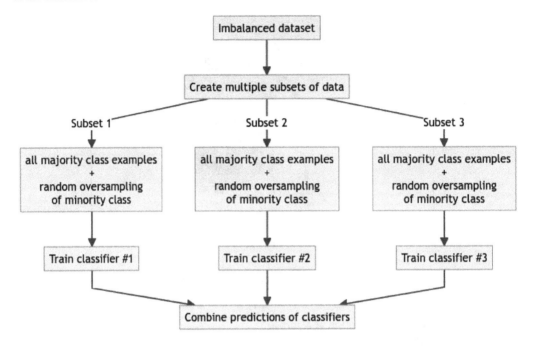

Figure 4.9 – Demonstrating how the OverBagging algorithm works

For OverBagging, we can use the same `BalancedBaggingClassifier` with `RandomOverSampler` in the `sampler` parameter.

We will see the following decision boundary:

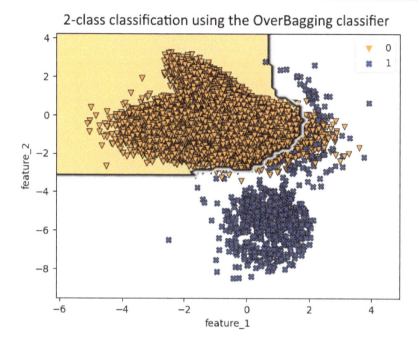

Figure 4.10 – The decision boundary of the OverBagging classifier on the training data

We will compare the performance metrics of these techniques after discussing the various bagging techniques.

SMOTEBagging

Can we use SMOTE at the time of bootstrapping instead of random oversampling of minority class examples? The answer is yes. The majority class will be bootstrapped with replacement, and the minority class will be sampled using SMOTE until a balancing ratio is reached.

The pseudocode for SMOTEBagging [2] is very similar to that for OverBagging, with the key difference being the use of the SMOTE algorithm instead of random oversampling to augment the minority class data.

Similar to OverBagging, we can implement `SMOTEBagging` using the `BalancedBagging Classifier` API with SMOTE as the `sampler` parameter.

The decision boundary is not very different from OverBagging:

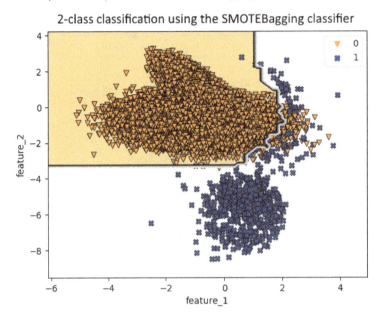

Figure 4.11 – The decision boundary of the SMOTEBagging classifier on the training data

A note about random forest and how it is related to bagging

Random forest [4] is another model that is based on the concept of bagging. The way the `RandomForestClassifier` and `BaggingClassifier` models from `sklearn` differ from each other is the fact that `RandomForestClassifier` considers a random subset of features while trying to decide the feature on which to split the nodes in the decision tree, while `BaggingClassifier` takes all the features.

Table 4.1 highlights the difference between random forest and bagging classifiers:

	RandomForestClassifier	**BaggingClassifier**
Base classifier	Decision trees	Any classifier.
Bootstrap sampling	Yes	Yes.
Take a subset of features	Yes (at each node)	No, by default. We can use the `max_features` hyperparameter to take subsets of features.
Works best with?	Any tabular data, but it shines with large feature sets	Any tabular data, but it's best when the base classifier is carefully chosen.

	RandomForestClassifier	**BaggingClassifier**
Handles missing values and outliers	Yes, inherently	Depends on the base classifier.

Table 4.1 – RandomForestClassifier versus BaggingClassifier

The `imbalanced-learn` library provides the `BalancedRandomForestClassifier` class to tackle the imbalanced datasets where each of the bootstraps is undersampled before the individual decision trees are trained. As an exercise, we encourage you to learn about `BalancedRandomForestClassifier`. See how it relates to the other techniques we just discussed. Also, try out the various sampling strategies and explore the parameters this class offers.

Comparative performance of bagging methods

Let's compare the performance of various bagging methods using the same dataset we've employed so far. We'll use the decision tree as a baseline and evaluate different techniques across several performance metrics. The highest values for each metric across all techniques are highlighted in bold:

TECHNIQUE	F2	PRECISION	RECALL	AVERAGE PRECISION	AUC-ROC
SMOTEBagging	**0.928**	0.754	0.985	0.977	**1.000**
OverBagging	0.888	0.612	**1.000**	0.976	**1.000**
UnderBagging	0.875	0.609	0.981	0.885	0.999
Bagging	0.891	0.967	0.874	0.969	**1.000**
Balanced random forest	0.756	0.387	0.993	0.909	0.999
Random forest	0.889	**0.975**	0.870	**0.979**	**1.000**
Decision tree	0.893	0.960	0.878	0.930	0.981

Table 4.2 – Performance comparison of various bagging techniques

Here are some conclusions we can draw from *Table 4.2*:

- For maximizing the F2 score, **SMOTEBagging** did the best
- For high precision, **bagging** and **random forest** performed exceptionally well
- For high recall, **OverBagging** and **balanced random forest** are strong choices
- For general performance across all metrics, **SMOTEBagging** and **bagging** proved to be solid options

In conclusion, although ensemble approaches such as bagging and random forest establish robust benchmarks that are challenging to outperform, incorporating imbalanced learning strategies such as SMOTEBagging can lead to notable gains.

This concludes our discussion of bagging techniques. If bagging is the wisdom of the crowd, boosting is the master sculptor, refining the previous art with each stroke. We'll try to understand how boosting works in the next section.

Boosting techniques for imbalanced data

Imagine two friends doing group study to solve their mathematics assignment. The first student is strong in most topics but weak in two topics: complex numbers and triangles. So, the first student asks the second student to spend more time on these two topics. Then, while solving the assignments, they combine their answers. Since the first student knows most of the topics well, they decided to give more weight to his answers to the assignment questions. What these two students are doing is the key idea behind boosting.

In bagging, we noticed that we could train all the classifiers in parallel. These classifiers are trained on a subset of the data, and all of them have an equal say at the time of prediction.

In boosting, the classifiers are trained one after the other. While every classifier learns from the whole data, points in the dataset are assigned different weights based on their difficulty of classification. Classifiers are also assigned weights that tell us about their predictive power. While predicting new data, the weighted sum of the classifiers is used.

Boosting begins by training the first classifier on the whole dataset, with each data point assigned the same weight. In the second iteration, the data points that were misclassified in the first iteration are given more weight, and a second classifier is trained with these new weights. A weight is also assigned to the classifiers themselves based on their overall performance. This process continues through multiple iterations with different classifiers. *Figure 4.12* illustrates this concept for a two-class dataset:

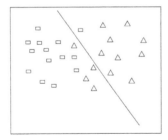 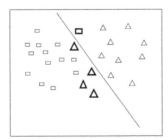 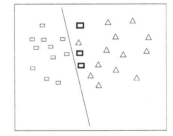

Figure 4.12 – Boosting idea: (left) the decision boundary from the first classifier; (middle) the weights of misclassified data points are bumped up for the second classifier; (right) the decision boundary from the second classifier

The kind of boosting we just described is called **AdaBoost**. There is another category of boosting algorithms called gradient boosting, where the main focus is on minimizing the residuals (the difference between the actual value and predicted output value) of the previous model, trying to correct the previous model's mistakes. There are several popular gradient boosting implementations, such as **XGBoost**, **LightGBM**, and **CatBoost**.

In this chapter, we will mostly focus on AdaBoost and modify it to account for data imbalance. However, swapping AdaBoost with XGBoost, for example, shouldn't be too difficult.

AdaBoost

AdaBoost, short for adaptive boosting, is one of the earliest boosting methods based on decision trees. Decision trees are classifiers that are easy to ensemble together:

Algorithm 1 AdaBoost Algorithm

1: **Input:** Training data and a fixed number of decision tree classifiers
2: **Output:** An aggregated classifier
3: **Initialize:** Equal weights for all samples in the training data
4: **for** each decision tree classifier **do**
5:     **Train:** Train classifier on data, giving more importance to samples with higher weights
6:     **Compute Error:** Compute error by comparing classifier predictions with actual outputs
7:     **Update Weights:** Increase weights of wrongly classified points for the next iteration
8: **end for**
9: **Combine Classifiers:** Combine all decision tree classifiers into a final classifier, where classifiers with smaller error values have a larger say

---

Figure 4.13 – AdaBoost pseudocode

The following code shows how to import the classifier from the `sklearn` library and train it on the data:

```
from sklearn.ensemble import AdaBoostClassifier
clf = AdaBoostClassifier(
    random_state=0, estimator = DecisionTreeClassifier(max_depth=6)
).fit(X_train, y_train)
```

Let's plot what the decision boundary looks like after the model gets trained on the data:

```
plot_decision_boundary(X_train, y_train, clf, 'AdaBoostClassifier')
plt.show()
```

Figure 4.14 shows the decision boundary of the model on the training data:

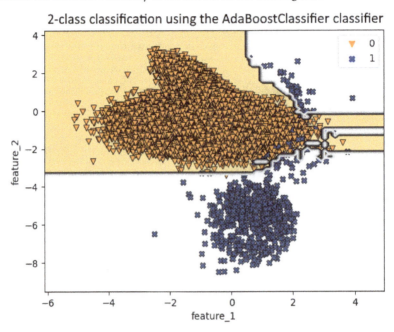

Figure 4.14 – The decision boundary of AdaBoostClassifier on the training data

We can make oversampling and undersampling an integral part of the boosting algorithm, similar to how we did for the bagging algorithm. We will discuss that next.

RUSBoost, SMOTEBoost, and RAMOBoost

As you might have guessed, we can combine AdaBoost with resampling techniques. Here is the main idea: at each boosting iteration, before training a classifier on the incorrect examples from the previous iteration, we sample the data (via some undersampling or oversampling variant). Here's the general pseudocode:

1. **Input**: The training data and some decision tree classifiers.

2. **Output**: An aggregated classifier.

3. Initialize the equal weights for all the samples of the training data.

4. Repeat this for each decision tree classifier:

   I.   Resample the data using a data sampling method:

         i.   If the sampling method used is **Random UnderSampling** (**RUS**), the method is called **RUSBoost** [5].

ii.   If the sampling method used is SMOTE, the method is called **SMOTEBoost** [6].

iii.   In **RAMOBoost** (short for **Ranked Minority Oversampling in Boosting** [7]), oversampling of the minority class is done based on the weight of the minority class examples. If the weight of an example is more (because the model didn't do well on that example in the previous iteration), then it's oversampled more, and vice versa.

II.   Train a classifier on the resampled data, giving more importance to samples with higher weights based on previous iterations.

III.   Compute the error for the classifier on the given data by comparing its predictions with the actual outputs.

IV.   Consider all the wrongly classified examples for the next iteration. Increase the weights of such wrongly classified examples.

5.   Combine all the decision tree classifiers into a final classifier, where the classifiers with smaller error values on the training data have a larger say in the final prediction.

In this pseudocode, *Step 4 (I)* is the only extra step we have added compared to the AdaBoost algorithm. Let's discuss the pros and cons of these techniques:

- In RUSBoost, as the data is reduced, we tend to have a faster training time.

- SMOTEBoost produces synthetic samples from the minority class. Thus, it adds diversity to the data and may improve the classifier's accuracy. However, it would increase the time to train and may not be scalable to very large datasets.

- RAMOBoost gives preference to the samples near the class boundaries. This can improve performance in some cases. However, like SMOTEBoost, this method may increase the training time and cost and may cause overfitting of the final model.

The `imbalanced-learn` library provides the implementation for `RUSBoostClassifier`:

```
from imblearn.ensemble import RUSBoostClassifier
rusboost_clf = RUSBoostClassifier(random_state=0, \
    estimator=DecisionTreeClassifier\
    (max_depth=6)).fit(X_train, y_train)
```

Let's examine the decision boundary of the trained model:

```
plot_decision_boundary(
    X_train, y_train, rusboost_clf, 'RUSBoostClassifier')
plt.show()
```

The resulting plot is shown here:

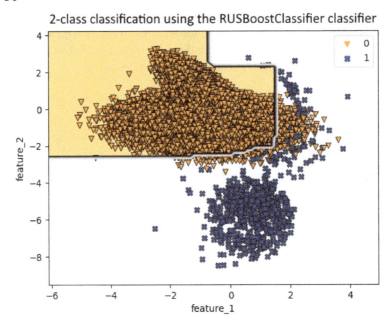

Figure 4.15 – The decision boundary of RUSBoostClassifier on training data

The `imbalanced-learn` library doesn't have the implementations of RAMOBoost and SMOTEBoost yet (as of version 0.11.0). You can check the open source repository at `https://github.com/dialnd/imbalanced-algorithms` for reference implementations.

Can we create multiple subsets of the majority class, train an ensemble from each of these subsets, and combine all weak classifiers in these ensembles into a final output? This approach will be explored in the next section, where we will utilize the ensemble of ensembles technique.

Ensemble of ensembles

Can we combine boosting and bagging? As we saw earlier, in bagging, we create multiple subsets of data and then train classifiers on those datasets. We can treat AdaBoost as a classifier while doing bagging. The process is simple: first, we create the bags and then train different AdaBoost classifiers on each bag. Here, AdaBoost is an ensemble in itself. Thus, these models are called an **ensemble of ensembles**.

On top of having an ensemble of ensembles, we can also do undersampling (or oversampling) at the time of bagging. This gives us the **benefits of bagging**, **boosting**, and **random undersampling** (or oversampling) in a single model. We will discuss one such algorithm in this section, called **EasyEnsemble**. Since random undersampling doesn't have significant overhead, both algorithms have training times similar to any other algorithm with the same number of weak classifiers.

EasyEnsemble

The EasyEnsemble algorithm [8] generates balanced datasets from the original dataset and trains a different AdaBoost classifier on each of the balanced datasets. Later, it creates an aggregate classifier that makes predictions based on the majority votes of the AdaBoost classifiers:

Algorithm 5 EasyEnsemble Algorithm

1: **Input:** Given a training set (with a minority class and a majority class) and some AdaBoost classifiers
2: **for** each AdaBoost classifier **do**
3:     **Create Sample:** Create a sample of training data by taking all the examples of the minority class and a subset (random sampling with replacement) of the majority class. Keep the sample size of the majority class the same as the size of the minority class
4:     **Train Classifier:** Train the AdaBoost classifier on the data from the previous step
5: **end for**
6: **Combine Classifiers:** Create an aggregated classifier by taking votes from all the AdaBoost classifiers

---

Figure 4.16 – EasyEnsemble pseudocode

Figure 4.17 summarizes the EasyEnsemble algorithm using three subsets of the training data:

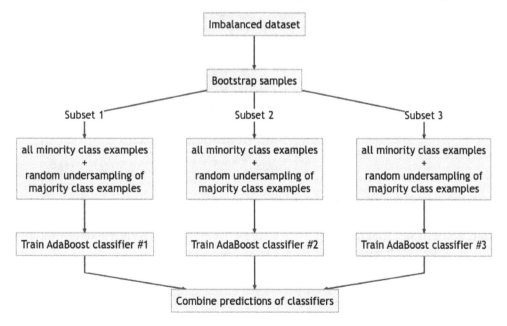

Figure 4.17 – EasyEnsemble algorithm explained

Instead of randomly undersampling the majority class examples, we can randomly oversample the minority class examples too.

The `imbalanced-learn` library provides the API for EasyEnsemble using `EasyEnsembleClassifier`. The `EasyEnsembleClassifier` API provides a `base_estimator` argument that can be used to set any classifier, with the default being `AdaBoostClassifier`:

```
from imblearn.ensemble import EasyEnsembleClassifier
clf = EasyEnsembleClassifier(n_estimators=70,random_state=42).fit(X,y)
```

Let's plot the decision boundary:

```
plot_decision_boundary(X, y, clf, 'EasyEnsembleClassifier')
plt.show()
```

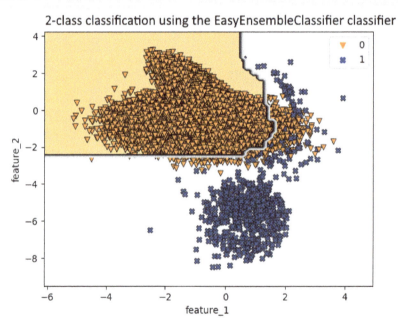

Figure 4.18 – The decision boundary of EasyEnsembleClassifier on the training data

By default, EasyEnsemble uses `AdaBoostClassifier` as the base estimator. However, we can use any other estimator as well, such as `XGBoostClassifier`, or tune it in other ways, say by passing another `sampling_strategy`.

This concludes our discussion of EasyEnsemble. Next, we will compare the various boosting methods that we've studied.

Comparative performance of boosting methods

Let's compare the performance of the various boosting methods we've discussed. We use a decision tree as a baseline and RUSBoost, AdaBoost, XGBoost, and EasyEnsemble, along with two variants. By default, `EasyEnsembleClassifier` uses `AdaBoostClassifier` as a baseline estimator. We use XGBoost instead as the estimator in the second variant of `EasyEnsembleClassifier`; in the third variant, we use `not majority` for our `sampling_strategy`, along with the XGBoost estimator:

Technique	F2 Score	Precision	Recall	Average Precision	AUC-ROC
EasyEnsemble (estimator=XGBoost and sampling_strategy = not_majority)	0.885	0.933	0.874	0.978	1.000
EasyEnsemble (estimator=XGBoost)	0.844	0.520	1.000	0.978	0.999
EasyEnsemble	0.844	0.519	1.000	0.940	0.999
RUSBoost	0.836	0.517	0.989	0.948	1.000
AdaBoost	0.907	0.938	0.900	0.978	1.000
XGBoost	0.885	0.933	0.874	0.968	1.000
Decision Tree	0.893	0.960	0.878	0.930	0.981

Table 4.3 – Performance comparison of various boosting techniques

Here are some conclusions from *Table 4.3*:

- For the highest F2 score, AdaBoost is the best choice
- For high precision, the plain decision tree beats all other techniques
- For perfect recall, EasyEnsemble (`estimator=XGBoost`) and EasyEnsemble perform perfectly
- For overall balanced performance, AdaBoost and EasyEnsemble (`estimator=XGBoost and sampling_strategy=not_majority`) are strong contenders

- The ensembling techniques such as RUSBoost and EasyEnsemble are specifically designed for handling data imbalance and improving recall compared to a baseline model such as the decision tree or even AdaBoost

Overall, the results indicate that while ensemble methods such as AdaBoost and XGBoost provide robust baselines that are hard to beat, leveraging imbalanced learning techniques can indeed modify the decision boundaries of the resulting classifiers, which can potentially help with improving the recall. The efficacy of these techniques, however, largely depends on the dataset and performance metric under consideration.

By wrapping up our journey through the ensemble of ensembles, we've added yet another powerful and dynamic tool to our machine learning arsenal.

Model performance comparison

The effectiveness of the techniques we've discussed so far can be highly dependent on the dataset they are applied to. In this section, we will conduct a comprehensive comparative analysis that compares the various techniques we have discussed so far while using the logistic regression model as a baseline. For a comprehensive review of the complete implementation, please consult the accompanying notebook available on GitHub.

The analysis spans four distinct datasets, each with its own characteristics and challenges:

- **Synthetic data with Sep: 0.5**: A simulated dataset with moderate separation between classes, serving as a baseline to understand algorithm performance in simplified conditions.

- **Synthetic data with Sep: 0.9**: Another synthetic dataset, but with a higher degree of separation, allowing us to examine how algorithms perform as class distinguishability improves.

- **Thyroid sick dataset**: A real-world dataset (available to import from `imblearn`) related to healthcare, chosen for its practical importance and the natural class imbalance often seen in medical datasets.

- **Abalone 19 dataset**: A challenging real-world dataset related to marine biology, with a high level of class imbalance (1:130). This can be imported from `imblearn` as well.

Our primary metric for evaluation is average precision, a summary measure that combines both precision and recall, thereby providing a balanced view of algorithm performance.

We'd like to emphasize that we are using the vanilla versions of the various ensemble models for comparison. With some additional effort in tuning the hyperparameters of these models, we could certainly enhance the performance of these implementations. We leave that as an exercise for you.

By comparing these diverse algorithms across a variety of datasets, this analysis aims to provide some valuable insights into the following aspects:

- How conventional and specialized techniques stack up against each other
- The dependency of algorithm effectiveness on dataset characteristics
- The practical implications of choosing one algorithm over another in different scenarios

Figure 4.19 compares the performance of various bagging and boosting techniques using the average precision score, while using the logistic regression model as a baseline, over two synthetic datasets:

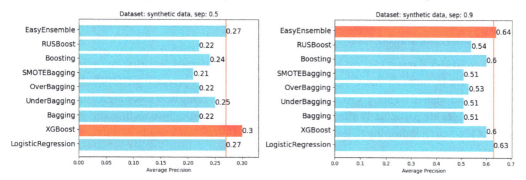

Figure 4.19 – Average precision scores on synthetic datasets

Figure 4.20 shows similar plots across two real-world datasets:

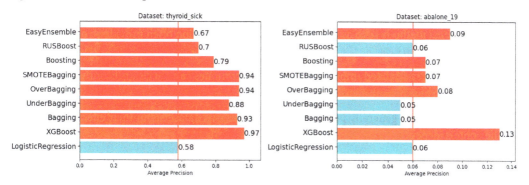

Figure 4.20 – Average precision scores on the thyroid_sick and abalone_19 datasets

Let's analyze these results for each of the datasets:

- **Synthetic data with Sep 0.5** (*Figure 4.19*, left): XGBoost and logistic regression performed the best in terms of average precision, scoring 0.30 and 0.27, respectively. Interestingly, ensemble methods designed specifically for imbalanced data, such as SMOTEBagging and OverBagging, perform comparably or even worse than conventional methods such as bagging. This suggests that specialized methods do not always guarantee an advantage in simpler synthetic settings.

- **Synthetic data with Sep 0.9** (*Figure 4.19*, right): EasyEnsemble takes the lead on this dataset with an average precision score of 0.64, closely followed by logistic regression and XGBoost. This higher separation seems to allow EasyEnsemble to capitalize on its focus on balancing, leading to better performance. Other ensemble methods such as UnderBagging and OverBagging perform reasonably but do not surpass the leaders.

- **Thyroid sick dataset** (*Figure 4.20*, left): In a real-world dataset focusing on thyroid sickness, XGBoost far outperforms all other methods with an average precision of 0.97. Other ensemble methods such as bagging, OverBagging, and SMOTEBagging also score high, suggesting that ensembles are particularly effective for this dataset. Interestingly, boosting and RUSBoost do not keep pace, indicating that not all boosting variants are universally effective.

- **Abalone 19 dataset** (*Figure 4.20*, right): For the Abalone 19 dataset, all methods perform relatively poorly, with XGBoost standing out with an average precision of 0.13. EasyEnsemble comes in second with a score of 0.09, while traditional methods such as logistic regression and bagging lag behind. This could indicate that the dataset is particularly challenging for most methods, and specialized imbalanced techniques can only make marginal improvements.

Here are some overall insights:

- Conventional methods such as XGBoost and logistic regression often provide strong baselines that are difficult to beat

- The efficacy of specialized imbalanced learning techniques can vary significantly, depending on the dataset and its inherent complexities

- Ensemble methods generally perform well across various datasets, but their effectiveness can be context-dependent

- The choice of performance metric – in this case, average precision – can significantly influence the evaluation, making it crucial to consider multiple metrics for a comprehensive understanding

We hope that this chapter has shown how you can incorporate sampling techniques with ensemble methods to achieve improved results, especially when dealing with imbalanced data.

Summary

Ensemble methods in machine learning create strong classifiers by combining results from multiple weak classifiers using approaches such as bagging and boosting. However, these methods assume balanced data and may struggle with imbalanced datasets. Combining ensemble methods with sampling methods such as oversampling and undersampling leads to techniques such as UnderBagging, OverBagging, and SMOTEBagging, all of which can help address imbalanced data issues.

Ensembles of ensembles, such as EasyEnsemble, combine boosting and bagging techniques to create powerful classifiers for imbalanced datasets.

Ensemble-based imbalance learning techniques can be an excellent addition to your toolkit. The ones based on KNN, viz., SMOTEBoost, and RAMOBoost can be slow. However, the ensembles based on random undersampling and random oversampling are less costly. Also, boosting methods are found to sometimes work better than bagging methods in the case of imbalanced data. We can combine random sampling techniques with boosting to get better overall performance. As we emphasized previously, it's empirical, and we have to try to know what would work best for our data.

In the next chapter, we will learn how to change the model to account for the imbalance in data and the various costs incurred by the model because of misclassifying the minority class examples.

Questions

1. Try using `RUSBoostClassifier` on the `abalone_19` dataset and compare the performance with other techniques from the previous chapters.

2. What is the difference between the `BalancedRandomForestClassifier` and `BalancedBaggingClassifier` classes in the `imbalanced-learn` library?

References

1. L. Breiman, *Bagging predictors*, Mach Learn, vol. 24, no. 2, pp. 123–140, Aug. 1996, doi: 10.1007/BF00058655, `https://link.springer.com/content/pdf/10.1007/BF00058655.pdf`.

2. (The paper that introduced OverBagging, UnderBagging, and SMOTEBagging) S. Wang and X. Yao, *Diversity analysis on imbalanced data sets by using ensemble models*, in 2009 IEEE Symposium on Computational Intelligence and Data Mining, Nashville, TN, USA: IEEE, Mar. 2009, pp. 324–331. doi: 10.1109/CIDM.2009.4938667, `https://www.cs.bham.ac.uk/~wangsu/documents/papers/CIDMShuo.pdf`.

3. *Live Site Incident escalation forecast* (2023), `https://medium.com/data-science-at-microsoft/live-site-incident-escalation-forecast-566763a2178`

4. L. Breiman, *Random Forests*, Machine Learning, vol. 45, no. 1, pp. 5–32, 2001, doi: 10.1023/A:1010933404324, `https://link.springer.com/content/pdf/10.1023/A:1010933404324.pdf`.

5. (The paper that introduced the RUSBoost algorithm) C. Seiffert, T. M. Khoshgoftaar, J. Van Hulse, and A. Napolitano, *RUSBoost: A Hybrid Approach to Alleviating Class Imbalance*, IEEE Trans. Syst., Man, Cybern. A, vol. 40, no. 1, pp. 185–197, Jan. 2010, doi: 10.1109/TSMCA.2009.2029559, `https://www.researchgate.net/profile/Jason-Van-Hulse/publication/224608502_RUSBoost_A_Hybrid_Approach_to_Alleviating_Class_Imbalance/links/0912f50f4bec299a8c000000/RUSBoost-A-Hybrid-Approach-to-Alleviating-Class-Imbalance.pdf`.

6. (The paper that introduced the SMOTEBoost algorithm) N. V. Chawla, A. Lazarevic, L. O. Hall, and K. W. Bowyer, *SMOTEBoost: Improving Prediction of the Minority Class in Boosting*, in Knowledge Discovery in Databases: PKDD 2003, N. Lavrač, D. Gamberger, L. Todorovski, and H. Blockeel, Eds., in Lecture Notes in Computer Science, vol. 2838. Berlin, Heidelberg: Springer Berlin Heidelberg, 2003, pp. 107–119. doi: 10.1007/978-3-540-39804-2_12, `https://www3.nd.edu/~dial/publications/chawla2003smoteboost.pdf`.

7. (The paper that introduced RAMOBoost algorithm) Sheng Chen, Haibo He, and E. A. Garcia, *RAMOBoost: Ranked Minority Oversampling in Boosting*, IEEE Trans. Neural Netw., vol. 21, no. 10, pp. 1624–1642, Oct. 2010, doi: 10.1109/TNN.2010.2066988, `https://ieeexplore.ieee.org/abstract/document/5559472`.

8. (The paper that introduced EasyEnsemble) Xu-Ying Liu, Jianxin Wu, and Zhi-Hua Zhou, *Exploratory Undersampling for Class-Imbalance Learning*, IEEE Trans. Syst., Man, Cybern. B, vol. 39, no. 2, pp. 539–550, Apr. 2009, doi: 10.1109/TSMCB.2008.2007853, `http://129.211.169.156/publication/tsmcb09.pdf`.

5
Cost-Sensitive Learning

So far, we have studied various sampling techniques and ways to oversample or undersample data. However, both of these techniques have their own unique set of issues. For example, oversampling can easily lead to overfitting of the model due to the exact or very similar examples being seen repeatedly. Similarly, with undersampling, we lose some information (that could have been useful for the model) because we discard the majority class examples to balance the training dataset. In this chapter, we'll consider an alternative to the data-level techniques that we learned about previously.

Cost-sensitive learning is an effective strategy to tackle imbalanced data. We will go through this technique and learn why it can be useful. This will help us understand some of the details of cost functions and how machine learning models are not designed to deal with imbalanced datasets by default. While machine learning models aren't equipped to handle imbalanced datasets, we will see how modern libraries enable this.

We will cover the following topics:

- The concept of **cost-sensitive learning (CSL)**
- Understanding costs in practice
- Cost-sensitive learning for logistic regression
- Cost-sensitive learning for decision trees
- Cost-sensitive learning using `scikit-learn` and XGBoost models
- MetaCost – making any classification model cost-sensitive
- Threshold adjustment

By the end of this chapter, you will understand what cost means in the context of classification problems, how to adjust model parameters to account for such costs, and how to prioritize minority class predictions to mitigate the cost of misclassification. We will also look at a generic meta-algorithm that can make any algorithm cost-sensitive and a post-processing technique for adjusting prediction thresholds.

Technical requirements

Similar to prior chapters, we will continue to utilize common libraries such as `numpy`, `scikit-learn`, `xgboost`, and `imbalanced-learn`. The code and notebooks for this chapter are available on GitHub at `https://github.com/PacktPublishing/Machine-Learning-for-Imbalanced-Data/tree/main/chapter05`. You can open this GitHub notebook using Google Colab by clicking on the **Open in Colab** icon at the top of this chapter's notebook or by launching it from `https://colab.research.google.com` using the GitHub URL of the notebook.

The concept of Cost-Sensitive Learning

Cost-Sensitive Learning (**CSL**) is a technique where the cost function of a machine learning model is changed to account for the imbalance in data. The key insight behind CSL is that we want our model's cost function to reflect the relative importance of the different classes.

Let's try to understand cost functions in machine learning and various types of CSL.

Costs and cost functions

A cost function estimates the difference between the actual outcome and the predicted outcome from a model. For example, the cost function of the logistic regression model is given by the log loss function:

$$LogLoss = -\tfrac{1}{N} * \sum_{i=1}^{N} \left(y_i * \log(\hat{y}_i) + (1 - y_i) * \log(1 - \hat{y}_i) \right)$$

Here, N is the total number of observations, y_i is the true label (0 or 1), and $\hat{y}_i$ is the probability value (between 0 and 1) predicted from the model.

One type of cost is called the cost of misclassification errors [1] – that is, the cost of predicting the majority class instead of the minority class or vice versa.

In practice, there can be other types of costs that we may incur, such as the following:

- Cost of labeling the dataset
- Cost of training or evaluating the model
- Cost of training data collection

Let's consider the confusion matrix:

	Predicted Negative	**Predicted Positive**
Actual Negative	True Negative	False Positive
Actual Positive	False Negative	True Positive

Table 5.1 – Confusion matrix for understanding the cost of classification errors

Psychological studies have suggested that loss hurts twice as much as gain. Similarly, in machine learning, the "cost" captures whenever the model makes a mistake (False Positive and False Negative) and does not worry about when it's right (True Positive and True Negative). This cost is the cost of misclassification errors.

Not all misclassifications are created equal. For instance, suppose we're attempting to predict whether a patient has cancer. If our model incorrectly indicates that the patient has cancer (a false positive), this could lead to additional testing. However, if our model incorrectly suggests that the patient is cancer-free (a false negative), the consequences could be far more severe as the disease could progress undiagnosed. Therefore, a false negative is significantly more detrimental than a false positive. Our cost function should take this discrepancy into account.

Unfortunately, most models treat the majority and minority classes equally by default. However, modern ML frameworks such as `scikit-learn`, Keras/TensorFlow, and PyTorch provide a way to weigh the various classes differently across a variety of learning algorithms.

Types of cost-sensitive learning

There are two major types of CSL approaches, namely weighting and meta-learning. In weighting approaches, we update the cost function of the machine learning model to reflect the importance of the different classes. In meta-learning, we can make the model cost-sensitive without changing its cost function.

In MetaCost, a type of meta-learning technique, for example, we alter the labels of training instances to minimize expected misclassification costs. Similarly, in the threshold adjustment method, we determine a probability threshold that minimizes total misclassification costs for predictions. *Figure 5.1* categorizes these methods at a high level [2][3]:

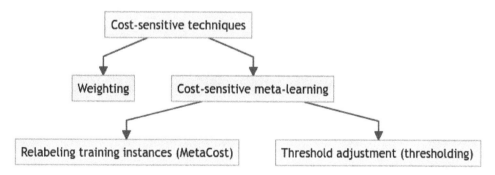

Figure 5.1 – Categorization of cost-sensitive learning methods

Difference between CSL and resampling

The key difference between previously discussed data-level techniques and CSL is that the data-level techniques adjust the frequency of the different error types, but they treat all misclassification errors the same. In certain cases, as we encountered earlier, the cost of misclassifying observations of different classes is not the same. For example, in cancer detection, the cost of misclassifying a patient who has cancer as healthy (False Negative) is much higher, as the patient is at high risk if not detected or treated early. Similarly, misclassifying a fraudulent booking as non-fraudulent can cost more money than wrongly classifying a legitimate transaction as fraud. Why? Because in the latter case, we can just call and verify with the user the legitimacy of the transaction. By applying resampling techniques such as upsampling or downsampling, we are implicitly changing the cost of different types of errors. So, CSL and resampling techniques can be considered to have an equivalent effect on the model at the end of the day.

However, resampling techniques may be problematic in certain cases, as we will discuss in the next section. In such cases, CSL can be more practical:

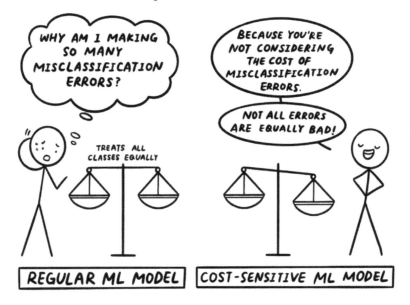

Figure 5.2 – Comic re-emphasizing the idea of misclassification errors

Problems with rebalancing techniques

In the previous chapters, we briefly touched on why in some cases, we would prefer not to apply any data sampling techniques. This could be because of the following reasons:

- We already have too much training data, and it might be quite expensive to deal with more data, or the training time can increase by many folds due to having more training data.

- Sometimes, we may not get the best results using sampling or data rebalancing techniques because of the dataset we are using.

- An additional consideration is that upon rebalancing the dataset, our model's predictive scores may become miscalibrated, necessitating a recalibration process. We will cover this topic in *Chapter 10, Model Calibration*, where we will learn about various model calibration techniques.

- Rebalancing techniques can lead to model overfitting or underfitting issues. Overfitting can especially happen when using oversampling since they produce repeated or similar training examples. Similarly, the model may be underfitted when using undersampling because the model did not get trained on the data thrown away during undersampling.

Next, let's try to understand what costs really mean.

Understanding costs in practice

We need to understand the various types of costs involved while creating weights for different classes. These costs change on a case-by-case basis. Let's discuss an example of cost calculations to understand what we should consider while thinking about cost calculations.

Let's take the example of pediatric pneumonia. According to UNICEF, a child dies of pneumonia every 43 seconds [4]. Imagine we are creating a new test for pediatric pneumonia – how will we decide the cost of different errors?

Let's review the confusion matrix from *Table 5.1*. There will usually be no extra cost for True Negatives and True Positives. But using a False Negative – that is, when a child has pneumonia and predicting the child to be healthy – will have a very high cost. On the flip side, when a healthy child is predicted as being affected by pneumonia, there will be a cost associated with the troubles the family of the child may have to go through, but there will be much less cost than in the previous case. Furthermore, the cost of misclassification can vary depending on the child's age. For example, younger kids will be at a higher risk than older kids. Thus, we will aim to penalize the model more if it makes an error in the case of younger kids.

The cost can vary depending on the duration of the symptoms. Consider it this way: if we make an error and misdiagnose a child who has only had flu symptoms for a day, it's not ideal, but it's not disastrous. However, if that child has been enduring flu symptoms for 2 weeks, that's a different scenario. That mistake will cost us significantly more.

While we've discussed real-world problems so far, this chapter will pivot to utilize a synthetic dataset. This approach is intended to reinforce concepts and methods in a controlled environment, thus enhancing the learning process:

```
X, y = make_classification(
    n_samples=50000, n_features=2, n_redundant=0, class_sep=2,\
    weights=[0.99], random_state=1, n_clusters_per_class=1)
```

```
X_train, X_test, y_train, y_test = train_test_split(X, y,\
    test_size = 0.2, random_state = 0, stratify=y)
print('y_train: ', Counter(y_train))
print('y_test: ', Counter(y_test))
plot_dataset(X_train, y_train)
```

The make_classification function produces some overlapping points that we cleaned up. To keep things simple, we've omitted that cleanup code here. You can refer to the full notebook on GitHub.

The preceding code produces the following output and scatter plot (*Figure 5.3*):

```
y_train:  Counter({0: 39404, 1: 596})
y_test:   Counter({0: 9851, 1: 149})
```

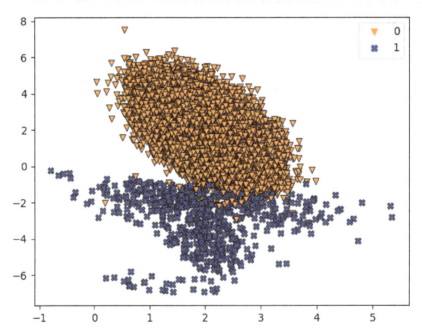

Figure 5.3 – Scatter plot showing the training dataset's distribution

We'll dive into how to apply CSL to logistic regression models next.

Cost-Sensitive Learning for logistic regression

Logistic regression is a simple classification algorithm. We train a model as a linear combination of the features. Then, we pass the result of that linear combination into a sigmoid function to predict the class probabilities for different classes.

The sigmoid function (also called a logit function) is a mathematical tool capable of converting any real number into a value between 0 and 1. This value can be interpreted as a probability estimate:

```python
import numpy as np
def sigmoid(x):
    s = 1/(1+np.exp(-x))
    return s
```

The graph of the sigmoid function has an S-shaped curve, and it appears like this:

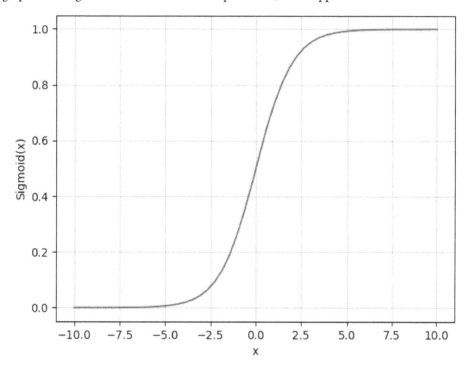

Figure 5.4 – Sigmoid function

The class with the highest predicted probability is taken as the prediction for a given sample.

Let's say we have an email to be classified as spam or non-spam, and our logistic regression model outputs the probabilities of 0.25 for non-spam and 0.75 for spam. Here, the class with the highest predicted probability is "spam" (1) since 0.75 is greater than 0.25. Therefore, the model would predict that this email is spam (*Figure 5.5*):

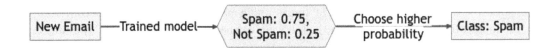

Figure 5.5 – Higher class probability determining the class for binary classification

For two-class classification, we just predict the probability of one class. The probability of the other class is one minus the probability of the first class.

The logistic regression model is trained using a loss function. The loss function for one example from a dataset with two classes would look like this:

$$cost = -y * log(classProbability) - (1 - y) * log(1 - classProbability)$$

For true positives and true negatives, this loss will be very low. For a false positive, y, the actual value would be 0; therefore, the first term will be 0, but the second term will be very high as the class probability approaches 1, and the term will approach negative infinity (since, $log(0) \rightarrow -\infty$). Since there is a negative sign at the front, the cost will approach positive infinity. A similar analysis can be done for the false negative case. One part of the cost can be seen as the false positive part, and another part of the cost can be seen as the false negative part:

$$cost = falsePositiveCost + falseNegativeCost$$

As discussed earlier, we don't want to weigh the two types of costs equally. So, all we do is add weights, W_{FP} and W_{FN}, for the respective costs:

$$cost = W_{FP} * falsePositiveCost + W_{FN} * falseNegativeCost$$

This is the crux of CSL with logistic regression. To get the overall costs of the model, we take the average cost across all the data points:

```
lr = LogisticRegression(random_state=0, max_iter=150).fit(
    X_train, y_train)
plot_decision_boundary(X_train, y_train, lr, 'LogisticRegression')
plt.show()
PrecisionRecallDisplay.from_estimator(
    lr, X_test, y_test, ax = plt.gca(),name = "LogisticRegression")
```

When all errors are equally costly, the model's decision boundary and the model's **Precision-Recall (PR)** curve will look like this:

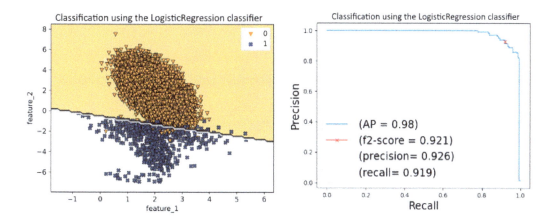

Figure 5.6 – The decision boundary (left) and PR curve (right) of the baseline regression model

```
compute_scores(lr, X_test, y_test)
```

The previous code outputs the following F2 score, precision, and recall values:

```
f2-score: 0.921 precision: 0.926 recall: 0.919
```

In this chapter, we will use the F2 score as our primary metric. What is the F2 score? In *Chapter 1, Introduction to Data Imbalance in Machine Learning*, we studied the F-beta score. The F2 score is the F-beta score with beta=2, while the F1 score is the F-beta score with beta=1. It's useful when recall is more important than precision – that is, false negatives are more costly (important) than false positives:

$$F_\beta = \frac{(1 + \beta^2) \times (precision \times recall)}{(\beta^2 \times precision) + recall} = \frac{(5 \times precision \times recall)}{(4 \times precision) + recall}$$

`LogisticRegression` from the `scikit-learn` library provides a `class_weight` parameter. When the value of this parameter is set to "balanced," the weight of each class is automatically computed by the following formula:

$$weightOfClass = \frac{totalNumberOfSamples}{numberOfClasses * numberOfSamplesPerClass}$$

For example, we have 100 examples in the dataset – 80 in class 0 and 20 in class 1. The weights of each class are computed as follows:

- Weight for class 0 = 100/(2*80) = 0.625

- Weight for class 1 = 100/(2*20) = 2.5

Given that the number of class 0 examples is four times that of class 1, the weight of class 1 is 2.5, which is four times the weight of class 0 – that is, 0.625. This makes sense since we would want to give more weight to class 1, which is smaller in number.

We can mention `class_weight` as a dictionary as well:

```
LogisticRegression(class_weight={0: 0.5, 1:0.5})
```

Let's try to use the `class_weight` parameter in the `LogisticRegression` function:

```
lr_weighted = LogisticRegression(class_weight='balanced', \
    random_state=0, max_iter=150).fit(X_train, y_train)
plot_decision_boundary(X_train, y_train, lr_weighted, \
    'LogisticRegression')
plt.show()
PrecisionRecallDisplay.from_estimator(lr_weighted, X_test,\
    y_test, ax = plt.gca(),name = "LogisticRegressionWeighted")
```

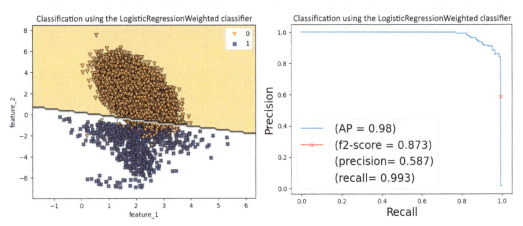

Figure 5.7 – The decision boundary (left) and PR curve (right) of the
"balanced" class-weighted logistic regression model

Let's calculate the F2 score, precision, and recall scores:

```
compute_scores(lr_weighted, X_test, y_test)
```

The scores of the "balanced" class-weighted logistic regression model are as follows:

```
f2-score: 0.873 precision: 0.587 recall: 0.993
```

Upon analyzing the results, we can see a decision boundary that correctly classifies most of the positive class examples. The precision comes down while the recall goes up. The decline in the F2 score can be attributed to changes in the recall and precision values. The model exhibits an improvement in recall, indicating its enhanced ability to correctly identify all positive class examples. However, this advancement results in a simultaneous drop in precision, suggesting an increased rate of mistakes made on the negative class examples (which we don't really care about as much!).

Let's try to tune the `class_weight` parameter using a grid search that optimizes our F2 score. We can always try to optimize any other objective, such as average precision, precision, or recall, and so on. The `np.linspace(0.05, 0.95, 20)` function is a numpy function that generates an array of 20 evenly spaced numbers between 0.05 and 0.95:

```
from sklearn.metrics import make_scorer, fbeta_score
def f2_func(y_true, y_pred):
    f2_score = fbeta_score(y_true, y_pred, beta=2.)
    return f2_score
def f2_scorer():
    return make_scorer(f2_func)


# Define the parameter grid
param_grid = {
    'class_weight': [
        {0: x, 1: 1.0-x} for x in np.linspace(0.05, 0.95, 20)]
}
# Instantiate the grid search model
grid_search =GridSearchCV(
    LogisticRegression(),param_grid,\
    cv=3, scoring=f2_scorer(), n_jobs=-1
)
# Fit the grid search to the data
grid_search.fit(X_train, y_train)
# Get the best parameters
best_params = grid_search.best_params_
best_params
```

This produces the following output:

```
{'class_weight': {0: 0.14473684210526316, 1: 0.8552631578947368}}
```

Our standard metrics are as follows:

```
f2-score: 0.930 precision: 0.892 recall: 0.940
```

After incorporating these class weights, our decision boundary attempts to strike a better balance between misclassifying positive and negative class examples, as illustrated in *Figure 5.8*. This results in a superior F2 score of 0.93, increasing the precision value while maintaining a modest recall:

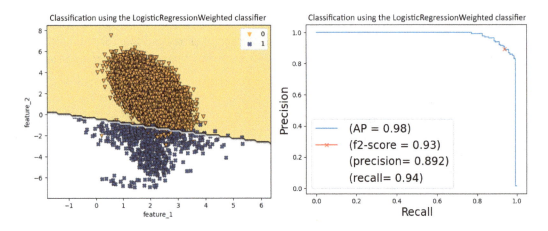

Figure 5.8 – The decision boundary (left) and PR curve (right) of
the class-weighted logistic regression model

> 🚀 **Cost-sensitive learning in production at Microsoft**
>
> In a practical application at Microsoft, the primary objective was to improve the **Click-Through Rate (CTR)** prediction for Bing ads [5]. Achieving accurate CTR prediction is vital for optimizing both user experience and revenue streams. A marginal improvement of just 0.1% in prediction accuracy has the potential to elevate profits by hundreds of millions of dollars. Through rigorous testing, an ensemble model that combines **Neural Networks (NNs)** and **Gradient-Boosted Decision Trees (GBDTs)** emerged as the most effective solution.
>
> For the training dataset, 56 million samples were randomly chosen from a month's log data, each containing hundreds of statistical features. To reduce training expenses, non-click cases were **downsampled** by 50% and assigned a **class weight** of 2 to maintain the original distribution. Model performance was then assessed using a test dataset of 40 million samples randomly drawn from the subsequent week's logs. Instead of recalibrating the model, class weighting was used to maintain the average CTR after downsampling.

In the next section, we will discuss how to do CSL with decision trees.

Cost-Sensitive Learning for decision trees

Decision trees are binary trees that use conditional decision-making to predict the class of the samples. Every tree node represents a set of samples corresponding to a chain of conditional statements based on the features. We divide the node into two children based on a feature and a threshold value. Imagine a set of students with height, weight, age, class, and location. We can divide the set into two parts according to the features of age and with a threshold of 8. Now, all the students with ages less than 8 will go into the left child, and all those with ages greater than or equal to 8 will go into the right child.

This way, we can create a tree by successively choosing features and threshold values. Every leaf node of the tree will contain nodes from only one class, respectively.

A question often arises during the construction of a decision tree: "Which feature and threshold pair should be selected to partition the set of samples at a given node?" The answer is straightforward: we opt for the pair that produces the most uniform (or homogeneous) subsets of data. Ideally, the two resulting subsets – referred to as the left and right children – should each contain elements predominantly from a single class.

The degree to which the nodes have a mixture of samples from different classes is known as the **impurity** of the node, which can be considered to be a measure of loss for decision trees. The more the impurity, the more heterogeneous the set of samples. Here are the two most common ways of calculating the impurity:

- Gini coefficient

- Entropy

Let's look at the formula for the Gini coefficient and entropy for two classes, c_1 and c_2:

$$Gini \ = \ 1- \ Proportion_{c1}{}^2- \ Proportion_{c2}{}^2$$

We will get the following:

$$Entropy \ = \ - \ Proportion_{c1} \ {}^*log\left(Proportion_{c1}\right)$$
$$- \ Proportion_{c2} \ {}^*log\left(Proportion_{c2}\right)$$

To do CSL with decision trees, we just multiply the class weights with the terms for each of the classes in the calculation of the Gini and entropy. If the weights for the two classes are W_1 and W_2, Gini and entropy will look as follows:

$$Gini \ = \ 1 - \ W_1 \ {}^* Proportion_{c1}{}^2 - \ W_2 \ {}^* Proportion_{c2}{}^2$$
$$Entropy \ = \ - \ W_1 \ {}^* Proportion_{c1} \ {}^* log(Proportion_{c1})$$
$$- \ W_2 \ {}^* Proportion_{c2} \ {}^* log(Proportion_{c2})$$

Now, the model prioritizes the class with a higher weight over the class with a lower weight. If we give more weight to the minority class, the model will make the decision that will prioritize nodes with homogeneous minority class samples.

In this section, we got some idea of how class weights can be accommodated into the loss function of decision trees to account for the misclassification error. In the next section, we will see how `scikit-learn` simplifies this process by integrating it into the model creation API, eliminating the need for us to manually adjust the loss function.

Cost-Sensitive Learning using scikit-learn and XGBoost models

scikit-learn provides a class_weight hyperparameter to adjust the weights of various classes for most models. This parameter can be specified in various ways for different learning algorithms in scikit-learn. However, the main idea is that this parameter specifies the weights to use for each class in the loss calculation formula. For example, this parameter specifies the values of *weigh t FP* and *weight FN* mentioned previously for logistic regression.

Similar to the LogisticRegression function, for DecisionTreeClassifier, we could use DecisionTreeClassifier(class_weight='balanced') or DecisionTreeClassifier(class_weight={0: 0.5, 1: 0.5}).

Regarding SVM, it can even be extended to multi-class classification by specifying a weight value for each class label:

```
svm.SVC(class_weight= {-1: 1.0, 0: 1.0, 1: 1.0})
```

The general guidance about coming up with the class_weight values is to use the inverse of the ratio of the majority class to the minority class. We can find even more optimal class_weight values by performing hyperparameter tuning using the GridSearch algorithm (use the GridSearchCV function from scikit-learn).

Similarly, XGBoost has the scale_pos_weight parameter to control the balance of positive and negative weights:

```
XGBClassifier(scale_pos_weight)
```

The default value of scale_pos_weight is 1. A recommended scale_pos_weight value is sum(negative_instances)/sum(positive_instances), which can be computed as float(np.sum(label == 0)) / np.sum(label==1).

XGBoost has a few other parameters, such as max_delta_step and min_child_weight, that can be tuned for imbalanced datasets. During the optimization process, max_delta_step determines the step size of updates, affecting learning speed and stability. min_child_weight controls overfitting and enhances generalization by influencing the size of leaf nodes in the decision tree. When dealing with imbalanced data scenarios, adjusting these parameters can strategically improve algorithm performance.

First, let's use `DecisionTreeClassifier` to solve our classification problem:

```
from sklearn.tree import DecisionTreeClassifier
from sklearn.metrics import PrecisionRecallDisplay
dt_clf = DecisionTreeClassifier(random_state=0, max_depth=6).fit(
    X_train, y_train)
plot_decision_boundary(X,y,dt_clf,'DecisionTreeClassifier')
plt.show()
PrecisionRecallDisplay.from_estimator(
    dt_clf, X_test, y_test, ax = plt.gca(),\
    name = "DecisionTreeClassifier")
print(classification_report_imbalanced(
    y_test,\
    dt_clf.predict(X_test), \
    target_names=['class 0', 'class 1']
    )
)
computescores(dt_clf, X_test, y_test)
```

The output decision boundary is more complex than that of logistic regression (*Figure 5.9*), separating the two classes better and giving an F2 score of 0.932:

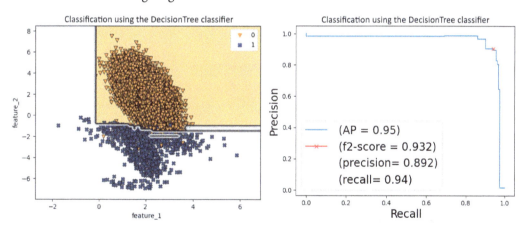

Figure 5.9 – The decision boundary (left) and PR curve (right) of the decision tree classifier model

We have reproduced the decision boundary and PR curve of the logistic regression model for comparison in *Figure 5.10*:

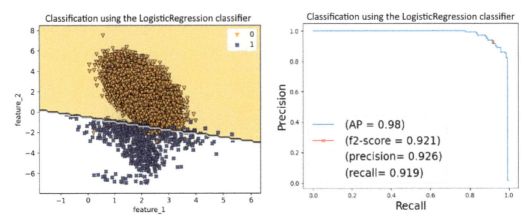

Figure 5.10 – The decision boundary (left) and PR curve (right) of logistic regression (for comparison)

Our standard metrics for the decision tree classifier are as follows:

```
f2-score: 0.932 precision: 0.892 recall: 0.94
```

Next, let's use the `class_weight='balanced'` parameter:

```
dt_clf_tuned = DecisionTreeClassifier(
    class_weight = 'balanced', random_state=0, max_depth=6
).fit(X_train, y_train)
```

After utilizing the code from before to plot the decision boundary, the PR curve, and compute the scores, the outputs are as follows:

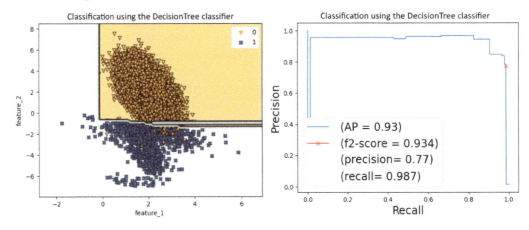

Figure 5.11 – The decision boundary (left) and PR curve (right) of the decision tree classifier model

```
f2-score: 0.934 precision: 0.770 recall: 0.987
```

The tuned weights improve the F2 score and recall values.

Popular frameworks such as `scikit-learn` also let us specify `sample_weight` as a list of weights for each observation in the dataset. The `sample_weight` and `class_weight` parameters can be quite confusing, and their purpose may not be very clear from their documentation on when to use what. The following table clarifies the difference between the two:

	sample_weight	class_weight
Purpose	Used to specify weights for individual examples. Can be useful when some examples are more important than others, regardless of their class. When some data is more trustworthy (say labeled using in-house human labelers), it can receive a higher weight. Can be useful when you don't have equal confidence in the samples in your batch.	Used to correct class imbalance. Should be used when the importance of examples depends on their class.

Usage	Can be used in training as well as testing.
	
	Especially useful when comparing multiple models on different test sets with metrics such as AUC, where it's often desirable to balance the test set:
	
	`sklearn.metrics.confusion_`
	`matrix(…, sample_weight)`
	
	`sklearn.linear_model`
	
	`.LogisticRegression()`
	
	`.score(…, sample_weight)`
		Mainly used during training to guide the training.
		
		Accounts for misclassification errors because certain classes are more important than others:
		
		`sklearn.linear_model`
		
		`.LogisticRegression(`
		
		`class_weight)`

Effect of setting the value to 0 during model training	Model will not take into account the examples for which `samples_weight=0` (irrespective of the example's class).	The model will not consider any example belonging to the class for which `class_weight = 0`. Also, the model will never predict that class.
Use case example	When predicting customer churn, if losing certain customers would have a larger impact on business because they tend to purchase more often or spend more, we would want to give these customers a higher weight using `sample_weight`.	If we have a dataset where one class significantly outnumbers the other(s), using `class_weight` can help the model pay more attention to the underrepresented class(es).

Table 5.2 – sample_weight versus class_weight in the scikit-learn library

> **Warning**
>
> If we use `sample_weight` along with `class_weight`, both will be multiplied, and we will see the effect of both parameters. The two can still be used together to balance class importance and individual instance importance with their intended purposes.

Using numpy makes it easier to create the list of weight values that are required by `sample_weight`: `sample_weight = np.where(label==1, 80, 20)`. However, `scikit-learn` has a function called `sklearn.utils.class_weight.compute_sample_weight()` that can be used to estimate the value of `sample_weight` automatically from `class_weight`.

`class_weight` can also be a dict of values for each label or balanced. If we set it to balanced, class weights are determined by `n_samples/(n_classes * np.bincount(y))`.

The returned value from `class_weight` is a dictionary: `{class_label: weight}` for each `class_label` value.

Similarly, you can use `sklearn.utils.class_weight.compute_sample_weight` if you have to do multi-label classification.

> 🚀 **Cost-sensitive learning in production at Airbnb**
>
> In a real-world application at Airbnb [6], the main problem to solve was improving the search and discoverability as well as personalization of their Experiences (handcrafted activities) platform. As the number of experiences grew, it became crucial to effectively rank these experiences to match user preferences and improve bookings.
>
> Airbnb aimed to improve its search ranking to provide users with the most relevant and high-quality experiences. To promote the quality of their ranking model, they used sample weights (discussed in the previous section) in their objective function.
>
> The data imbalance in terms of quality tiers was addressed by using sample weighting (discussed in the previous section) in the training data. High-quality experiences were given higher weights, and low-quality experiences were given lower weights in the objective function. This was done to promote high-quality experiences in the search rankings, and they successfully improved the ranking of high-quality experiences and reduced low-quality ones without affecting overall bookings, as confirmed by A/B tests.
>
> Airbnb iteratively developed and tested its machine learning model, eventually integrating it into its production system to rank "Experiences" in real time. They went through multiple stages, from building a strong baseline to personalization and online scoring to handle various business rules.

In the next section, we will learn about a technique that can convert any model into its cost-sensitive version without us knowing about its loss function or the inner workings of the model.

MetaCost – making any classification model cost-sensitive

MetaCost was first introduced in a paper by Pedro Domingos [7] in 1999. MetaCost acts as a wrapper around machine learning algorithms that converts the underlying algorithm into a cost-sensitive version of itself. It treats the underlying algorithm as a black box and works best with unstable algorithms (defined below). When MetaCost was first proposed, CSL was in its early stages. Only a few algorithms, such as decision trees, had been converted into their cost-sensitive versions. For some models, creating a cost-sensitive version turned out to be easy while for others it was a non-trivial task. For algorithms where defining cost-sensitive versions of the model turned out to be difficult, people mostly relied upon data sampling techniques such as oversampling or undersampling. This was when Domingos came up with an approach for converting a large range of algorithms into their cost-sensitive versions. MetaCost can work for multi-class classification and with all types of cost matrices.

> **Unstable algorithms**
>
> An algorithm is called unstable [8] if a slight change in its initial conditions (for example, training data or initial weights) can create a big change in the model. Assume you are given a dataset of 1,000 items. A stable model such as a **K-Nearest Neighbor** (**KNN**) will not change much if you remove one item from the dataset. However, a model such as a decision tree might get completely restructured if you train it on 999 items instead of 1,000 items.

Let's delve into the mechanics of the MetaCost algorithm, as illustrated in *Figure 5.12*:

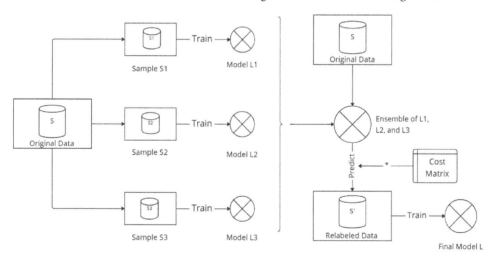

Figure 5.12 – The MetaCost algorithm

MetaCost works by combining the concept of bagging with a misclassification cost matrix:

1. First, we create multiple bootstrap samples of the original data.

2. We train one new copy of the given model for each bootstrap sample. So far, the process is the same as bagging. You can see the first two steps in *Figure 5.12* on the left-hand side. First, we create bootstrap samples S1, S2, and S3 from the original data. Then, we train models L1, L2, and L3 on the samples (S1, S2, and S3), respectively.

3. Next, we send the original data, S, into the ensemble of L1, L2, and L3.

4. We multiply the misclassification costs obtained from the cost matrix with the class probabilities predicted by the ensemble to get the actual cost. This is shown on the right-hand side of *Figure 5.12*.

5. Then, we relabel the data so that the new class labels minimize the actual cost.

6. Finally, we train a new copy of the model on the relabeled data. This copy of the model is used as the final model.

We can see the process of relabeling data using MetaCost in *Figure 5.13*:

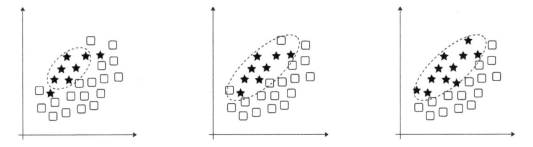

Figure 5.13 – Process of relabeling data using MetaCost

On the left of *Figure 5.13*, we have the original data. Stars are the minority class examples and squares are the majority class examples. Here, all the samples inside the oval are predicted as stars, and all the samples outside it are predicted as squares. The oval on the left is drawn by assuming the same misclassification cost for all errors. In the center, we create a new class boundary based on the actual misclassification cost drawn as an elongated oval. Notice that all the stars are now classified correctly. Also, notice that some squares are now misclassified as stars. This is expected as the misclassification cost for the stars is much higher than that of squares. At this point, MetaCost relabels these misclassified squares as stars. Finally, MetaCost trains a model on the relabeled data. Because the majority class examples that are easily mistaken for the minority class have been relabeled as belonging to the minority class, the final model is less likely to mislabel instances of the minority class.

To save space, we have omitted the implementation of the MetaCost algorithm. You can find it in the GitHub repository for this chapter.

We will apply the algorithm to the logistic regression model. MetaCost uses a cost matrix, which is a hyperparameter. The values in the cost matrix correspond to the weight or cost of items in the confusion matrix (the transpose of the confusion matrix from *Table 5.1*):

$$C = \begin{pmatrix} TN & FN \\ FP & TP \end{pmatrix}$$

Let's say we use a cost matrix with equal costs for false positives and false negatives (that is, an identity matrix):

```
C = np.array([[0, 1], [1, 0]])
```

Figure 5.14 shows the decision boundary and metrics, which are very close to the ones from the logistic regression classifier (*Figure 5.10*):

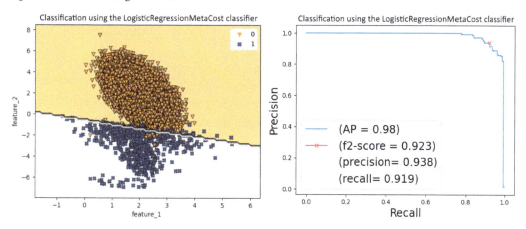

Figure 5.14 – The decision boundary (left) and PR curve (right) of the MetaCost variant of the logistic regression model with an identity cost matrix

We can estimate the cost matrix based on the imbalance ratio of the training data:

```
C = np.array([[0, 66], [1, 0]])
```

Figure 5.15 shows the output decision function and PR curve:

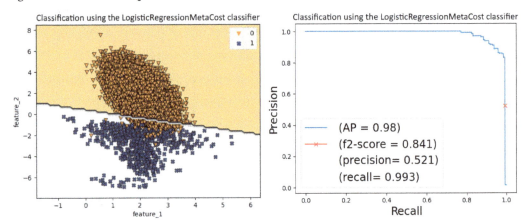

Figure 5.15 – The decision boundary (left) and PR curve (right) of the MetaCost
variant of the logistic regression model with a more optimal cost matrix

Although the F2 score dropped compared to the baseline, the recall did improve drastically.

The various steps in the MetaCost algorithm, such as relabeling the whole training set, can be quite an expensive operation, and that might deter us from using this technique when our training dataset is large.

> **Cost-sensitive ensemble techniques**
>
> AdaCost [9], AdaUBoost [10], and AsymBoost [11] are cost-sensitive modifications of the AdaBoost model. AdaCost minimizes misclassification costs during iterative training. AdaUBoost handles imbalanced datasets by emphasizing the minority class. AsymBoost focuses on reducing the costliest misclassifications. They all adjust weights while considering misclassification costs.
>
> The underlying principle behind these algorithms is that besides allocating high initial weights to instances where the cost of misclassification is large, the rule for updating weights should also consider costs. This means that the weights of expensive misclassifications should be increased while the weights of correct classifications should be reduced.

In the next section, we will learn about another cost-sensitive meta-learning technique, called threshold adjustment.

Threshold adjustment

The decision threshold is a very important concept to keep track of. By default, we have the following:

- Prediction probability >= 0.5 implies Class 1
- Prediction probability < 0.5 implies Class 0

However, the threshold is a powerful meta-parameter that we are free to adjust. *Table 5.3* shows predictions from a model versus the true labels.

If we use the default threshold of 0.5, the accuracy is 2/4 = 50%. If, on the other hand, the threshold chosen is 0.80, the accuracy is 100%. This shows how important the chosen threshold can be:

Predicted Output	True Output
0.65	0
0.75	0
0.85	1
0.95	1

Table 5.3 – A table showing the predicted output from a model versus the true output (labels)

Most of the metrics, such as accuracy, precision, recall, and F1 score, are all threshold-dependent metrics.

On the other hand, metrics such as the ROC curve and the PR curve are threshold-independent, which means that these plots evaluate the performance of a model at all possible thresholds rather than a single, fixed threshold.

When dealing with machine learning metrics such as F1 or accuracy, it's important to understand the role of the threshold value. These metrics, by default, utilize a threshold of 0.5. Therefore, a misconception arises, particularly among novice and intermediate machine learning practitioners, that these metrics are inevitably linked to this particular threshold.

However, this can lead to an inaccurate interpretation of the model's performance, particularly in scenarios involving imbalanced datasets. The selection of the metric and the decision threshold are separate choices and should be treated as such. Establishing an appropriate threshold is a crucial step in the process, which should be considered independently of the chosen metric.

Furthermore, relying solely on the default threshold of 0.5 can be misleading. The threshold should be set based on the specific requirements of the project and the nature of the data. Therefore, it's integral that machine learning practitioners understand the interplay between the threshold and the selected metric to accurately assess the performance of their models.

In binary classification, altering the threshold will easily change the threshold-dependent metrics such as accuracy, F1 score, TPR, or FPR. Many pieces of research [12][13] have mentioned the value of threshold adjustment, especially in the case when training data is imbalanced. A paper by Provost [14] states that using models without adjusting the output thresholds may be a critical mistake. Among deep learning domains, Buda et al. [15] show that using **random oversampling (ROS)** along with thresholding outperforms plain ROS on imbalanced datasets created from CIFAR and MNIST. Regardless of whether the data is imbalanced or not, choosing an optimal threshold can make a lot of difference in the performance of the model.

Many times, we would want to find the threshold that optimizes our threshold-dependent metric, say F1 score. Here, find the threshold at which the F1 score is the maximum (*Figure 5.16*):

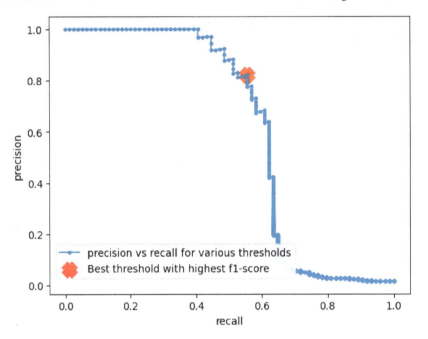

Figure 5.16 – A PR curve with the best threshold that finds the max F1 score (see the notebook in this chapter's GitHub repository)

Figure 5.17 presents a plot that illustrates the impact of modifying the decision threshold on various classification metrics for an imbalanced dataset: **True Positive Rate (TPR** or recall), **True Negative Rate (TNR), False Positive Rate (FPR)**, and precision. The model that was used was logistic regression without any class weighting or sensitivity to the minority class. For the full notebook, please refer to the GitHub repository for this chapter:

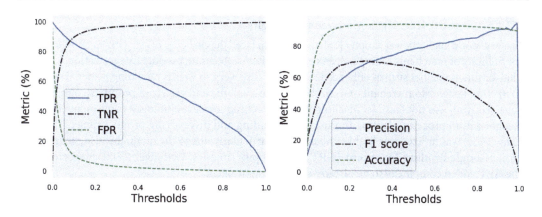

Figure 5.17 – A plot of the different classification metrics (TPR, TNR, FPR, precision, F1 score, and accuracy) as a function of the decision threshold

Here are some observations about these plots:

- **Precision**: If the threshold is increased, precision ($\frac{TP}{Total\ number\ of\ positive\ predictions}$) typically goes up as well. Why? Because as the threshold is increased, the total number of positive predictions would come down, and hence, as the denominator decreases, precision increases. Similarly, the opposite is true as well: if the threshold goes down, the precision goes down too.

- **Recall**: Let's see the impact of threshold change on recall. The recall is defined as $\frac{TP}{Total\ number\ of\ positives}$ and the denominator is a constant value. As the threshold is lowered, TP may increase and would typically increase the recall.

- **True Negative Rate** (TNR): TNR measures the proportion of actual negatives that are correctly identified as such. In imbalanced datasets, where the negative class is the majority, a naive or poorly performing classifier might have a high TNR simply because it predicts the majority class for all or most instances. In such cases, the TNR could be misleadingly high.

- **False Positive Rate** (FPR): This is the rate at which negative instances are incorrectly classified as positive. In imbalanced datasets, a naive classifier that predicts everything as the majority (negative) class would have an FPR close to 0.

Usually, we have a trade-off between TPR and TNR that must be taken into account while selecting an optimal decision threshold, as shown in the plot in *Figure 5.17*.

🚀 Cost-sensitive learning in production at Shopify

In a real-world application at Shopify [16], the platform faced the challenge of categorizing products for millions of merchants selling a diverse array of items. Accurate product categorization was vital for functionalities such as enhanced search and discovery, as well as providing personalized marketing insights to merchants. Given the immense volume and variety of products, manual categorization was not feasible. Machine learning techniques were employed to automate the categorization process, adapting to the ever-expanding and diversifying product range. The dataset that was utilized was highly imbalanced, particularly due to the hierarchical structure of the **Google Product Taxonomy** (**GPT**) that Shopify employs. With over 5,500 categories, the GPT added complexity to an already challenging problem.

To address the issue of data imbalance, class weights were implemented. By assigning the class weights, the model could impose higher penalties for incorrect predictions in underrepresented classes, effectively mitigating the lack of data in those categories. The model was fine-tuned to strike a balance between hierarchical precision and recall. This fine-tuning was informed by specific business use cases and aimed at enhancing the merchant experience by minimizing negative interactions and friction. Manual adjustments were made to the confidence thresholds (this shows that threshold tuning is so relevant in the real world!) to ensure optimal performance in sensitive categories such as "Religious and Ceremonial." Various metrics such as hierarchical accuracy, precision, recall, and F1 score were balanced to tailor the model to business requirements. The model is now actively used by multiple internal teams and partner ecosystems to develop derivative data products.

Next, we'll look at various ways of tuning these thresholds.

Methods for threshold tuning

Most of the time, we aim to optimize specific business metrics or standard machine learning metrics, requiring us to select a threshold that maximizes the metric of interest. In literature, various methods for threshold tuning are discussed, such as setting a threshold equal to the priority probability of observing a positive example, using the ROC curve to optimize for high TPR and low FPR, or employing the PR curve to maximize the F1 score or F_{beta} score (see *Figure 5.18*):

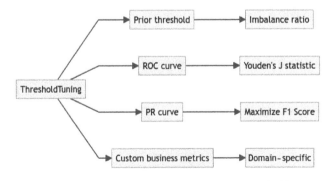

Figure 5.18 – Popular ways of tuning the threshold

We will discuss these methods one by one.

We will continue to use the same dataset we created earlier. The following code block fits a logistic regression model and obtains predicted probabilities for the test set:

```
lr = LogisticRegression(max_iter=1000)
lr.fit(X_train, y_train)
y_pred = lr.predict_proba(X_test)
y_pred = y_pred[:, 1]
```

Threshold tuning using the prior threshold

An obvious threshold that can be used is equal to the probability of the positive class in the training dataset [10]. Let's implement this idea:

```
num_pos, num_neg = Counter(y)[1], Counter(y)[0]
prior_threshold = num_pos /(num_pos + num_neg)
print('Prior threshold=%f'% prior_threshold)

# Find the closest threshold from thresholds from ROC curve
fpr, tpr, thresholds = roc_curve(y_test, y_pred)
min_threshold_index = np.absolute( \
    thresholds-prior_threshold).argmin()
print('Best threshold using prior threshold from ROC \
    function=%f'% thresholds[min_threshold_index])
print("TPR at threshold=%f" % tpr[min_threshold_index])
print("FPR at threshold=%f" % fpr[min_threshold_index])
print("TNR at threshold=%f" % (1-fpr[min_threshold_index]))
```

This prints the following threshold:

```
Prior threshold=0.014900
Best threshold using prior threshold from ROC function=0.014232
TPR value at the threshold=0.675676
FPR value at the threshold=0.147990
TNR value at the threshold=0.852010
```

Threshold tuning using the ROC curve

For the ROC curve, Youden's J statistic [17] can be used to find the optimal threshold. Youden's J statistic has roots in the clinical field and is a single statistic that captures the performance of a diagnostic test. In the context of binary classification, the statistic, J, is defined as follows:

$$J = Sensitivity + Specificity - 1 = TPR + TNR - 1 = TPR - FPR$$

Its value can range from -1 (TPR=0 and TNR=0 – that is, always wrong results) to 1 (TPR=1 and FPR=0 – that is, perfect results). This is a common choice for selecting a threshold in an ROC analysis since it balances both sensitivity (TPR) and specificity (TNR). Please note that TNR = 1-FPR.

The reason that maximizing Youden's J is equivalent to choosing the optimal threshold is that it essentially finds the point on the ROC curve that is farthest from the line of no discrimination (the diagonal). This means that it selects a threshold that achieves a balance between TPR and FPR, which is often what we want in a classifier.

The "optimal" threshold can depend heavily on the cost of false positives versus false negatives in our specific application. The following code block identifies the optimal classification threshold using the Youden index, which is calculated from the ROC curve:

```
fpr, tpr, thresholds = roc_curve(y_test, y_pred)
youden_index = tpr - fpr
max_youden_index = np.argmax(youden_index)
best_thresh = thresholds[max_youden_index]
print('Best threshold using Youden index=%f'% best_thresh)
print('Max Youden index value=%f'% youden_index[max_youden_index])
print("TPR value at the threshold=%f" % tpr[max_youden_index])
print("FPR value at the threshold=%f" % fpr[max_youden_index])
print("TNR value at the threshold=%f" % (1-fpr[max_youden_index]))
```

This outputs the following values:

```
Best threshold using Youden index=0.098879
Max Youden index value=0.622143
TPR value at the threshold=0.635135
FPR value at the threshold=0.012992
TNR value at the threshold=0.987008
```

Another threshold adjustment method that uses ROC curves that's often used in literature is maximizing the geometric mean of TPR (also known as sensitivity) and TNR (also known as specificity):

$$G - mean = \sqrt{Sensitivity * Specificity} = \sqrt{TPR * TNR} = \sqrt{TPR * (1 - FPR)}$$

Maximizing the geometric mean is equivalent to finding a good balance between TPR and TNR. The following code block calculates the best threshold for classification using the G-mean metric, along with its corresponding TPR, FPR, and TNR values. We import `roc_curve` from `sklearn.metrics`:

```
fpr, tpr, thresholds = roc_curve(y_test, y_pred)
gmean = np.sqrt(tpr*(1-fpr))
max_gmean_index = np.argmax(gmean)

best_thresh = thresholds[max_gmean_index]
print('Best threshold using G-mean=%f'% (best_thresh))
print('Max G-mean value=%f'% (gmean[max_gmean_index]))
print("TPR value at the threshold=%f" % tpr[max_gmean_index])
print("FPR value at the threshold=%f" % fpr[max_gmean_index])
print("TNR value at the threshold=%f" % (1 - fpr[max_youden_index]))
```

This outputs the following optimal values:

```
Best threshold using G-mean=0.098879
Max G-mean value=0.791760
TPR value at the threshold=0.635135
FPR value at the threshold=0.012992
TNR value at the threshold=0.987008
```

Threshold tuning using the PR curve

As we discussed in *Chapter 1, Introduction to Data Imbalance in Machine Learning*, the PR curve is generally preferred over ROC curves for imbalanced datasets when the positive class is more important than the negative class. As a reminder, the simple reason for this is that the PR curve ignores the true negatives, and hence, it can represent a stark difference between model performance when using imbalanced datasets in comparison to a balanced dataset. While ROC curves won't change much as an imbalance in the data increases, they can be a preferred option if both classes are equally important.

We want the maximum possible values for both precision and recall, ideally both being 1. Thus, the point of optimality on a PR curve is (1,1).

When we move away from this point of optimality, both the precision and recall values decrease, and we are less optimal.

One measure that captures this trade-off between precision and recall is the F1 score. The F1 score is defined as the harmonic mean of the precision and recall:

$$F1 = 2 * (Precision * Recall) / (Precision + Recall)$$

If we analyze this equation, we will see that the F1 score is highest (reaching its maximum at 1) when both precision and recall are 1, which is exactly the optimal point we defined on the PR curve.

Therefore, optimizing for the maximum F1 score would ensure that we are striving to maximize both precision and recall, effectively pushing us toward the optimal point on the PR curve.

Maximizing the F1 score is a common and effective method for determining the optimal threshold. The following code block calculates the best threshold using the F1 score metric derived from the PR curve:

```
from numpy import argmax
from sklearn.metrics import precision_recall_curve
precision, recall, thresholds = precision_recall_curve(y_test, y_pred)
fscore = 2*precision*recall/(precision+recall)
max_fscore_idx = argmax(fscore)
print('max_fscore_idx==%d' % max_fscore_idx)
print('best threshold using PR curve=%f' % thresholds[max_fscore_idx])
```

This outputs the following optimal values:

```
max_fscore_idx==4950
best threshold using PR curve=0.258727
max(fscore)= 0.661290
```

Let's plot the PR curve with the optimal threshold value:

```
pyplot.plot(recall, precision, marker='.', \
    label='precision vs recall for various thresholds')
result = pyplot.scatter(recall[max_fscore_idx], \
    precision[max_fscore_idx], \
    marker='x', color='red', \
    label='Best threshold with highest\
    f1-score')
plt.legend(handles=result.legend_elements()[0], \
    labels="legend", loc='upper center', \
    bbox_to_anchor=(1, 1))
pyplot.xlabel('recall')
pyplot.ylabel('precision')
```

The PR curve looks like this:

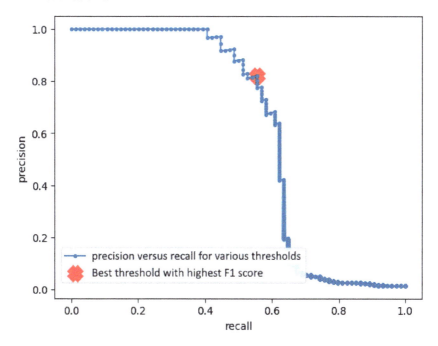

Figure 5.19 – The PR curve with the best F1 score threshold value

General threshold tuning

As a general method, we may have to optimize any metric, such as average precision, accuracy, and so on, or any other business metric. In such cases, we can write a function to optimize that metric directly. Let's take the example of the **Index of Union** (IU) metric defined by I. Unal et al. in their research [18], where the metric is defined by the threshold value, c, at which $IU(c)$ is minimized:

$$IU(c) = (|Sensitivity(c) - ROC\_AUC| + |Specificity(c) - ROC\_AUC|)$$

Here, *Sensitivity*(c) is the sensitivity at c, *Specificity* is the specificity at c, and *ROC_AUC* is the **Area Under the Curve** (**AUC**) of the ROC plot.

Let's implement the IU metric, as defined here, as a custom metric to find the optimal threshold that minimizes it:

```
from sklearn.metrics import f1_score, auc
def custom_metric(y_test, y_pred):
    fpr, tpr, thresholds = roc_curve(y_test, y_pred)
    sensitivity = tpr
    specificity = 1-fpr #same as tnr
```

```
    roc_auc = auc(fpr, tpr)
    index_of_union = abs(sensitivity-roc_auc) + \
        abs(specificity-roc_auc)
    return index_of_union

scores = custom_metric(y_test, y_pred)
min_score_idx = np.argmin(scores)
print('max_score_idx=%d' % min_score_idx)
print('best threshold=%f'% thresholds[min_score_idx])
print('minimum IU-value at the best threshold=%f' % \
    scores[min_score_idx])
```

This produces the following optimal values:

```
max_score_idx=34
best threshold=0.000042
minimum IU-value at the best threshold=0.112514
```

This wraps up our discussion on classical modeling techniques. We are now ready to venture into studying data imbalance in the realm of deep learning. We'll explore how the insights gained from the general techniques learned from previous chapters can be adapted to enhance our deep learning models when dealing with imbalanced data.

Summary

In this chapter, we delved into CSL, an alternative to oversampling and undersampling. Unlike data-level techniques that treat all misclassification errors equally, CSL adjusts the cost function of a model to account for the significance of different classes. It includes class weighting and meta-learning techniques.

Libraries such as scikit-learn, Keras/TensorFlow, and PyTorch support cost-sensitive learning. For instance, scikit-learn offers a class_weight hyperparameter to adjust class weights in loss calculation. XGBoost has a scale_pos_weight parameter for balancing positive and negative weights. MetaCost transforms any algorithm into its cost-sensitive version using bagging and a misclassification cost matrix. Additionally, threshold adjustment techniques can enhance metrics such as F1 score, precision, and recall by post-processing model predictions.

Experiments with various data sampling and CSL techniques can help determine the best approach. We'll extend these concepts to deep learning models in *Chapter 8, Algorithm-Level Deep Learning Techniques*. This concludes our discussion of classical machine learning models, and we have graduated to move on to deep learning techniques. In the next chapter, we will briefly introduce deep learning concepts and see how imbalanced datasets could be a problem in the deep learning world.

Questions

1. Apply the CSL technique to the SVM model from `scikit-learn` while utilizing the dataset that was used in this chapter. Use the `class_weight` and `sample_weight` parameters, similar to how we used them for other models in this chapter. Compare the performance of this model with the ones that we already encountered in this chapter.

2. LightGBM is another gradient-boosting framework similar to XGBoost. Apply the cost-sensitive learning technique to a LightGBM model while utilizing the dataset we used in this chapter. Use the `class_weight` and `sample_weight` parameters similar to how we used them for other models in this chapter. Compare the performance of this model with the ones that we already encountered in this chapter.

3. AdaCost [10] is a variant of AdaBoost that combines boosting with CSL. It updates the training distribution for successive boosting rounds by utilizing the misclassification cost. Extend `AdaBoostClassifier` from `scikit-learn` to implement the AdaCost algorithm. Compare the performance of AdaCost with MetaCost on the dataset that was used in this chapter.

4. Tune the hyperparameters, specifically `max_depth`, `max_delta_step`, and `min_child_weight`, for the XGBoost model using the dataset that we used in this chapter. After tuning, evaluate whether the weighted XGBoost model outperforms the non-weighted version.

References

1. P. Turney, *Types of cost in inductive concept learning*, Proc. Workshop on CostSensitive Learning at the 17th Int. Conf. Mach. Learn., Stanford University, CA (2000), pp. 15–21.

2. C. X. Ling and V. S. Sheng, *Cost-Sensitive Learning and the Class Imbalance Problem*.

3. Sheng, V. S., & Ling, C. X. (2006). *Thresholding for making classifiers cost-sensitive*. AAAI'06: Proceedings of the 21st national conference on artificial intelligence, vol. 6, pp. 476–481.

4. *Pneumonia in Children Statistics* – UNICEF data: `https://data.unicef.org/topic/child-health/pneumonia/`.

5. X. Ling, W. Deng, C. Gu, H. Zhou, C. Li, and F. Sun, Model Ensemble for Click Prediction in Bing Search Ads, in Proceedings of the 26th International Conference on World Wide Web Companion – WWW '17 Companion, Perth, Australia: ACM Press, 2017, pp. 689–698. doi: `10.1145/3041021.3054192`.

6. *Machine Learning-Powered Search Ranking of Airbnb Experiences* (2019), `https://medium.com/airbnb-engineering/machine-learning-powered-search-ranking-of-airbnb-experiences-110b4b1a0789`.

7. P. Domingos, MetaCost: A general method for making classifiers cost-sensitive, in Proceedings of International Conference on Knowledge Discovery and Data Mining, pp. 155–164, 1999.

8. *Unstable Learner.* In: Sammut, C., Webb, G.I. (eds) Encyclopedia of Machine Learning and Data Mining. Springer, Boston, MA. doi: `https://doi.org/10.1007/978-1-4899-7687-1_866`.

9. W. Fan, S. J. Stolfo, J. Zhang, and P. K. Chan, *AdaCost: Misclassification Cost-sensitive Boosting.*

10. G. I. Karakoulas and J. Shawe-Taylor, *Optimizing Classifiers for Imbalanced Training Sets.*

11. P. Viola and M. Jones, *Fast and Robust Classification using Asymmetric AdaBoost and a Detector Cascade.*

12. J. M. Johnson and T. M. Khoshgoftaar, *Output Thresholding for Ensemble Learners and Imbalanced Big Data*, in 2021 IEEE 33rd International Conference on Tools with Artificial Intelligence (ICTAI), Washington, DC, USA: IEEE, Nov. 2021, pp. 1449–1454. doi: `10.1109/ICTAI52525.2021.00230`.

13. J. M. Johnson and T. M. Khoshgoftaar, *Deep Learning and Thresholding with Class-Imbalanced Big Data*, in 2019 18th IEEE International Conference On Machine Learning And Applications (ICMLA), Boca Raton, FL, USA, Dec. 2019, pp. 755–762. doi: 10.1109/ICMLA.2019.00134.

14. F. Provost, *Machine Learning from Imbalanced Data Sets 101.*

15. M. Buda, A. Maki, and M. A. Mazurowski, *A systematic study of the class imbalance problem in convolutional neural networks*, Neural Networks, vol. 106, pp. 249–259, Oct. 2018, doi: `10.1016/j.neunet.2018.07.011`.

16. *Using Rich Image and Text Data to Categorize Products at Scale* (2021), `https://shopify.engineering/using-rich-image-text-data-categorize-products`.

17. W. J. Youden, *Index for rating diagnostic tests*, Cancer, vol. 3, no. 1, pp. 32–35, 1950, doi: 10.1002/1097-0142(1950)3:1<32::AID-CNCR2820030106>3.0.CO;2-3.

18. I. Unal, *Defining an Optimal Cut-Point Value in ROC Analysis: An Alternative Approach*, Computational and Mathematical Methods in Medicine, vol. 2017, pp. 1–14, 2017, doi: `10.1155/2017/3762651`.

19. X. Ling, W. Deng, C. Gu, H. Zhou, C. Li, and F. Sun, *Model Ensemble for Click Prediction in Bing Search Ads*, in Proceedings of the 26th International Conference on World Wide Web Companion – WWW '17 Companion, Perth, Australia: ACM Press, 2017, pp. 689–698. doi: `10.1145/3041021.3054192`.

Data Imbalance in Deep Learning

Class imbalanced data is a common issue for deep learning models. When one or more classes have significantly fewer samples, the performance of deep learning models can suffer as they tend to prioritize learning from the majority class, resulting in poor generalization for the minority class(es).

A lot of real-world data is imbalanced, which presents challenges to deep learning classification tasks. *Figure 6.1* shows some common categories of imbalanced data problems in various deep learning applications:

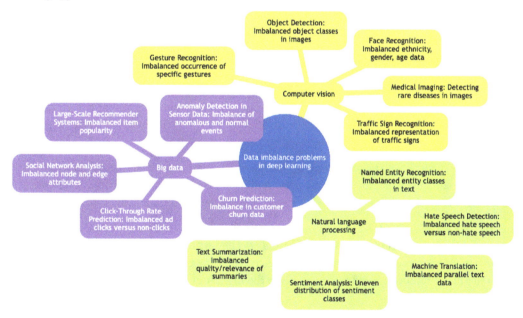

Figure 6.1 – Some common categories of imbalanced data problems

We will cover the following topics in this chapter:

- A brief introduction to deep learning

- Data imbalance in deep learning

- Overview of deep learning techniques to handle data imbalance

- Multi-label classification

By the end of this chapter, we'll have a foundational understanding of deep learning and neural networks. We'll have also grasped the impact of data imbalance on these models and gained a high-level overview of various strategies to address the challenges of imbalanced data.

Technical requirements

In this chapter, we will utilize common libraries such as `numpy`, `scikit-learn`, and `PyTorch`. `PyTorch` is an open source machine learning library that's used for deep learning tasks and has grown in popularity recently because of its flexibility and ease of use.

You can install `PyTorch` using `pip` or `conda`. Visit the official PyTorch website (`https://pytorch.org/get-started/locally/`) to get the appropriate command for your system configuration.

The code and notebooks for this chapter are available on GitHub at `https://github.com/PacktPublishing/Machine-Learning-for-Imbalanced-Data/tree/main/chapter06`.

A brief introduction to deep learning

Deep learning is a subfield of machine learning that focuses on artificial neural networks with multiple layers (deep models typically have three or more layers, including input, output, and hidden layers). These models have demonstrated remarkable capabilities in various applications, including image and speech recognition, natural language processing, and autonomous driving.

The prevalence of "big data" (large volumes of structured or unstructured data, often challenging to manage with traditional data processing software) problems greatly benefited from the development of **Graphical Processing Units** (**GPUs**), which were initially designed for graphics processing.

In this section, we will provide a concise introduction to the foundational elements of deep learning, discussing only what is necessary for the problems associated with data imbalance in deep learning. For a more in-depth introduction, we recommend referring to a more dedicated book on deep learning (please refer to the resources listed as [1] and [2] in the *References* section).

Neural networks

Neural networks are the foundation of deep learning. Inspired by the structure and function of the human brain, neural networks consist of interconnected nodes or artificial neurons organized in layers.

The core data structure in PyTorch is tensors. Tensors are multi-dimensional arrays, similar to NumPy arrays, but with GPU acceleration support and capabilities for automatic differentiation. Tensors can be created, manipulated, and operated using PyTorch functions, as shown here:

```
import torch
# Create a tensor with specific data
t1 = torch.tensor([[1, 2], [3, 4]])

# Create a 2x3 tensor filled with zeros
t2 = torch.zeros(2, 3)

# Create a 2x3 tensor filled with random values
t3 = torch.randn(2, 3)
```

Mixing CUDA tensors with CPU-bound tensors will lead to errors:

```
# moving the tensor to GPU (assuming a GPU with CUDA support is available)
x = torch.rand(2,2).to("cuda")
y = torch.rand(2,2) # this tensor remains on the CPU
x+y      # adding a GPU tensor & a CPU tensor will lead to an error
```

Here's the output:

```
----------------------------------------------------------------------
-----
RuntimeError Traceback (most recent call last)
----> 1 x+y

RuntimeError: Expected all tensors to be on the same device, but found
at least two devices, cuda:0 and cpu!
```

autograd is a powerful feature in PyTorch that allows automatic differentiation for tensor operations. This is particularly useful for backpropagation (discussed later) in neural networks:

```
# Create a tensor with autograd enabled
x = torch.tensor([[1., 2.], [3., 4.]], requires_grad=True)

# Perform operations on the tensor
y = x + 2
z = y * y * 3
```

```
# Compute gradients with respect to the input tensor x
z.backward(torch.ones_like(x))

# Display the gradients
print(x.grad)
```

We will see the following output:

```
tensor([[18., 24.],
        [30., 36.]])
```

Let's review how this code works. It creates a PyTorch tensor, x, performs some operations to compute y and z, and then computes the gradient of z concerning x using the backward() method. The gradients are stored in x.grad. The operations are as follows:

- y = x + 2 increases each element in x by 2

- z = y * y * 3 squares each element in y and then multiplies by 3

The gradient calculation, in this case, involves applying the chain rule to these operations to compute $\frac{dz}{dx}$:

$$\frac{dz}{dx} = \frac{dz}{dy} \cdot \frac{dy}{dx}$$

Ok, let's calculate each piece in this equation:

1. First, let's compute $\frac{dz}{dy}$:

$$\frac{dz}{dy} = 2 * y * 3 = 6 * y = 6 * \left(x + 2 \right)$$

2. $\frac{dy}{dx} = 1$ because y is a linear function of x:

3. Finally, let's compute $\frac{dz}{dx}$:

$$\frac{dz}{dx} = \frac{dz}{dy} \cdot \frac{dy}{dx} = 6 \cdot (x + 2) \cdot 1 = 6 \cdot (x + 2)$$

Given x = [[1., 2.], [3., 4.]], the output when we print x.grad should be as follows:

```
tensor([[18., 24.],
        [30., 36.]])
```

The output tensor corresponds to the evaluated gradients of z concerning x at the specific values of x.

Perceptron

The perceptron is the most basic unit of a neural network. It is a simple, linear classifier that takes a set of input values, multiplies them by their corresponding weights, adds a bias term, sums the results, and applies an activation function to produce an output:

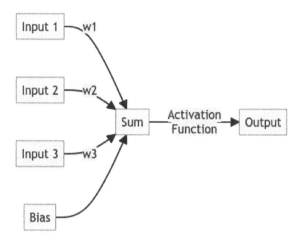

Figure 6.2 – A simple perceptron

So, what's an activation function, then?

Activation functions

Activation functions introduce non-linearity into neural networks and help determine the output of a neuron. Common activation functions include sigmoid, tanh, **Rectified Linear Unit** (**ReLU**), and softmax. These functions enable the network to learn complex, non-linear patterns in the data.

Let's get into the various components of an artificial neural network.

Layers

A neural network typically consists of an input layer, one or more hidden (intermediate) layers, and an output layer. The input layer receives the raw data, while the hidden layers perform various transformations, and the output layer produces the final result.

The number of layers in a neural network is called the **depth** of the network, while the number of neurons in each layer is called the **width** of the network.

Counterintuitively, deeper and wider neural networks, though they have more capacity to learn complex patterns and representations in the training data, are not necessarily more robust to imbalanced datasets than shallower and narrower networks.

Deeper and wider networks are more prone to overfitting, especially in the context of imbalanced datasets, because large networks can memorize the patterns of the majority class(es), which can hamper the performance of minority class(es).

Feedforward neural networks

A feedforward neural network is a kind of neural network that has a unidirectional flow of information, starting from the input layer, progressing through any hidden layers, and ending at the output layer.

There are no feedback loops or connections between layers that cycle back to previous layers, hence the name feedforward. These networks are widely used for tasks such as image classification, regression, and others.

PyTorch provides the nn module for creating and training neural networks – the nn.Module class is the base class for all neural network modules. The following code snippet defines a simple feedforward neural network:

```python
import torch
import torch.optim as optim

class Net(torch.nn.Module):
    def __init__(self):
        super(Net, self).__init__()
        self.fc1 = torch.nn.Linear(4, 10)
        self.fc2 = torch.nn.Linear(10, 3)

    def forward (self, x):
        x = torch.relu(self.fc1(x))
        x = self.fc2(x)
        return x

# Create an instance of the network
net = Net()

# Define a loss function and an optimizer
criterion = torch.nn.CrossEntropyLoss()
optimizer = optim.SGD(net.parameters(), lr=0.01)
```

Loss functions quantify the difference between the predicted output and target values. Common loss functions include **Mean Squared Error** (**MSE**), cross-entropy, and hinge loss.

The most commonly used loss function, CrossEntropyLoss, which we used in the previous snippet, tends to favor the majority class examples in imbalanced datasets. This occurs because the majority class examples significantly outnumber those of the minority class. As a result, the loss function becomes biased toward the majority class and fails to account for the error in the minority classes adequately.

We will learn about several loss function modifications more suited to class imbalance problems in *Chapter 8, Algorithm-Level Deep Learning Techniques.*

MultiLayer Perceptron

A MultiLayer Perceptron (MLP) is a feedforward neural network consisting of an input layer, one or more hidden layers, and an output layer. Each layer is fully connected, meaning every neuron in one layer is connected to all neurons in the next layer. MLPs can be used for various tasks, including classification, regression, and feature extraction. They are particularly suited for problems where the input data can be represented as a fixed-size vector, such as tabular data or flattened images. *Figure 6.3* shows a multilayer perceptron with two input nodes, two hidden nodes, and one output node, using the specified weights w1 to w6:

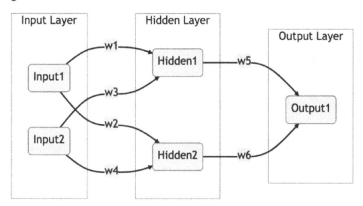

Figure 6.3 – A multilayer perceptron

Training neural networks

Training neural networks involves finding the optimal weights and biases that minimize a loss function. Two essential algorithms are used in this process – gradient descent and backpropagation:

- **Gradient descent**: Gradient descent is an optimization algorithm that minimizes the loss function by iteratively updating the weights and biases.

- **Backpropagation**: Backpropagation is a critical algorithm for training neural networks. It computes the gradient of the loss function concerning each weight using the chain rule (a method for finding the derivative of composite functions), efficiently calculating the gradients from the output layer back to the input layer.

Training a neural network involves iterating through a dataset, feeding the data into the network, computing the loss, and updating the weights using backpropagation, as shown here:

```
# Example dataset
inputs = torch.randn(100, 4)
targets = torch.randint(0, 3, (100,))
```

```
# Train for 100 epochs
for epoch in range(100):
    # Forward pass
    outputs = net(inputs)

    # Compute loss
    loss = criterion(outputs, targets)

    # Backward pass and optimization
    # reset gradients of model parameters
    optimizer.zero_grad()
    # compute the gradient of loss w.r.t model parameters
    loss.backward()
    # update model parameters based on computed gradients
    optimizer.step()

    # Print the loss for this epoch
    print(f"Epoch {epoch + 1}, Loss: {loss.item()}")
```

This code produces the following output, which shows the loss for each epoch (note that the loss goes down as the training progresses):

```
Epoch 1, Loss: 1.106634497642517
Epoch 2, Loss: 1.1064313650131226
...
Epoch 100, Loss: 1.026018738746643
```

In the previous code snippet, the line containing `loss.backward()` maps to the backpropagation process. The `optimizer.zero_grad()` and `optimizer.step()` lines both represent one step of the gradient descent process. `optimizer.zero_grad()` clears old gradients from the last step (otherwise, they will accumulate), while `optimizer.step()` performs the actual update of the parameters (weights and biases) in the direction that reduces the loss the most.

The following flowchart depicts the training logic in PyTorch:

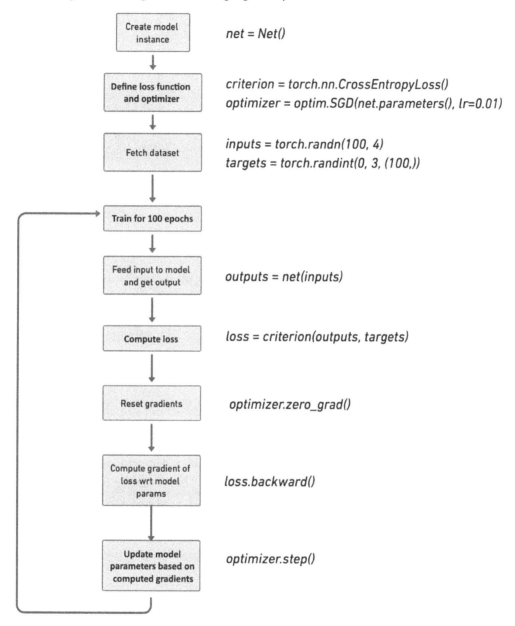

Figure 6.4 – PyTorch training logic flowchart

Overfitting is a common problem in machine learning, where a model performs well on the training data but fails to generalize to unseen data.

Underfitting happens when the model is too simple (think about when we used a linear regression model when we needed a decision tree regressor model) and does not capture the underlying patterns in the data.

Both overfitting and underfitting lead to poor performance on unseen data.

Regularization

Regularization techniques help mitigate overfitting by adding additional constraints the model must meet beyond merely optimizing the loss function. If L is the loss function, the most commonly used types of regularization are L1 and L2, which add a penalty term to the loss function, discouraging overly complex models:

$$L1\text{-}loss = L + \lambda \sum_{i=1}^{n} |w_i|$$
$$L2\text{-}loss = L + \lambda \sum_{i=1}^{n} w_i^2$$

Here, λ is the regularization strength and w_i are the model parameters (weights).

There are a few other regularization techniques as well:

- **Dropout**: Dropout is another regularization technique to prevent overfitting in neural networks. During training, dropout randomly "drops" or deactivates a fraction of neurons in a layer, preventing them from contributing to the output. This forces the network to learn more robust and generalized features as it cannot rely on any single neuron. In `PyTorch`, the `torch.nn.Dropout` class implements dropout and takes the dropout rate (the probability of the neuron being zeroed) as a parameter.

- **Batch normalization**: Batch normalization (implemented in PyTorch using `torch.nn.BatchNorm1d` and `torch.nn.BatchNorm2d`) is a technique that's used to improve the training of deep neural networks. It normalizes the inputs to each layer by adjusting their mean and standard deviation, which helps stabilize and accelerate the training process, allowing the use of higher learning rates and reducing sensitivity to weight initialization.

- **Early stopping**: Early stopping is a technique that's used to prevent overfitting during the training of neural networks. It involves monitoring the model's performance on a validation set and stopping the training process when the performance stops improving or starts to degrade. This helps with finding the point at which the model generalizes well to new data without the need to memorize the training set:

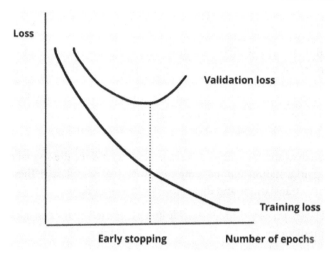

Figure 6.5 – Applying the early stopping technique when
validation loss starts to increase with more epochs

The effect of the learning rate on data imbalance

We have seen that gradient descent takes a step in the direction of the negative gradient – the size of that step is called the **learning rate**.

Choosing the right learning rate is crucial for models operating on imbalanced datasets.

The learning rate should be selected so that the model learns patterns from both majority and minority classes effectively. Monitoring training and validation loss and other evaluation metrics such as precision, recall, and F1-score can help fine-tune the learning rate.

A high learning rate means that the model's weights are updated more drastically during each iteration of training. When applied to the minority class, these rapid, large updates can cause the model to skip over the optimal set of weights that minimize the loss for that class. It's often beneficial to use techniques such as adaptive learning rates [3][4] or even class-specific learning rates [5] to ensure that the model learns effectively from both the majority and minority classes.

Now, let's review some particular kinds of neural networks that have been quite useful for image and text domains.

Image processing using Convolutional Neural Networks

Convolutional Neural Networks (CNNs) is a deep learning model designed for image and video processing tasks. It consists of convolutional layers, pooling layers, and fully connected layers:

- Convolutional layers apply filters to the input data, learning to detect local features such as edges or textures. These filters slide across the input data, performing element-wise multiplication and summing the results, which creates a feature map representing the presence of specific features.

- Pooling layers, such as max-pooling or average pooling, reduce the spatial dimensions of the data, aggregating information and reducing computational complexity. These layers help build invariance to small translations and distortions in the input data.

- Fully connected layers process the high-level features extracted by the convolutional and pooling layers to make predictions. Fully connected layers are traditional neural network layers where each neuron is connected to every neuron in the previous layer.

CNNs tend to overfit minority classes, which is in contrast with traditional machine learning algorithms, which usually underfit these minority classes [6]. The intuition here is that CNNs, with their multiple layers and a large number of parameters, are designed to capture complex patterns. Additionally, being data-hungry, CNNs can learn intricate details from the data. When faced with imbalanced data, CNNs may focus excessively on the minority class, essentially "memorizing" the minority class instances.

We will discuss this in more detail in *Chapter 8, Algorithm-Level Deep Learning Techniques*, in the *Class-Dependent Temperature (CDT) loss* section.

The imbalance problems in the computer vision domain can be categorized as shown in *Figure 6.6* [7]:

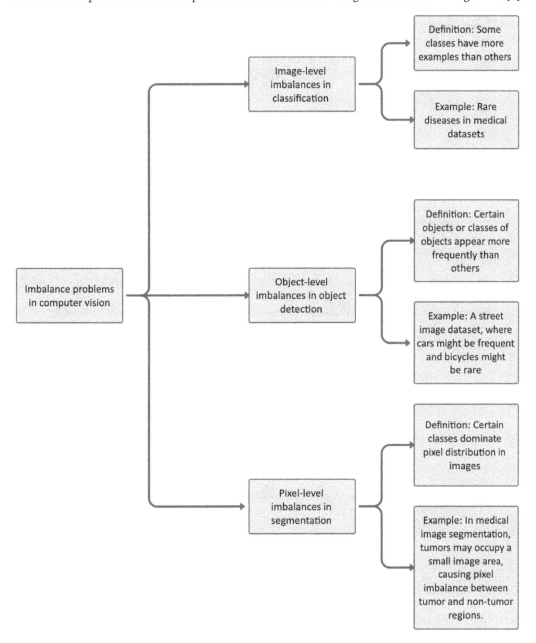

Figure 6.6 – Categorization of imbalance problems in computer vision (adapted from [7])

Text analysis using Natural Language Processing

Natural Language Processing (**NLP**) is another branch of AI that helps computers understand and analyze human language for extracting insights and organizing information. *Figure 6.7* shows the categorization of imbalance problems in text based on data complexity levels, while *Figure 6.8* shows the categorization based on some of the popular NLP application areas:

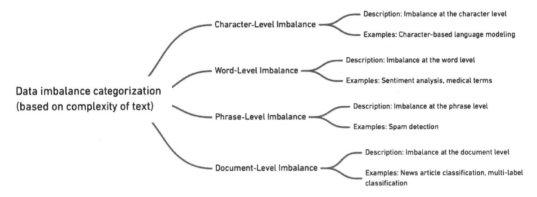

Figure 6.7 – Categorization of imbalance problems in NLP based on the form of textual data

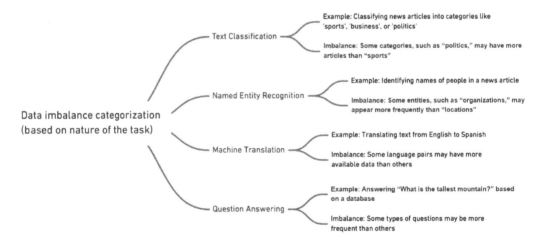

Figure 6.8 – Categorization of imbalance problems in NLP based on applications

With the basics out of the way, let's see how data imbalance affects deep learning models.

Data imbalance in deep learning

While many classical machine learning problems that use tabular data are limited to binary classes and are interested in predicting the minority class, this is not the norm in domains where deep learning is often applied, especially computer vision or NLP problems.

Even benchmark datasets such as MNIST (a collection of handwritten digits containing grayscale images from 0 to 9) and CIFAR10 (color images with 10 different classes) have 10 classes to predict. So, we can say that **multi-class classification** is typical in problems that use deep learning models.

This data skew or imbalance can severely impact the model performance. We should review what we discussed about the typical kinds of imbalance in datasets in *Chapter 1, Introduction to Data Imbalance in Machine Learning*. To simulate real-world data imbalance scenarios, two types of imbalance are usually investigated in the literature:

- **Step imbalance**: All the minority classes have the same or almost the same number of examples, as do all the majority classes:

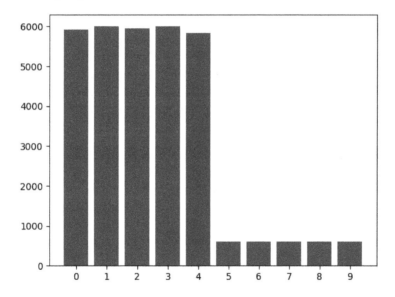

Figure 6.9 – Step imbalance

- **Long-tailed imbalance**: The number of examples across different classes follows an exponential decay. The plot usually has a long tail toward the left or the right:

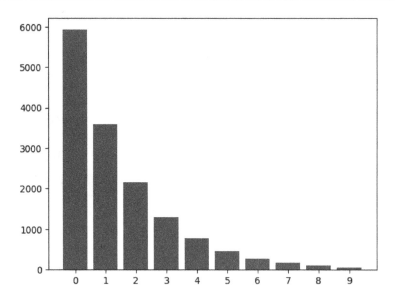

Figure 6.10 – Long-tailed imbalance

Generally, when comparing two datasets, the one with a higher imbalance ratio is likely to yield a lower ROC-AUC score [8]. There can be issues of class overlap, noisy labels, and concept complexity in imbalanced datasets [9][10]. These issues can significantly impact the performance of deep learning models:

- **Class overlap**: Class overlap occurs when instances from different classes are close to each other in the feature space. Deep learning models often rely on complex decision boundaries to separate classes. When instances from different classes are close in the feature space, as is common in imbalanced datasets, the majority class can dominate these decision boundaries. This makes it especially challenging for deep learning models to accurately classify minority class instances.

- **Noisy labels**: Noisy labels refers to instances in a dataset that have incorrect or ambiguous class labels. In imbalanced datasets, noisy labels can disproportionately affect the minority class as the model has fewer instances to learn from. Deep learning models are data-hungry and highly sensitive to the quality of the training data. This can lead to poor generalization in deep learning models, affecting their performance on new, unseen data.

- **Concept complexity**: Concept complexity is the inherent difficulty in distinguishing between classes based on the given features. Deep learning models excel at capturing intricate patterns in the data. However, the complexity of the relationships between features and class labels in imbalanced datasets can make it difficult for these models to effectively learn the minority class. The limited number of instances available for the minority class often compounds this issue.

The impact of data imbalance on deep learning models

Let's also review how data imbalance affects deep learning models compared to classical machine learning models:

- **Model sensitivity**: The performance of deep learning models can be significantly impacted as the imbalance ratio of a dataset increases (*Figure 6.11*):

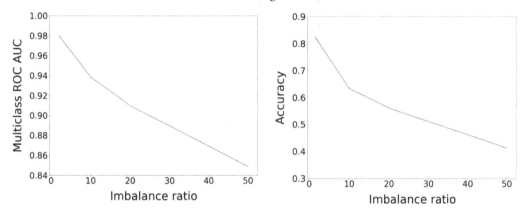

Figure 6.11– Model performance on an imbalanced version of CIFAR-10
with a fixed number of minority classes (adapted from [8])

- **Feature engineering**: Classical machine learning models usually require manual feature engineering, which can help address data imbalance by creating new features or transforming existing ones to highlight the minority class. In deep learning models, feature engineering is typically performed automatically through the learning process, making it less reliant on human intervention to address the imbalance.

- **Techniques to handle imbalance**: In classical machine learning, standard techniques for handling data imbalance include resampling (oversampling the minority class or undersampling the majority class), generating synthetic samples (for example, using the **Synthetic Minority Over-Sampling Technique (SMOTE)**), and using cost-sensitive learning (assigning different misclassification costs to different classes).

    Some techniques from classical machine learning can also be applied in deep learning, but additional methods have been developed specifically for deep learning models. These include transfer learning (leveraging pre-trained models to learn from imbalanced data), using focal loss (a loss function that focuses on hard-to-classify examples), and employing data augmentation techniques to generate more varied and balanced training data. These data augmentation techniques will be discussed in detail in *Chapter 7, Data-Level Deep Learning Methods*.

- **Model interpretability**: Classical machine learning models are often more interpretable, which can help us understand the impact of data imbalance on the model's decision-making process.

Deep learning models, on the other hand, are often referred to as "black boxes" due to their lack of interpretability. This lack of interpretability can make it harder to understand how the model handles imbalanced data and whether it is learning meaningful patterns or simply memorizing the majority class.

- **Training data size**: Deep learning models typically require large amounts of training data to achieve optimal performance. In cases of severe data imbalance, gathering sufficient data for the minority class may be more challenging, hindering the performance of deep learning models. Additionally, if a large dataset is available, it is more likely that instances of the minority class will be found within that vast amount of data. In contrast, in a smaller dataset, the minority class might never appear at all! On the other hand, classical machine learning algorithms can often achieve decent performance with smaller datasets, which is an advantage when dealing with imbalanced data.

- **The impact of depth (number of layers) on deep learning models trained on imbalanced data problems**: The pros of more layers are the improved capacity to learn complex patterns and features in the data and improved generalization of the model. The cons of adding more layers can be the model overfitting and the problem of vanishing or exploding gradients worsening (as depth increases, the gradients during backpropagation can become very small (vanish) or very large (explode), making it challenging to train the model). This is summarized in *Figure 6.12*:

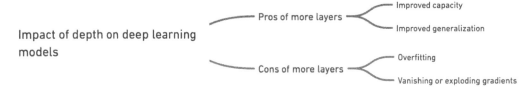

Figure 6.12 – Summarizing the impact of depth on deep learning models

Overall, the influence of depth on a deep learning model varies with the data and model architecture requiring empirical evaluation.

- **Oversampling and undersampling**: The study titled *A systematic study of the class imbalance problem in convolutional neural networks*, by Mateusz Buda [8], thoroughly examined how class imbalance affects the performance of CNNs. The research utilized three well-known datasets – MNIST, CIFAR-10, and ImageNet – and employed models such as LeNet-5, All-CNN, and ResNet-10 for the experiments. Their key findings were as follows:

  - In almost all analyzed cases, oversampling proved to be the most effective technique for mitigating class imbalance

  - Oversampling was more effective when the imbalance was eliminated while undersampling yielded better results when only reducing the imbalance partially

- Contrary to some traditional machine learning algorithms, CNNs did not overfit when oversampling was applied

- In some cases, undersampling performs on par with oversampling, even when using less data

- Undersampling generally showed poor performance compared to the baseline and never showed a notable advantage over oversampling

- If the focus is on correctly classifying examples from minority classes, undersampling may be preferable to oversampling

If there's too much data, undersampling might be the preferred or only option to save time, resources, and the cost of training.

- **Threshold adjustment**: We discussed threshold adjustment in detail in *Chapter 5, Cost-Sensitive Learning*. As a refresher, a decision threshold is a value that determines the boundary between different classes or outcomes in a classification problem. The paper by Johnson et al. [11] emphasized that the optimal threshold is linearly correlated with the minority class size (that is, the lower the minority class size, the lower the threshold). They trained and tested for fraud detection using deep learning models with two and four hidden layers on CMS Medicare data [12]. The default threshold often leads to poor classification, especially for the minority class, highlighting the need for threshold adjustment based on a validation set.

A note about the datasets used in the second half of this book

In the remainder of this book, we will primarily use imbalanced versions of the MNIST and CIFAR10-LT ("LT" stands for "long-tailed") datasets for training:

- **MNIST**: A small grayscale image dataset with 10 classes containing digits from 0 to 9. It consists of 60,000 training images and 10,000 test images, each 28 pixels x 28 pixels. It's faster to train/test compared to CIFAR-10.

- **CIFAR-10**: Used for object recognition, this color image dataset also has 10 classes. It includes 50,000 training images and 10,000 test images, each 32 pixels x 32 pixels.

Though the training sets are imbalanced, the corresponding test sets have an equal number of examples in each class. This balanced test set approach provides several benefits:

- **Comparability**: Balanced test sets allow unbiased comparison across various classes and models

- **Repeatability and reproducibility**: Using simple datasets such as MNIST and CIFAR-10 ensures ease of code execution and understanding

- **Efficiency**: Smaller datasets enable quicker iterations, allowing us to try, test, and retry running the code in a reasonable timeframe

- **Alignment with research**: This approach is consistent with most research studies on long-tailed learning and imbalanced datasets, providing a common framework for comparison

The next section will give us an overview of deep learning strategies for managing data imbalance. We will also see how various techniques for handling imbalanced datasets that were initially developed for classical machine learning techniques can be easily extended to deep learning models.

Overview of deep learning techniques to handle data imbalance

Much like the first half of this book, where we focused on classical machine learning techniques, the major categories typically include sampling techniques, cost-sensitive techniques, threshold adjustment techniques, or a combination of these:

- The sampling techniques comprise either undersampling the majority class or oversampling the minority class data. Data augmentation is a fundamental technique in computer vision problems that's used to increase the diversity of the training set. While not directly an oversampling method aimed at addressing class imbalance, data augmentation does have the effect of expanding the training data. We will discuss these techniques in more detail in *Chapter 7, Data-Level Deep Learning Methods*.

- Cost-sensitive techniques usually involve changing the model loss function in some way to accommodate the higher cost of misclassifying the minority class examples. Some standard loss functions, such as `CrossEntropyLoss` in PyTorch, support the weight parameter to accommodate such costs. We will cover many of those, including several custom loss functions, in detail in *Chapter 8, Algorithm-Level Deep Learning Techniques*.

- Hybrid deep learning techniques integrate the data-level and algorithm-level approaches. This fusion allows for more nuanced and effective solutions to tackle class imbalance. We'll discuss this in *Chapter 9, Hybrid Deep Learning Methods*.

- Threshold adjustment techniques are applied to the scores produced from the model after the model has been trained. These techniques can help adjust the threshold so that the model metric, say, F1-score or geometric mean, gets optimized. This was discussed in *Chapter 5, Cost-Sensitive Learning*:

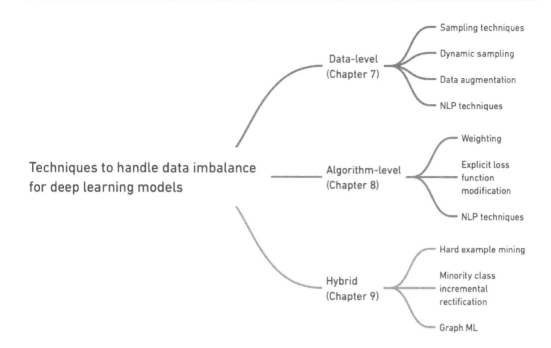

Figure 6.13 – Categorization of deep learning techniques covered

We will not use deep learning methods for tabular data from this chapter onwards because classical models such as XGBoost, LightGBM, and CatBoost tend to perform well on such structured data. Several studies ([13] and [14]) have shown that traditional machine learning models often outperform deep learning models in supervised learning tasks involving tabular data. However, an ensemble of an XGBoost model and a deep learning model can outperform the XGBoost model alone [13]. Therefore, tasks using tabular datasets can still benefit from deep learning models. It's likely only a matter of time before deep learning models catch up to the performance of classical models on tabular data. Nevertheless, we will focus our implementation and examples on vision and NLP problems when using deep learning models.

This concludes our high-level discussion of various techniques for dealing with imbalanced datasets when using deep learning models.

Multi-label classification

Multi-label classification is a classification task where each instance can be assigned to multiple classes or labels simultaneously. In other words, an instance can belong to more than one category or have multiple attributes. For example, a movie can belong to multiple genres, such as action, comedy, and romance. Similarly, an image can have multiple objects in it (*Figure 6.14*):

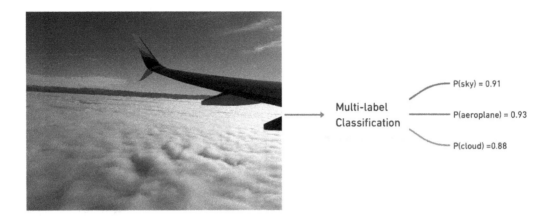

Figure 6.14 – Multi-label image classification with prediction probabilities shown

But how is it different from multi-class classification? Multi-class classification is a classification task where each instance can be assigned to only one class or label. In this case, the classes or categories are mutually exclusive, meaning an instance can belong to just one category. For example, a handwritten digit recognition task would be multi-class since each digit can belong to only one class (0-9).

In summary, the main difference between multi-label and multi-class classification is that in multi-label classification, instances can have multiple labels. In contrast, in multi-class classification, instances can have only one label. This is summarized in *Figure 6.15*:

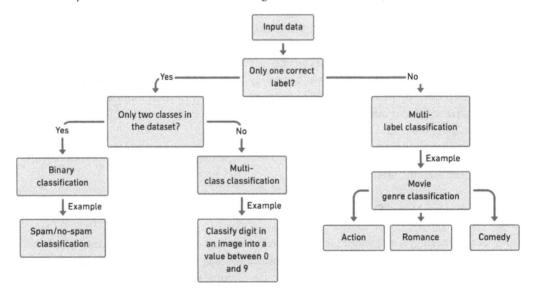

Figure 6.15 – Distinction between multi-label and multi-class classification

Many real-world problems are inherently multi-labeled and experience class imbalance. Deep learning models are particularly useful here, especially when the data involved is unstructured, such as images, videos, or text.

In **Multi-Label Datasets** (**MLDs**), there can be tens or hundreds of labels, and each instance can be associated with a subset of those labels. The more different labels exist, the more possibilities there are that some have a very low presence, leading to a significant imbalance.

The data imbalance in multi-label classification can occur at many levels [15]:

- **Imbalance within labels**: A large disparity between negative and positive instances in each label can happen, causing classification models to struggle with minority classes

- **Imbalance between labels**: Unequal distribution of positive instances among labels, leading to poor performance for minority classes

- **Imbalance among label sets**: Sparse frequency of label sets (a combination of various labels) due to label sparseness, making it challenging for classification models to learn effectively

Figure 6.16 sums up these kinds of imbalances when classifying multi-label datasets:

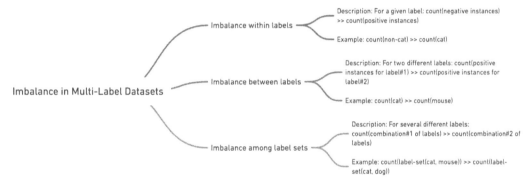

Figure 6.16 – Kinds of imbalances in multi-label datasets

The imbalance handling approaches and metrics are similar to those used for imbalanced multi-class classification methods. Typical approaches include resampling methods, ensemble approaches, and cost-sensitive methods.

The most straightforward approach is to convert the multi-label dataset into the multi-class dataset and then apply various re-sampling methods such as random oversampling, random undersampling, **Edited Nearest Neighbors** (**ENN**), and others. Similar strategies have been used in the literature to adapt the cost-sensitive approaches to fit multi-label classification problems.

Summary

Deep learning has become essential in many fields, from computer vision and natural language processing to healthcare and finance. This chapter has provided a brief introduction to the core concepts and techniques in deep learning. We talked about PyTorch, the fundamentals of deep learning, activation functions, and data imbalance challenges. We also got a bird's-eye view of the various techniques we will discuss in the following few chapters.

Understanding these fundamentals will equip you with the knowledge necessary to explore more advanced topics and applications and ultimately contribute to the ever-evolving world of deep learning.

In the next chapter, we will look at data-level deep learning methods.

Questions

1. What are some challenges in porting data imbalance handling methods from classical machine learning models to deep learning models?

2. How could an imbalanced version of the MNIST dataset be created?

3. Use the MNIST dataset to train a CNN model with varying degrees of imbalance in the data. Record the model's overall accuracy on a fixed test set. Plot how the overall accuracy changes as the imbalance in the training data increases. Observe whether the overall accuracy declines as the training data becomes more imbalanced.

4. What is the purpose of using random oversampling with deep learning models?

5. What are some of the data augmentation techniques that can be applied when dealing with limited or imbalanced data?

6. How does undersampling work in handling data imbalance, and what are its limitations?

7. Why is it important to ensure that the data augmentation techniques preserve the original labels of the dataset?

References

1. A. W. Trask, Grokking Deep Learning (Manning, Shelter Island, NY, 2019).

2. F. Chollet, *Deep Learning with Python*. Manning Publications, 2021.

3. Y. Cui, M. Jia, T.-Y. Lin, Y. Song, and S. Belongie, "*Class-Balanced Loss Based on Effective Number of Samples*," p. 10.

4. K. Cao, C. Wei, A. Gaidon, N. Arechiga, and T. Ma, *Learning Imbalanced Datasets with Label-Distribution-Aware Margin Loss* [Online]. Available at `https://proceedings.neurips.cc/paper/2019/file/621461af90cadfdaf0e8d4cc25129f91-Paper.pdf`.

5. R. Jantanasukon and A. Thammano, *Adaptive Learning Rate for Dealing with Imbalanced Data in Classification Problems*. In 2021 Joint International Conference on Digital Arts, Media and Technology with ECTI Northern Section Conference on Electrical, Electronics, Computer and Telecommunication Engineering, Cha-am, Thailand: IEEE, Mar. 2021, pp. 229–232, doi: `10.1109/ECTIDAMTNCON51128.2021.9425715`.

6. H.-J. Ye, H.-Y. Chen, D.-C. Zhan, and W.-L. Chao, *Identifying and Compensating for Feature Deviation in Imbalanced Deep Learning*. arXiv, Jul. 10, 2022. Accessed: Dec. 14, 2022. [Online]. Available at `http://arxiv.org/abs/2001.01385`.

7. V. Sampath, I. Maurtua, J. J. Aguilar Martín, and A. Gutierrez, *A survey on generative adversarial networks for imbalance problems in computer vision tasks*. J Big Data, vol. 8, no. 1, p. 27, Dec. 2021, doi: `10.1186/s40537-021-00414-0`.

8. M. Buda, A. Maki, and M. A. Mazurowski, *A systematic study of the class imbalance problem in convolutional neural networks*. Neural Networks, vol. 106, pp. 249–259, Oct. 2018, doi: `10.1016/j.neunet.2018.07.011`.

9. K. Ghosh, C. Bellinger, R. Corizzo, B. Krawczyk, and N. Japkowicz, *On the combined effect of class imbalance and concept complexity in deep learning*. arXiv, Jul. 29, 2021. Accessed: Mar. 28, 2023. [Online]. Available at `http://arxiv.org/abs/2107.14194`.

10. K. Ghosh, C. Bellinger, R. Corizzo, B. Krawczyk, and N. Japkowicz, *On the combined effect of class imbalance and concept complexity in deep learning*. arXiv, Jul. 29, 2021. Accessed: Mar. 28, 2023. [Online]. Available at `http://arxiv.org/abs/2107.14194`.

11. J. M. Johnson and T. M. Khoshgoftaar, *Medicare fraud detection using neural networks*. J Big Data, vol. 6, no. 1, p. 63, Dec. 2019, doi: `10.1186/s40537-019-0225-0`.

12. *Medicare fraud & abuse: prevention, detection, and reporting*. Centers for Medicare & Medicaid Services. 2017. `https://www.cms.gov/Outreach-and-Education/Medicare-Learning-Network-MLN/MLNProducts/MLN-Publications-Items/MLN4649244`.

13. R. Shwartz-Ziv and A. Armon, *Tabular Data: Deep Learning is Not All You Need*. arXiv, Nov. 23, 2021. Accessed: Apr. 10, 2023. [Online]. Available at `http://arxiv.org/abs/2106.03253`.

14. V. Borisov, T. Leemann, K. Sessler, J. Haug, M. Pawelczyk, and G. Kasneci, *Deep Neural Networks and Tabular Data: A Survey*. IEEE Trans. Neural Netw. Learning Syst., pp. 1–21, 2022, doi: `10.1109/TNNLS.2022.3229161`.

15. A. N. Tarekegn, M. Giacobini, and K. Michalak, *A review of methods for imbalanced multi-label classification*. Pattern Recognition, vol. 118, p. 107965, Oct. 2021, doi: `10.1016/j.patcog.2021.107965`.

7

Data-Level
Deep Learning Methods

You learned about various sampling methods in the previous chapters. Collectively, we call these methods *data-level methods* in this book. These methods include random undersampling, random oversampling, NearMiss, and SMOTE. We also explored how these methods work with classical machine learning algorithms.

In this chapter, we'll explore how to apply familiar sampling methods to deep learning models. Deep learning offers unique opportunities to enhance these methods further. We'll delve into elegant techniques to combine deep learning with oversampling and undersampling. Additionally, we'll learn how to implement various sampling methods with a basic neural network. We'll also cover dynamic sampling, which involves adjusting the data sample across multiple training iterations, using varying balancing ratios for each iteration. Then, we will learn to use some data augmentation techniques for both images and text. We'll end the chapter by highlighting key takeaways from a variety of other data-level techniques.

We will cover the following topics in this chapter:

- Preparing data
- Sampling techniques for deep learning models
- Data-level techniques for text classification
- A discussion of other data-level deep learning methods and their key ideas

It is not always straightforward to port methods to handle data imbalance, which worked well on classical ML models, into the deep learning world. The challenges and opportunities of deep learning models differ from the classical ML models primarily because of the difference in the type of data these models have to deal with. While classical ML models mostly deal with tabular and structured data, deep learning models typically deal with unstructured data, such as images, text, audio, and video, which is fundamentally different from tabular data.

We will discuss various techniques to deal with imbalance problems in computer vision. In the first part of the chapter, we will focus on various techniques, such as sampling and data augmentation, to handle class imbalance when training convolutional neural networks on image and text data.

In the latter half of the chapter, we will discuss common data-level techniques that can be applied to text problems. A lot of computer vision techniques can be successfully applied to NLP problems, too.

Technical requirements

Similar to prior chapters, we will continue to utilize common libraries such as torch, torchvision, numpy, and scikit-learn. We will also use nlpaug for NLP-related functionalities. The code and notebooks for this chapter are available on GitHub at https://github.com/PacktPublishing/Machine-Learning-for-Imbalanced-Data/tree/main/chapter07. You can open the GitHub notebooks using Google Colab by clicking on the **Open in Colab** icon at the top of the chapter's notebook, or by launching it from https://colab.research.google.com, using the GitHub URL of the notebook.

Preparing the data

In this chapter, we are going to use the classic MNIST dataset. This dataset contains 28-pixel x 28-pixel images of handwritten digits. The task for the model is to take an image as input and identify the digit in the image. We will use PyTorch, a popular deep-learning library, to demonstrate the algorithms. Let's prepare the data now.

The first step in the process will be to import the libraries. We will need NumPy (as we deal with numpy arrays), torchvision (to load MNIST data), torch, random, and copy libraries.

Next, we can download the MNIST data from torchvision.datasets. The torchvision library is a part of the PyTorch framework, which contains datasets, models, and common image transformers for computer vision tasks. The following code will download the MNIST dataset from this library:

```
img_transform = torchvision.transforms.ToTensor()
trainset = torchvision.datasets.MNIST(\
    root='/tmp/mnist', train=True,\
    download=True, transform=img_transform)
testset = torchvision.datasets.MNIST(root='/tmp/mnist',\
    train=False, transform=img_transform)
```

Once the data is downloaded from `torchvision`, we can load it into the `Dataloader` utility of PyTorch, which creates batches of data and provides us with a Python-style iterator over the batches. The following code does exactly that. Here, we are creating batches of size 64 for `train_loader`.

```
train_loader = torch.utils.data.DataLoader(trainset,\
    batch_size=64, shuffle=True)
test_loader = torch.utils.data.DataLoader(dataset=testset,\
    batch_size=500)
```

Since we are interested in imbalanced datasets, we will convert our MNIST dataset, which is a balanced dataset, into a long-tailed version of itself by deleting examples from various classes. We are omitting that implementation here to save space; you can refer to the chapter's GitHub repository for details. We assume that you have the `imbalanced_train_loader` class created from the imbalanced trainset.

Figure 7.1 shows the distribution of samples in the imbalanced MNIST dataset:

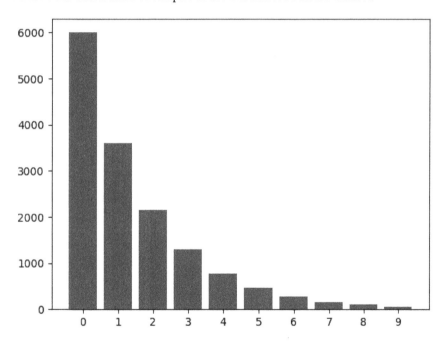

Figure 7.1 – A bar chart of the counts of examples from each digit class

Next, we will learn to create a training loop in PyTorch.

Creating the training loop

Before creating the training loop, we should import the `torch.nn` and `torch.optim` packages. The `torch.nn` package provides all the building blocks to create a neural network graph, while the `torch.optim` package provides us with most of the common optimization algorithms.

```
import torch.nn as nn
import torch.optim as optim
```

Since we will need some hyperparameters, let's define them:

```
input_size = 28 * 28 # 784
num_classes = 10
num_epochs = 20
learning_rate = 0.01
```

After setting up the hyperparameters, we can define the `train` function, which will take PyTorch's data loader as input and return a model fitted to the data. To create a trained model, we will need a model, a loss criterion, and an optimizer. We will use a single-layer linear neural network as the model here. You can design your own neural network architecture based on your requirements. For the loss criterion, we will use `CrossEntropyLoss`, and we will use **Stochastic Gradient Descent (SGD)** as the optimizer.

We will train the model for num_epochs epochs. We will discuss how the model is trained during a single epoch in the next paragraph. For now, we will abstract that part out in the run_epoch function:

```
def train(trainloader):
    model = nn.Linear(input_size, num_classes)
    criterion = nn.CrossEntropyLoss()
    optimizer = optim.SGD(model.parameters(), learning_rate)
    for epoch in range(num_epochs):
        run_epoch(trainloader, model, criterion, optimizer, \
            total_step, epoch)
    return model
```

During every epoch, we will train our model over the whole training data once. As discussed earlier, dataloader divides the data into multiple batches. First, we will have to match the shape of the images in the batch with the input dimension of our model. We will take the current batch and do a forward pass over the model, calculating the predictions and loss over the predictions in one go. Then, we will backpropagate the loss to update the model weights:

```
def run_epoch(
    trainloader, model, criterion, optimizer, total_step, epoch
):
    for i, (images, labels) in enumerate(trainloader):
        # Reshape images to (batch_size, input_size)
```

```
        images = images.reshape(-1, input_size)

        # Forward pass
        outputs = model(images)
        loss = criterion(outputs, torch.tensor(labels))

        # Backward and optimize
        optimizer.zero_grad()
        loss.backward()
        optimizer.step()
```

To get a trained model, we can now send the data loader to the `train` function:

```
model = train(imbalanced_train_loader)
```

For all image-related methods in this chapter, we'll employ the model code detailed next. We will create a `PyTorch` neural network named `Net` that features two convolutional layers, a dropout mechanism, and a pair of fully connected layers. Through the `forward` function, the model seamlessly integrates these layers using ReLU activations and max-pooling, manipulating the input, x. The result is `log_softmax` of the computed output:

```
class Net(torch.nn.Module):
    def __init__(self):
        super(Net, self).__init__()
        self.conv1 = torch.nn.Conv2d(1, 10, kernel_size=5)
        self.conv2 = torch.nn.Conv2d(10, 20, kernel_size=5)
        self.conv2_drop = torch.nn.Dropout2d()
        self.fc1 = torch.nn.Linear(320, 50)
        self.fc2 = torch.nn.Linear(50, 10)

    def forward(self, x):
        x = F.relu(F.max_pool2d(self.conv1(x), 2))
        x = F.relu(F.max_pool2d(
            self.conv2_drop(self.conv2(x)),2))
        x = x.view(-1, 320)
        x = F.relu(self.fc1(x))
        x = F.dropout(x, training=self.training)
        x = self.fc2(x)
        return F.log_softmax(x, dim=1)
```

Next, let's break down some of these terms:

- **Conv2d Layers (convolutional layers)**: These are the primary layers you'd find in a **Convolutional Neural Network (CNN)**, which is especially popular for image data. The main function of these layers is to scan the input data (such as an image) with a filter to detect patterns (such as edges or textures). In our `Net` class, there are two such layers – `conv1` and `conv2`. The numbers (`1, 10`) and (`10, 20`) are simply the input and output channels. The term `kernel_size=5` means that a 5 x 5 grid (or filter) is used to scan the input.

- **Dropout2d (Dropout for 2D Data)**: Dropout is a technique to prevent overfitting (a scenario where our model performs exceptionally well on training data but poorly on unseen data). By "dropping out" or turning off certain neurons during training, the model becomes more robust. `conv2_drop` is a dropout layer of type `Dropout2d`, specifically designed for 2D data (such as images).

- **Linear layers**: These are fully connected layers where each neuron is connected to every neuron in the previous layer. Our class has two linear layers, `fc1` and `fc2`, which further process the patterns recognized by the convolutional layers to make predictions.

- **Activation and pooling functions**:
  - `F.relu` is an activation function that introduces non-linearity to the model, enabling it to learn complex patterns
  - `F.max_pool2d` is a pooling function that reduces the spatial dimensions of the data while retaining important features
  - Finally, `F.log_softmax` is an activation function commonly used for classification tasks to produce probabilities for each class

In essence, the `Net` class defines a neural network that first detects patterns in data using convolutional layers, reduces overfitting using dropout, and then makes predictions using fully connected layers. The forward method is a sequence of operations that define how data flows through this network.

In the next section, we will learn how to use the `train` function with oversampling methods.

Sampling techniques for deep learning models

In this section, we'll explore some sampling methods, such as random oversampling and weighted sampling, for deep learning models. We'll then transition into data augmentation techniques, which bolster model robustness and mitigate dataset limitations. While large datasets are ideal for deep learning, real-world constraints often make them hard to obtain. We will also look at some advanced augmentations, such as CutMix and MixUp. We'll start with standard methods before discussing these advanced techniques.

Random oversampling

Here, we will apply the plain old random oversampling we learned in *Chapter 2, Oversampling Methods*, but using image data as input to a neural network. The basic idea is to duplicate samples from the minority classes randomly until we end up with an equal number of samples from each class. This technique often performs better than no sampling.

> **Tip**
> Make sure to train the model for enough epochs so that it has fully been fitted to the data. Under-training will likely lead to suboptimal model performance.

Let's spend some time working with the code. There are a few simple steps we need to follow. First, we need to convert data from the data loaders into tensors. Our RandomOverSampler API from imbalanced-learn doesn't work directly with data loaders:

```
X=torch.stack(tuple(imbalanced_train_loader.dataset.data))
y=torch.tensor(imbalanced_train_loader.dataset.targets)
```

We also need to reshape the X tensor for RandomOverSampler to work with two-dimensional inputs, as each of our images is a 28 x 28 matrix:

```
reshaped_X = X.reshape(X.shape[0],-1)
```

Now, we can import the RandomOverSampler class from the imbalanced-learn library, define an oversampler object, and resample our data using it:

```
from imblearn.over_sampling import RandomOverSampler
oversampler = RandomOverSampler()
oversampled_X, oversampled_y = oversampler.fit_resample(reshaped_X, y)
```

After resampling the data, we need to reshape it again back to the original form:

```
oversampled_X = oversampled_X.reshape(-1,28,28)
```

We can now create a new data loader using the oversampled data:

```
balanced_train_dataset = copy.deepcopy(imbalanced_train_dataset)
balanced_train_dataset.targets = torch.from_numpy(oversampled_y)
balanced_train_dataset.data = torch.from_numpy(oversampled_X)
balanced_train_loader = torch.utils.data.DataLoader( \
    balanced_train_dataset, batch_size=100, shuffle=True)
```

Finally, we can train our model using the new data loader. For this step, we can use the train function defined in the previous section:

```
balanced_data_model = train(balanced_train_loader)
```

That's all we need to do to use the random oversampling technique with deep learning models.

A similar strategy can be used for RandomUnderSampling from the imbalanced-learn library.

PyTorch provides a WeightedRandomSampler API, which is similar to the sample_weight parameter from scikit-learn (found in many of the fit methods in scikit-learn estimators (such as RandomForestClassifier and LogisticRegression) and serves a similar purpose of assigning a weight to each sample of the training dataset. We had a detailed discussion of the differences between class_weight and sample_weight in *Chapter 5, Cost-Sensitive Learning*.

We can specify weights as a parameter to WeightedRamdomSampler so that it can automatically weigh the examples in the batch, according to the weight of each sample. The weights parameter values are typically the inverse of the frequency of various classes in the dataset:

```
class_counts = pd.Series(\
    imbalanced_train_loader.dataset.targets.numpy()).value_counts()
class_weights = 1.0/class_counts
```

class_weights is more for the minority class labels than the majority class labels. Let's compute the weightedRamdomSampler values:

```
weightedRandomSampler = \
    WeightedRandomSampler(weights=class_weights, \
    num_samples=len(imbalanced_train_dataset), \
    replacement=True)
weightedRandomSampler_dataloader = \
    torch.utils.data.DataLoader(imbalanced_train_dataset,\
    sampler=weightedRandomSampler, batch_size=64)
```

In the next section, we will learn how to sample data dynamically.

Dynamic sampling

Dynamic sampling [1] is an advanced technique that can self-adjust the sampling rate as training progresses. It promises to adapt according to the problem's complexity and class imbalance, with almost no hyperparameter tuning. It is just one more tool in your arsenal to try on your dataset, especially when you have imbalanced image data at hand, and see whether it gives a better performance than the other techniques we've discussed so far in this chapter.

The basic idea of dynamic sampling is to dynamically adjust the sampling rate for various classes, depending on whether they are doing well or worse in a particular training iteration when compared to the prior iteration. If a class is performing comparatively poorly, then the class is oversampled in the next iteration, and vice versa.

The details of the algorithm

These are the core components of dynamic sampling:

- **Real-time data augmentation**: Apply various kinds of image transformations to the images of each training batch. These transformations can be rotation, flipping, adjusting brightness, translation, adjusting contrast/color, noise injection, and so on. As discussed earlier, this step helps to reduce model overfitting and improves generalization.

- **Dynamic sampling method**: In each iteration, a sample size (given by a certain formula) is chosen, and a model is trained with that sample size. The classes with lower F1 scores are sampled at a higher rate in the next iteration, forcing the model to focus more on previously misclassified examples. The number of images, c_j, for the next iteration is updated according to the following formula:

$$UpdateSampleSize\left(F1_i, c_j \right) = \frac{1 - fl_{i,j}}{\sum_{c_i \in C} 1 - fl_{i,k}} \times N$$

Here:

- $fl_{i,j}$ is the F1-score of class c_j in iteration i
- N = the average number of samples in all classes

For a particular training epoch, let's say we got the following F1 score for each of the three classes, **A**, **B**, and **C**, on our validation dataset:

Class	F1 score
A	0.1
B	0.2
C	0.3

Table 7.1 – Sample F1-scores of each class after some epoch

Here is how we would compute the weight of each class for the next epoch of training:

$$Weight\ (class\ A) = \frac{N * (1 - fl_a)}{(1 - fl_a) + (1 - fl_b) + (1 - fl_c)} = \frac{N * 0.9}{0.9 + 0.8 + 0.7}$$

$$= N * 0.375$$

$$Weight\ (class\ B) = N * 0.8/2.4 = N*0.33$$

$$Weight\ (class\ C) = N * 0.7/2.4 = N * 0.29$$

This means that we will sample class A at a higher rate than class B and class C, which makes sense because the performance on class A was weaker than that on classes B and C.

A second model is trained through transfer learning, without sampling, to prevent the minority classes from overfitting. At inference time, the model output is a function of both models.

There are additional details about the **DynamicSampling** algorithm that we have omitted here due to space constraints. You can find the complete implementation code in the corresponding GitHub repository for this chapter.

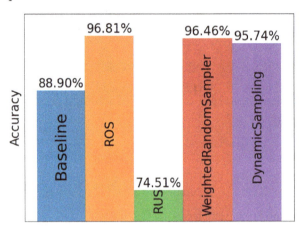

Figure 7.2 – An overall model accuracy comparison of various sampling techniques

Table 7.2 shows the per-class model accuracy using various sampling techniques, including the baseline, where no sampling is done.

Class	Baseline	Weighted random sampler	Dynamic sampler	Random oversampling	Random undersampling
0	**99.9**	99.0	92.4	99.1	97.2
1	**99.7**	99.2	96.8	99.2	90.7
2	**98.5**	98.3	93.5	**98.5**	70.8
3	97.3	97.4	96.8	**98.3**	74.4
4	98.3	98.0	91.9	**98.6**	79.6
5	96.2	96.0	97.3	**98.1**	52.8
6	94.5	97.6	**98.7**	97.3	77.6
7	89.7	94.7	**96.5**	94.1	81.1
8	63.3	91.5	**96.9**	93.0	60.2
9	50.7	92.6	**97.7**	91.8	56.5

Table 7.2 – A per-class model accuracy comparison of various sampling techniques (the highest value for a class is in bold)

Here are some insights from the results:

- In terms of overall performance, **Random OverSampling (ROS)** performed the best, while **Random Undersampling (RUS)** did the worst.

- Although ROS did the best, it can be computationally very expensive due to data cloning, making it less suitable for large datasets and industrial settings.

- Dynamic sampling did a little worse than ROS; it did best on the minority classes 6–9 and would be our preferred choice here. However, due to its increased complexity, our second choice will be the weighted random sampler.

- The baseline and weighted random sampler techniques are stable across classes; RUS is notably variable and performs poorly on most classes.

Similarly, we can apply SMOTE in the same way as `RandomOverSampler`. Please note that while SMOTE can be applied to images, its use of a linear subspace of the original data is often limiting.

This ends our discussion of the various sampling techniques. In the next section, we will focus on data augmentation techniques specifically designed for images to achieve more effective oversampling.

Data augmentation techniques for vision

Today, a variety of custom augmentation techniques are used for various kinds of data, such as images, audio, video, and even text data. In the vision realm, this includes techniques such as rotating, scaling, cropping, blurring, adding noise to an image, and a host of other techniques, including combining those techniques all at once in some appropriate sequence. Image data augmentation is not really a recent innovation. Some image augmentation techniques can also be found in the LeNet-5 model paper [2] from 1998, for example. Similarly, the AlexNet model [3] from 2012 uses random cropping, flipping, changing the color intensity of RGB channels, and so on to reduce errors during model training.

Let's discuss why data augmentation can often be helpful:

- In problems where we have limited data or imbalanced data, it may not always be possible to gather more data. This could be because either gathering more data is difficult in the first place (for example, waiting for more fraud to occur when dealing with credit card fraud, or gathering satellite images where we have to pay satellite operators, which can be quite expensive) or labeling the data is difficult or expensive (for example, to label medical image datasets, we need domain experts).

- Data augmentation can help reduce overfitting and improve the overall performance of a model. One motivation for this practice is that attributes such as lighting, noise, color, scale, and focus in the training set may not align with those in the real-world images on which we run inference. Additionally, augmentation diversifies a dataset to help the model generalize better. For example, if the model is trained only on images of cats facing right, it may not perform well on images where the cat faces left. Therefore, it's advisable to always apply valid transformations to augment image datasets, as most models gain performance with more diverse data.

Data augmentation is widely used for computer vision tasks such as object detection, classification, and segmentation. It can be very useful for NLP tasks as well. In the computer vision world, there are lots of open source libraries that help standardize the various image augmentation techniques, while the NLP tools for data augmentation space have yet to mature.

While there are several popular open source libraries for image augmentation, such as `imgaug`, Facebook's `AugLy`, and `Albumentations`, we will use `torchvision` in this book. As a part of the PyTorch ecosystem, it offers seamless integration with PyTorch workflows, a range of common image transformations, as well as pre-trained models and datasets, making it a convenient and comprehensive choice for computer vision tasks. If you need more advanced augmentations, or if speed is a concern, `Albumentations` may be a better choice.

We can use `torchvision.transforms.Pad` to add some padding to the image boundaries:

```
padded_imgs = [torchvision.transforms.Pad(padding=90)(orig_img)]
plot(padded_imgs)
```

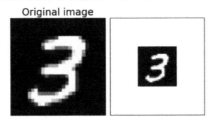

Figure 7.3 – The results of applying the Pad function to the image

The `torchvision.transforms.FiveCrop` class transforms and crops the given image into four corners and the central crop:

```
(top_left, top_right, bottom_left, bottom_right, center) =\
    torchvision.transforms.FiveCrop(size=(100,100))(orig_img)
plot([top_left, top_right, bottom_left, bottom_right, center])
```

Figure 7.4 – The results of applying the FiveCrop function on the image

`torchvision.transforms.CenterCrop` is a similar class to crop images from the center.

The `torchvision.transforms.ColorJitter` class changes the brightness, saturation, and other similar properties of the image:

```
jitter = torchvision.transforms.ColorJitter(brightness=.7, hue=.5)
jitted_imgs = [jitter(orig_img) for _ in range(3)]
plot(jitted_imgs)
```

Figure 7.5 – The results of applying the ColorJitter function on the image

`GaussianBlur` can add some blurring to the images:

```
gaussian_blurrer = \
    torchvision.transforms.GaussianBlur(kernel_size=(9,\
    11), sigma=(0.1, 5))
blurred_imgs = [gaussian_blurrer(orig_img) for _ in \
    range(4)]
plot(blurred_imgs)
```

Figure 7.6 – The results of applying the GaussianBlur function on the image

The `torchvision.transforms.RandomRotation` class transform rotates an image at a random angle:

```
rotater = torchvision.transforms.RandomRotation(degrees=(0, 50))
rotated_imgs = [rotater(orig_img) for _ in range(4)]
plot(rotated_imgs)
```

Figure 7.7 – The results of random rotation on the original image (leftmost)

Consider exploring the other image transformation functionalities supported by the `torchvision.transforms` class that we didn't discuss here.

Cutout masks out random square regions of input images during training. While it may seem like this technique removes unnecessary portions of the image, it's important to note that the areas to be masked are typically selected at random. The primary aim is to force the neural network to generalize better by ensuring it does not overly rely on any specific set of pixels within a given image.

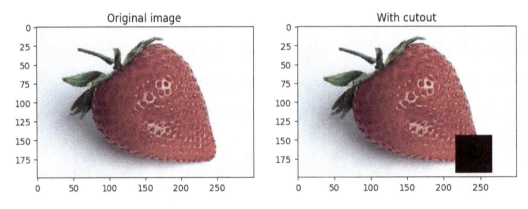

Figure 7.8 – The result of applying the cutout function on an image

Deep learning data-level techniques in production at Etsy/Booking/Wayfair

🎯 **Problem being solved:**

Etsy, `Booking.com`, and Wayfair leveraged user behavior to enhance personalization. Etsy focused on item recommendations based on browsing history [4], `Booking.com` tailored search results to boost bookings [5], and Wayfair optimized product image angles to improve CTRs [6]. All aimed to utilize data-driven strategies for better user experience and performance.

⚖️ **Data imbalance issue:**

Etsy, `Booking.com`, and Wayfair each grappled with data imbalance issues in their machine learning projects. Etsy faced a power law distribution in user sessions, where most users interacted with only a few listings within a one-hour window. `Booking.com` dealt with imbalanced classes in hotel images, as photos of bedrooms and bathrooms vastly outnumbered those of other facilities such as saunas or table tennis. Wayfair encountered an imbalance in real-world images of furniture, with a majority of images showing the "front" angle, leading to poor performance for other angles. All three companies had to address these imbalances to improve the performance and fairness of their models.

🎨 **Data augmentation strategy:**

Etsy, `Booking.com`, and Wayfair each had unique data augmentation strategies to address their specific challenges. Etsy used image random rotation, translation, zoom, and color contrast transformation to augment their dataset. `Booking.com` employed a variety of techniques, including mirroring, random cropping, affine transformation, aspect ratio distortion, color manipulation, and contrast enhancement. They increased their labeled data by 10 times through these methods, applying distortions on the fly during training. Wayfair took a different approach by creating synthetic data with 3D models, generating 100 views for each 3D model of chairs and sofas, thus providing granular angle information for training.

Next, let's look at some of the more advanced techniques, such as CutMix, MixUp, and AugMix, which are types of **Mixed Sample Data Augmentation (MSDA)** techniques.

MSDA is a set of techniques that involve mixing data samples to produce an augmented dataset, used to train a model (*Figure 7.9*).

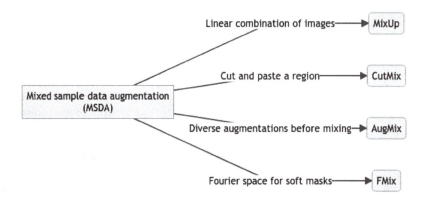

Figure 7.9 – Common MSDA techniques

CutMix

CutMix [7] is an image data augmentation technique where patches are cut and pasted among training images. Specifically, a portion of an image is replaced by a portion of another image, as shown here:

Figure 7.10 – The result of applying the CutMix function to the images (image 1 and image 2)

It's designed to encourage a model to make more localized, fine-grained predictions, thus improving overall generalization. CutMix also enforces consistent predictions outside the mixed regions, further enhancing model robustness.

`torchvision` also offers an in-built API for CutMix, `torchvision.transforms.v2.CutMix`, so we don't have to implement it from scratch.

The full notebook with CutMix implementation from scratch can be found in the GitHub repo.

CutMix often shows improvements over traditional augmentation techniques on benchmark datasets, such as CIFAR-10, CIFAR-100, and ImageNet [7].

MixUp

MixUp [8] creates virtual training examples by forming combinations of pairs of inputs and their corresponding labels.

If (x_i, y_i) and (x_j, y_j) is an arbitrary pair of images in dataset D, where x is the image while y is its label, a mixed sample $\tilde{x}, \tilde{y}$ can be generated using the following equations:

$$\tilde{x} = \lambda x_i + (1 - \lambda) x_j$$

$$\tilde{y} = \lambda y_i + \left(1 - \lambda\right) y_j$$

where λ is the mixing factor sampled from the beta distribution. The Beta distribution is a flexible, continuous probability distribution defined on the interval [0, 1].

MixUp acts as a regularizer, preventing overfitting and enhancing the generalization capabilities of models. The following implementation shuffles the data and targets, and then combines them using a weighted average, based on a value sampled from the Beta distribution, creating mixed data and targets for augmentation:

```
def mixup(data, target, alpha):
    indices = torch.randperm(data.size(0))
    shuffled_data = data[indices]
    shuffled_target = target[indices]

    lamda = np.random.beta(alpha, alpha)
    data = lamda * data + (1 - lamda) * shuffled_data
    target = lamda * target + (1 - lamda) * shuffled_target

    return data, target
```

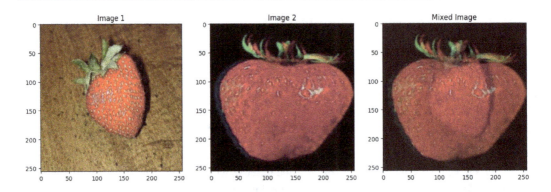

Figure 7.11 – The result of applying MixUp on the images (image 1 and image 2)

On datasets such as CIFAR-100, MixUp has been found to provide significant gains in test accuracy compared to models trained without MixUp [8].

Similar to CutMix, `torchvision` provides a built-in API called `torchvision.transforms.v2.MixUp`, eliminating the need for manual implementation.

AugMix

The augmentation techniques that we have studied so far have all been fixed augmentations, but deep learning models can memorize them [9] and their performance can plateau. This is where AugMix [10] can be helpful, as it produces a diverse set of augmented images by performing several random augmentations in a sequence.

AugMix improves model robustness and uncertainty without requiring any changes to the model architecture. The full AugMix algorithm also uses a special kind of loss function, but we will skip that for simplicity.

The following code presents a simplified version of AugMix's core logic:

```python
from torchvision.transforms import transforms
def simple_augmix(image):
    # Our box of magic tricks
    magic_tricks = [
        transforms.RandomHorizontalFlip(),
        transforms.RandomAffine(degrees=30)
        # other transforms here
    ]

    # Pick a random number of tricks to use
    num_tricks = np.random.randint(0, len(magic_tricks) + 1)

    # Create a new picture by mixing transformed ones
```

```
new_picture = torch.zeros_like(image)

# Let's use 4 mixed images for our example
for _ in range(4):
    transformed_picture = image.clone()
    for _ in range(num_tricks):
        trick = np.random.choice(magic_tricks)
        transformed_picture = trick(transformed_picture)

        # Add the transformed picture to our new picture
        new_picture += (1/4) * transformed_picture

return new_picture
```

At the end of the function, we combine images by using equal weight for each of the four transformed pictures. The actual AugMix implementation uses a Dirichlet distribution function to combine the images. A Dirichlet distribution is a generalization of the beta distribution that we saw in the MixUp technique.

Figure 7.12 – The result of applying the Augmix function to four different images

In *Figure 7.12*, the top row shows the original image, while the bottom row shows the result of applying AugMix. Images 1 and 3 don't seem to have changed, but images 2 and 4 have noticeable changes.

According to the AugMix paper [10], in experiments with ImageNet and CIFAR, AugMix achieved reduced test errors while providing improved robustness against corruption.

We don't need to create AugMix from scratch, as `torchvision` provides a built-in API called `torchvision.transforms.AugMix` for this purpose.

Remix

Standard data augmentation techniques such as MixUp and CutMix may not be sufficient to handle class imbalances, as they do not take the distribution of class labels into account. Remix [11] addresses the challenges of training deep learning models on imbalanced datasets.

MixUp and CutMix utilize the same mixing factor to combine samples in both the feature space and the label space. In the context of imbalanced data, the authors of the Remix paper [11] argued that this approach may not be optimal. Therefore, they proposed to separate the mixing factors, allowing for more flexibility in their application. By doing so, greater weight can be assigned to the minority class, enabling the creation of labels that are more favorable to the underrepresented class.

If $(x_i, y_i; x_j, y_j)$ is an arbitrary pair of images in dataset D, a mixed sample x^{RM}, y^{RM} can be generated using the following equations:

$$x^{RM} = \lambda_x x_i + (1 - \lambda_x)x_j$$

$$y^{RM} = \lambda_y y_i + (1 - \lambda_y)y_j$$

λ_x and λ_y are the mixing factors sampled from the beta distribution.

Here is a simplified implementation:

```
def remix_data(inputs, labels, class_counts, alpha=1.0):
    lambda_x = np.random.beta(alpha, alpha) if alpha > 0 else 1
    # Constants for controlling the remixing conditions.
    K = 3
    tau = 0.5

    # Shuffle the indices randomly.
    random_indices = torch.randperm(inputs.size()[0])

    # Determine lambda_y values based on class counts and lambda_x.
    lambda_y_values = []
    for i, j in enumerate(random_indices):
        class_count_ratio = (
            class_counts[labels[i]] / class_counts[labels[j]]
        )
        if class_count_ratio >= K and lambda_x < tau:
            lambda_y_values.append(0)
```

```
        else:
            lambda_y_values.append(lambda_x)

    lambda_y = torch.tensor(lambda_y_values)
    # Mix inputs, labels based on lambda_x, lambda_y, and shuffled
indices.
    mixed_inputs = (
        lambda_x * inputs + (1 - lambda_x) * inputs[random_indices, :]
    )
    mixed_labels = (
        lambda_y * labels + (1 - lambda_y) * labels[random_indices]
    )
    return mixed_inputs, mixed_labels
```

Combining previous techniques

It's possible to combine these methods to introduce even more diversity to the training data, such as the following:

- **CutMix and MixUp**: These can be alternated or used in tandem, creating regions in images that are replaced with parts of other images while also blending images pixel-wise

- **Sequential**: You could sequentially apply these techniques (e.g., use MixUp first and then CutMix) to further diversify the augmented dataset

When combining these methods, it's important to carefully manage the probabilities and strengths of each method, thus avoiding introducing too much noise or making the training data too divergent from the original distribution.

Also, while combining these methods might improve model robustness and generalization in certain scenarios, it can also make training more computationally intensive and complex. It's essential to balance the benefits against the potential trade-offs.

Remember, always validate the effectiveness of combined augmentations on a validation set to ensure they are beneficial for the task at hand.

Let's use a long-tailed version of a different dataset called Fashion-MNIST for the techniques we just discussed (*Figure 7.13*). Fashion-MNIST is another MNIST variant, consisting of 60,000 training and 10,000 testing images of 10 different clothing items, such as shoes, shirts, and dresses, each represented in a grayscale image of 28x28 pixels.

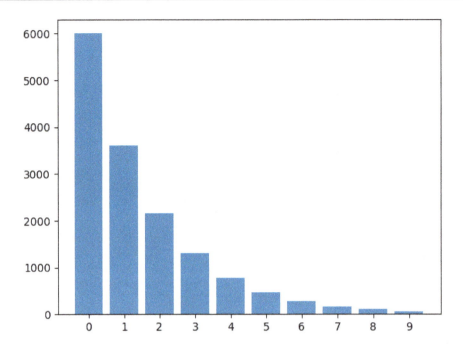

Figure 7.13 – Imbalanced FashionMNIST

Figure 7.14 shows the overall model accuracy when trained using CutMix, MixUp, a combination of both, and Remix on the imbalanced FashionMNIST dataset.

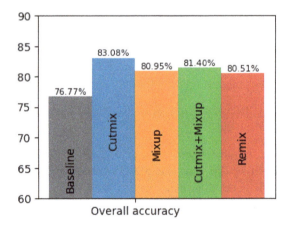

Figure 7.14 – Overall model accuracy (FashionMNIST)

The difference in the performance of these techniques is more apparent when looking at the class-wise accuracy numbers (*Figure 7.15*).

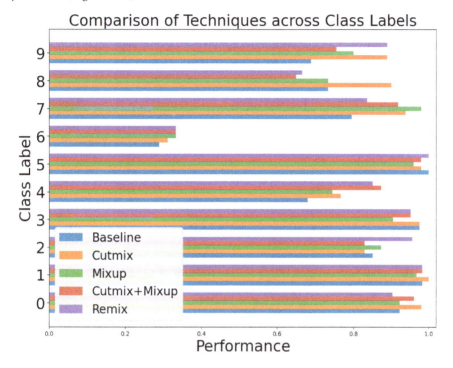

Figure 7.15 – Class-wise model accuracy (the FashionMNIST dataset)

Based on the given data, here are some insightful conclusions that can be drawn for the various techniques, especially in the context of imbalanced data:

- **Overall performance**: **Cutmix** and **Remix** generally offer the highest performance across most classes, followed closely by **Mixup** and **Cutmix+Mixup**. **Baseline** seems to be the least effective in general.

- **Performance on minority classes**: For the minority class labeled as "6," all techniques show relatively low performance compared to other classes. However, **Mixup** and **Cutmix+Mixup** offer a slight improvement over the baseline.

- **Consistency across classes**: **Cutmix** and **Mixup** are more consistent across different classes, excluding class "6," where they are only marginally better. **Baseline**, on the other hand, shows significant variability, performing extremely well on some classes (such as "0" and "5") but poorly on others (such as "6").

- **Techniques suited for specific classes**: **Cutmix** performs exceptionally well for the classes labeled "1" and "8," where it outperforms all other techniques.

  Remix is particularly strong for the class labeled "2," where it outshines all other techniques.

- **Complexity versus benefit**: **Cutmix+Mixup** does not offer a significant improvement over **Cutmix** or **Mixup** individually, raising questions about whether the additional computational complexity is justified.

- **Generalizability**: **Cutmix** and **Mixup** appear to be the most robust techniques, showing high performance across most classes. These techniques would likely perform well on unseen data and are potentially good choices for imbalanced datasets.

- **Trade-offs**: **Cutmix** offers high performance but may not be the best for minority classes. **Mixup**, although slightly less effective overall, offers more balanced performance across classes, including minority ones.

The following are some points to be careful about while performing these image augmentations:

- We must ensure that data augmentations preserve the original labels. For instance, rotating digits such as 6 and 9 can be problematic in digit recognition tasks. Similarly, cropping an image could invalidate its label, such as removing a cat from a "cat" image. This is especially crucial in complex tasks, such as image segmentation in self-driving cars, where augmentations can alter output labels or masks.

- While geometric and color transformations often increase memory usage and training time, they are not inherently problematic. Although color alterations can sometimes remove important details and affect label integrity, smart manipulation can also be beneficial. For instance, tweaking the color space to mimic different lighting or camera lenses can improve model performance.

To overcome some of the increased memory, time, and cost issues, as mentioned, a technique called `AutoAugment` is available in `PyTorch`, which can automatically search for the best augmentation policies on the dataset being used.

Deep learning data-level techniques in production at Grab

🎯 **Problem being solved:**

Grab, a ride-hailing and food delivery company in South-East Asia, faced the primary challenge of anonymizing faces and license plates in images collected for their geotagged imagery platform, KartaView [12]. This was essential to ensure user privacy.

⚖️ **Data imbalance issue:**

The dataset used by Grab was imbalanced, particularly in terms of the object sizes. Larger regions of interest, such as close-ups of faces or license plates, were underrepresented. This skewed distribution led to poor model performance in detecting these larger objects.

🎨 **Data augmentation strategy:**

Grab employed a multi-pronged data augmentation approach to address the imbalance:

- **Offline augmentation**: One key method they used was the "image view splitting," where each original image is divided into multiple "views" with predefined properties. This was crucial to accommodate different types of images such as perspective, wide field of view, and 360-degree equirectangular images. Each "view" was treated as a separate image with its tags, which helped the model generalize better. They also implemented oversampling for images with larger tags, addressing the imbalance in their dataset. This was vital for their anchor-based object detection model, as the imbalance was affecting the model's performance in identifying larger objects.

- **Online augmentation**: They used YOLOv4 for object detection, which allowed for a variety of online augmentations, such as saturation, exposure, hue, flip, and mosaic.

Modern techniques such as autoencoders and adversarial networks, specifically **Generative Adversarial Networks (GANs)**, have recently gained traction in creating synthetic data to enhance image datasets. A GAN comprises two neural networks – the generator, which produces synthetic data, and the discriminator, which evaluates the authenticity of this data. Together, they work to create realistic and high-quality synthetic samples. GANs have also been applied to generate synthetic tabular data. For example, they've been used to create synthetic medical images that significantly improve diagnostic models. We'll explore these cutting-edge techniques in greater detail toward the end of the chapter. In the next section, we will learn about applying data-level techniques to NLP problems.

Data-level techniques for text classification

Data imbalance, wherein certain classes in a dataset are underrepresented, is not just an issue confined to image or structured data domains. In NLP, imbalanced datasets can lead to biased models that might perform well on the majority class but are likely to misclassify underrepresented ones. To address this challenge, numerous strategies have been devised.

In NLP, data augmentation can boost model performance, especially with limited training data. *Table 7.3* categorizes the various data augmentation techniques for text data:

Level	Method	Description	Example techniques
Character level	Noise	Introducing randomness at the character level	Jumbling characters
	Rule-based	Transformations based on predefined rules	Capitalization
Word level	Noise	Random word changes	"cat" to "dog"
	Synonyms	Replacing words with their synonyms	"happy" to "joyful"
	Embeddings	Using word embeddings for replacement	"king" to "monarch"
	Language models	Leveraging advanced language models for word replacement	BERT
Phrase level	Structure	Altering the structure of phrases	Changing word order
	Interpolation	Merging features of two phrases	"The cat sat" + "The dog barked" = "The cat barked"
Document level	Translation	Translating the document to another language and back	English to French to English
	Generative	Using models to generate new content	GPT-3

Table 7.3 – The categorization of different data augmentation methods (adapted from [13])

Data augmentation techniques for text can be categorized into character, word, phrase, and document levels. Techniques vary from jumbling characters to using models such as BERT and GPT-3. This taxonomy guides us through NLP data augmentation methods.

Table 7.3 shows various data augmentation methods used in NLP. We will break down the methods based on the level at which the data is manipulated – character, word, phrase, and document. Each level has its unique set of methods, such as introducing "noise" at the character level or leveraging "language models" at the word level. These methods are not just random transformations; they are often carefully designed to preserve the semantic meaning of the text while introducing variability.

What sets this categorization apart is its multilayered approach, which allows a more targeted application of data augmentation methods. For instance, if you're dealing with short text snippets, methods at the character or word level may be more appropriate. On the other hand, if you're working with longer documents or need to generate entirely new content, then methods at the document level, such as "generative" techniques, come into play.

In the subsequent sections, we will explore a text classification dataset that is imbalanced and illustrate various data augmentation techniques using it. These methodologies are designed to synthesize additional data, thereby enhancing a model's ability to learn and generalize from the imbalanced information.

Dataset and baseline model

Let's take the spam text message classification dataset available on Kaggle (`https://www.kaggle.com/datasets/team-ai/spam-text-message-classification`). This dataset, primarily used to distinguish spam from legitimate messages, presents an imbalance with a majority of "ham" (legitimate) messages and a minority of "spam" messages. We are skipping the code here to save space. You can find the notebook in the GitHub repo with the name `Data_level_techniques_NLP.ipynb`.

With a baseline model, we have the following results:

	precision	recall	f1-score	support
ham	0.97	1.00	0.98	1216
spam	0.97	0.80	0.88	177
accuracy			0.97	1393
macro avg	0.97	0.90	0.93	1393
weighted avg	0.97	0.97	0.97	1393

Random oversampling

One basic technique to handle data imbalance is random oversampling, where instances of the minority class are replicated to balance out the class distribution. While this technique is easy to implement and often shows improved performance, it's essential to be wary of overfitting:

	precision	recall	f1-score	support
ham	0.99	0.99	0.99	1216
spam	0.93	0.91	0.92	177
accuracy			0.98	1393
macro avg	0.96	0.95	0.95	1393
weighted avg	0.98	0.98	0.98	1393

Random oversampling shows a slight improvement in overall accuracy, rising from 0.97 to 0.98. The most notable gain is in the recall for the spam class, which increased from 0.80 to 0.91, indicating better identification of spam messages. However, the precision for spam dropped a bit from 0.97 to 0.93.

The macro average F1-score also improved from 0.93 to 0.95, suggesting that the model is now better at handling both classes (ham and spam) more equally. The weighted average metrics remain strong, reinforcing that the model's overall performance has improved without sacrificing its ability to correctly classify the majority class (ham).

Similarly, undersampling can be useful to reduce the size of the majority class, particularly by eliminating exact duplicate sentences. For example, you might not need 500 copies of "Thanks very much!" However, sentences with similar semantic meaning but different wording, such as "Thanks very much!" and "Thanks so much!", should generally be retained. Exact duplicates can be identified, using methods such as string matching, while sentences with similar meanings can be detected using cosine similarity or the Jaccard similarity of sentence embeddings.

🚀 **Deep learning data-level techniques in production at Cloudflare**

🎯 **Problem being solved**:

Cloudflare [14] aimed to enhance its **Web Application Firewall (WAF)** to better identify malicious HTTP requests and protect against common attacks, such as SQL injection and **cross-site scripting (XSS)**.

⚖️ **Data imbalance issue**:

Creating a quality dataset to train the WAF model was difficult, due to strict privacy regulations and the absence of labeled data for malicious HTTP requests. The heterogeneity of samples also presented challenges as the requests came in various formats and encodings. There was a significant lack of samples for specific types of attacks, making the dataset imbalanced and leading to the risk of false positives or negatives.

🎨 **Data augmentation strategy**:

To tackle this, Cloudflare employed a combination of data augmentation and generation techniques. These included mutating benign content in various ways, generating pseudo-random noise samples, and using language models for synthetic data creation. The focus was on increasing the diversity of negative samples while maintaining the integrity of the content, thereby forcing the model to consider a broader spectrum of structural, semantic, and statistical properties for better classification.

🚀 **Model deployment**:

The model that they used significantly improved after employing these data augmentation techniques, with a remarkable F1 score of 0.99 after augmentation compared to 0.61 before. The model has been validated against Cloudflare's signature-based WAF and was found to perform comparably, making it production-ready.

Document-level augmentation

In document-level augmentation, entire documents are modified to create new examples, in order to preserve the broader semantic context or narrative flow of the document. One such technique is back translation.

Back translation

Back translation involves translating a sentence to a different language and then reverting it back to the original (*Figure 7.16*). This produces sentences that are syntactically different but semantically similar to the original text, providing a form of augmentation.

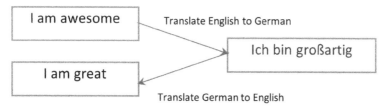

Figure 7.16 – Demonstrating the back translation technique

We generate the back-translated text and append it to the original dataset. Then, we use the full dataset to train the logistic regression model. Note that this can be a time-consuming process, since the translation model binaries are resource-intensive. It may also introduce errors, since some words may not be exactly translatable across languages. In the GitHub notebook, we used the `BackTranslationAug` API from the `nlpaug` library [15].

The following results show the classification metrics on the test set. The precision of the spam class shows improvement over the random oversampling technique, while recall is a bit worse:

	precision	recall	f1-score	support
ham	0.98	1.00	0.99	1216
spam	0.96	0.86	0.91	177
accuracy			0.98	1393
macro avg	0.97	0.93	0.95	1393
weighted avg	0.98	0.98	0.98	1393

Back translation maintains an overall accuracy of 0.98, similar to random oversampling. It slightly improves `spam` precision to 0.96 but lowers recall to 0.86. Both methods outperform the baseline, with back translation favoring precision over recall for the `spam` class.

Character and word-level augmentation

Let's briefly go over a few character and word-level augmentation techniques that can be applied to NLP problems.

Easy Data Augmentation techniques

Easy Data Augmentation (EDA) is a suite of data augmentation techniques specific to text data. It includes simple operations such as synonym replacement, random insertion, random swap, and random deletion. These operations, being simple, ensure that the augmented data remains meaningful. The following table shows various metrics when using EDA on the dataset:

```
                precision       recall      f1-score     support
   ham            0.98          0.99          0.99        1216
   spam           0.96          0.88          0.91         177

   accuracy                                   0.98        1393
   macro avg      0.97          0.93          0.95        1393
   weighted avg   0.98          0.98          0.98        1393
```

After applying EDA, the model retains an overall accuracy of 0.98, consistent with both random oversampling and back translation. The precision for spam is high at 0.96, similar to back translation, while the recall is slightly better at 0.88 compared to 0.86 with Back Translation. The macro and weighted averages remain robust at 0.95 and 0.98, respectively.

EDA offers a balanced improvement in both precision and recall for the spam class, making it a strong contender among the data augmentation techniques we've tried.

	Precision	Recall	F1-Score	Accuracy
Baseline model	**0.97**	0.80	0.88	0.97
Random oversampling	0.93	**0.91**	**0.92**	**0.98**
Back translation	0.96	0.86	0.91	**0.98**
EDA	0.96	0.88	0.91	**0.98**

Table 7.4 – Comparing the results of the various NLP data-level
techniques for the spam class (max per metric in bold)

Overall, as we can see in *Table 7.4*, for our dataset, random oversampling excels in recall for spam but slightly lowers precision. Back translation boosts precision at a minor recall trade-off. EDA offers a balanced improvement in both. It's important to note that these results are empirical and specific to the dataset used for this analysis. Data augmentation techniques can yield different outcomes, depending on the nature of the data, its distribution, and the problem being addressed. Therefore, while these techniques show promise in this context, their effectiveness may vary when applied to different datasets or NLP tasks.

We will not be covering phrase-level augmentation techniques in this book due to space constraints, but we recommend exploring them on your own.

Next, we will look at some miscellaneous data-level deep learning techniques at a high level.

Discussion of other data-level deep learning methods and their key ideas

In addition to the methods previously discussed, there is a rich array of other techniques specifically designed to address imbalanced data challenges. This section provides a high-level overview of these alternative approaches, each offering unique insights and potential advantages. While we will only touch upon their key ideas, we encourage you to delve deeper into the literature and explore them further if you find these techniques intriguing.

Two-phase learning

Two-phase learning [16][17] is a technique designed to enhance the performance of minority classes in multi-class classification problems, without compromising the performance of majority classes. The process involves two training phases:

1. In the first phase, a deep learning model is first trained on the dataset, which is balanced with respect to each class. Balancing can be done using sampling techniques such as random oversampling or undersampling.

2. In the second phase, we freeze all the layers except the last one, and then the model is fine-tuned using the entire dataset.

The first phase ensures that all layers are trained on a balanced dataset. The second phase calibrates the output probabilities by retraining the last layer with the entire dataset, reflecting the original imbalanced class distribution.

The order of the two phases can be reversed – that is, the first model is trained on the full imbalanced data and then fine-tuned on a balanced dataset in the second phase. This is called **deferred sampling**, since sampling is done later.

Expansive Over-Sampling

Introduced in a paper by Damien Dablain et al. [18], **Expansive Over-Sampling** (EOS) is another data augmentation technique used within a three-phase CNN training framework, designed for imbalanced data. It can be considered to incorporate both two-phase learning and data augmentation techniques.

EOS works by creating synthetic training instances as combinations between the minority class samples and their nearest "enemies" in the embedded space. The term "nearest enemies" refers to instances of other classes that are closest in the feature space to a given instance. By creating synthetic instances in this way, EOS aims to reduce the generalization gap, which is wider for minority classes.

The paper's authors [18] claimed that this method improves accuracy and efficiency over common imbalanced learning techniques, requiring fewer parameters and less training time.

Using generative models for oversampling

Generative models, including GANs, **Variational AutoEncoders (VAEs)**, diffusion models, and their derivatives, such as StyleGAN, StyleGAN2, and GPT-based models, have become prominent tools for producing data points that resemble training data.

VAEs, a specific type of generative model, consist of an encoder and decoder that work together to create new instances of data, such as realistic images, and can be used to balance imbalanced datasets. On the long-tailed version of MNIST, we got a decent performance improvement by using a VAE-augmented model when compared to the baseline model on the most imbalanced classes. *Figure 7.17* shows the performance comparison after 50 epochs. You can find the notebook in the corresponding chapter of the GitHub repo.

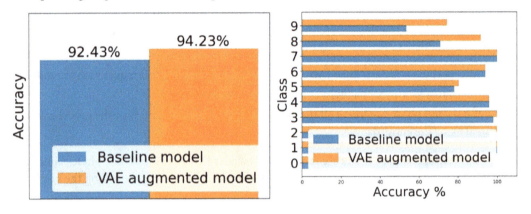

Figure 7.17 – VAE-augmented model performance on the long-tailed MNIST dataset

Diffusion models operate by progressively corrupting an image with noise and then reconstructing it, with applications in areas such as medical imaging. Examples include DALLE-2 and the open source stable diffusion model.

Recent studies [19] highlight the utility of synthetic data in enhancing zero-shot and few-shot image classification tasks. Specifically, text-to-image generation models, when used in conjunction with large-scale pre-trained models such as DALL-E and Stable Diffusion, significantly improve performance in scenarios where real-world data is sparse or unavailable. These generative models have gained prominence for their ability to create high-quality images based on natural language prompts, offering a potential solution for imbalanced datasets. For example, if there is a scarcity of images featuring a monkey seated in a car, these models can generate hundreds or even thousands of such images to augment training datasets. However, it's worth noting that models trained solely on synthetic data may still underperform compared to those trained on real data.

These models often require significant computational resources, making them time-consuming and expensive to scale up, especially for vast datasets. Diffusion models, in particular, are computationally intensive, and potential overfitting can compromise model generalizability. Therefore, it is crucial to balance the benefits of data augmentation with the computational cost and potential challenges when employing these advanced generative models.

DeepSMOTE

The **Deep Synthetic Minority Oversampling (DeepSMOTE)** technique [20] is essentially SMOTE adapted for deep learning models using an encoder-decoder architecture, with minor tweaks for image data. DeepSMOTE consists of three major components:

- **An encoder/decoder framework to handle complex and high-dimensional data**: An encoder/decoder framework is used to learn a compact feature representation of the image data. It is trained to reconstruct the original images from this compact form, ensuring that essential features are captured.

- **SMOTE-based oversampling for generating synthetic instances**: Once the feature representation is learned, SMOTE is applied in this feature space to generate synthetic instances of the minority class. This is particularly useful for image data where the raw data is high-dimensional and complex. SMOTE creates these synthetic instances by finding the k-nearest neighbors in the feature space and generating new instances that are interpolations between the instance under consideration and its neighbors.

- **A dedicated loss function**: DeepSMOTE introduces a specialized loss function that not only focuses on the reconstruction error (how well the decoder can reconstruct the original image from the encoded form) but also includes a penalty term, ensuring that the synthetic instances are useful for the classification task.

Unlike GAN-based oversampling, DeepSMOTE does not require a discriminator. It claims to generate high-quality, information-rich synthetic images that can be visually inspected.

Deep oversampling

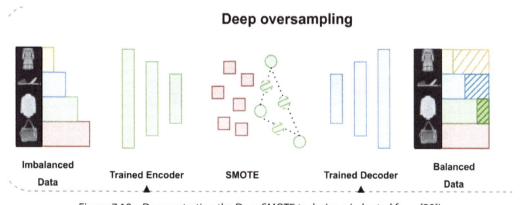

Figure 7.18 – Demonstrating the DeepSMOTE technique (adapted from [20])

Neural style transfer

Neural style transfer is a technique in deep learning that artistically blends the content of one image with the style of another (*Figure 7.19*). While its primary application is in art and image processing, the concept of generating synthetic data samples can be adapted to address data imbalance in machine learning. By drawing inspiration from style transfer, one could potentially generate synthetic samples for the minority class, blend features of different classes, or adapt domain-specific knowledge. However, care must be taken to ensure that synthetic data authentically represents real-world scenarios to avoid overfitting and poor generalization of real data.

Figure 7.19 – Demonstrating the neural style transfer technique

We hope that this provides a thorough understanding of data-level deep learning methods to address imbalanced data, including oversampling, data augmentation, and various other strategies.

Summary

The transition of methods to handle data imbalance from classical machine learning models to deep learning models can pose unique challenges, primarily due to the distinct types of data that these models have to work with. Classical machine learning models typically deal with structured, tabular data, whereas deep learning models often grapple with unstructured data, such as images, text, audio, and video. This chapter explored how to adapt sampling techniques to work with deep learning models. To facilitate this, we used an imbalanced version of the MNIST dataset to train a model, which is then employed in conjunction with various oversampling methods.

Incorporating random oversampling with deep learning models involves duplicating samples from minority classes randomly, until each class has an equal number of samples. This is usually performed using APIs from libraries such as imbalanced-learn, Keras, TensorFlow, or PyTorch, which work together seamlessly for this purpose. Once data is oversampled, it can be sent for model training in PyTorch or TensorFlow.

The chapter also delved into different data augmentation techniques, which can be especially beneficial when dealing with limited or imbalanced data. Augmentation techniques include rotating, scaling, cropping, blurring, and adding noise, among other advanced techniques such as AugMix, CutMix, and MixUp. However, care must be taken to ensure these augmentations preserve the original labels and do not inadvertently alter vital information in the data. We discussed other methods, such as two-phase learning and dynamic sampling, as potential strategies to improve model performance on imbalanced data. We also learned about some data-level techniques applicable to text, such as back translation and EDA, while running them on a spam/ham dataset.

In the next chapter, we will look at some algorithm-based methods to deal with imbalanced datasets.

Questions

1. Apply Mixup interpolation to the Kaggle spam detection NLP dataset used in the chapter. See if Mixup helps to improve the model performance. You can refer to the paper *Augmenting Data with Mixup for Sentence Classification: An Empirical Study* by Guo et al. (`https://arxiv.org/pdf/1905.08941.pdf`) for further reading.

2. Refer to the FMix paper [21] and implement the FMix augmentation technique. Apply it to the Caltech101 dataset. See whether model performance improves by using FMix over the baseline model performance.

3. Apply the EOS technique described in the chapter to the CIFAR-10-LT (the long-tailed version of CIFAR-10) dataset, and see whether the model performance improves for the most imbalanced classes.

4. Apply the MDSA techniques we studied in this chapter to the CIFAR-10-LT dataset, and see whether the model performance improves for the most imbalanced classes.

References

1. Samira Pouyanfar, Yudong Tao, Anup Mohan, Haiman Tian, Ahmed S. Kaseb, Kent Gauen, Ryan Dailey, Sarah Aghajanzadeh, Yung-Hsiang Lu, Shu-Ching Chen, and Mei-Ling Shyu. 2018. *Dynamic Sampling in Convolutional Neural Networks for Imbalanced Data Classification*. In 2018 IEEE Conference on Multimedia Information Processing and Retrieval (MIPR), pages 112–117, Miami, FL, April. IEEE.

2. LeNet-5 paper, *Gradient-based learning applied to document classification*: `http://vision.stanford.edu/cs598_spring07/papers/Lecun98.pdf`.

3. AlexNet paper, *ImageNet Classification with Deep Convolutional Neural Networks*: `https://papers.nips.cc/paper/2012/hash/c399862d3b9d6b76c8436e924a68c45b-Abstract.html`.

4. *Leveraging Real-Time User Actions to Personalize Etsy Ads* (2023): `https://www.etsy.com/codeascraft/leveraging-real-time-user-actions-to-personalize-etsy-ads`.

5. Automated image tagging at `Booking.com` (2017): `https://booking.ai/automated-image-tagging-at-booking-com-7704f27dcc8b`.

6. *Shot Angle Prediction: Estimating Pose Angle with Deep Learning for Furniture Items Using Images Generated from 3D Models (2020)*: `https://www.aboutwayfair.com/tech-innovation/shot-angle-prediction-estimating-pose-angle-with-deep-learning-for-furniture-items-using-images-generated-from-3d-models`.

7. S. Yun, D. Han, S. Chun, S. J. Oh, Y. Yoo, and J. Choe, "*CutMix: Regularization Strategy to Train Strong Classifiers With Localizable Features*," in 2019 IEEE/CVF International Conference on Computer Vision (ICCV), Seoul, Korea (South): IEEE, Oct. 2019, pp. 6022–6031. doi: `10.1109/ICCV.2019.00612`.

8. H. Zhang, M. Cisse, Y. N. Dauphin, and D. Lopez-Paz, "*mixup: Beyond Empirical Risk Minimization*." arXiv, Apr. 27, 2018. Accessed: Feb. 11, 2023. [Online]. Available: `http://arxiv.org/abs/1710.09412`.

9. R. Geirhos, C. R. M. Temme, J. Rauber, H. H. Schütt, M. Bethge, and F. A. Wichmann, "*Generalisation in humans and deep neural networks*."

10. D. Hendrycks, N. Mu, E. D. Cubuk, B. Zoph, J. Gilmer, and B. Lakshminarayanan, "*AugMix: A Simple Data Processing Method to Improve Robustness and Uncertainty*." arXiv, Feb. 17, 2020. Accessed: Aug. 01, 2023. [Online]. Available: `http://arxiv.org/abs/1912.02781`.

11. H.-P. Chou, S.-C. Chang, J.-Y. Pan, W. Wei, and D.-C. Juan, "*Remix: Rebalanced Mixup*." arXiv, Nov. 19, 2020. Accessed: Aug. 15, 2023. [Online]. Available: `http://arxiv.org/abs/2007.03943`.

12. *Protecting Personal Data in Grab's Imagery* (2021): `https://engineering.grab.com/protecting-personal-data-in-grabs-imagery`.

13. M. Bayer, M.-A. Kaufhold, and C. Reuter, "*A Survey on Data Augmentation for Text Classification*," ACM Comput. Surv., vol. 55, no. 7, pp. 1–39, Jul. 2023, doi: `10.1145/3544558`.

14. *Improving the accuracy of our machine learning WAF using data augmentation and sampling* (2022), Vikram Grover: `https://blog.cloudflare.com/data-generation-and-sampling-strategies/`.

15. *Data augmentation for NLP*: `https://github.com/makcedward/nlpaug`.

16. B. Kang *et al.*, "*Decoupling Representation and Classifier for Long-Tailed Recognition*." arXiv, Feb. 19, 2020. Accessed: Dec. 15, 2022. [Online]. Available: `http://arxiv.org/abs/1910.09217`.

17. K. Cao, C. Wei, A. Gaidon, N. Arechiga, and T. Ma, "*Learning Imbalanced Datasets with Label-Distribution-Aware Margin Loss*", [Online]. Available: `https://proceedings.neurips.cc/paper/2019/file/621461af90cadfdaf0e8d4cc25129f91-Paper.pdf`.

18. D. Dablain, C. Bellinger, B. Krawczyk, and N. Chawla, "*Efficient Augmentation for Imbalanced Deep Learning*." arXiv, Oct. 17, 2022. Accessed: Jul. 23, 2023. [Online]. Available: `http://arxiv.org/abs/2207.06080`.

19. R. He *et al.*, "*Is synthetic data from generative models ready for image recognition?*" arXiv, Feb. 15, 2023. Accessed: Aug. 06, 2023. [Online]. Available: `http://arxiv.org/abs/2210.07574`.

20. D. Dablain, B. Krawczyk, and N. V. Chawla, "*DeepSMOTE: Fusing Deep Learning and SMOTE for Imbalanced Data*," IEEE Transactions on Neural Networks and Learning Systems, pp. 1–15, 2022, doi: `10.1109/TNNLS.2021.3136503`.

21. E. Harris, A. Marcu, M. Painter, M. Niranjan, A. Prügel-Bennett, and J. Hare, "*FMix: Enhancing Mixed Sample Data Augmentation*." arXiv, Feb. 28, 2021. Accessed: Aug. 08, 2023. [Online]. Available: `http://arxiv.org/abs/2002.12047`.

8

Algorithm-Level Deep Learning Techniques

The data-level deep learning techniques have problems very similar to classical ML techniques. Since deep learning algorithms are quite different from classical ML techniques, we'll explore some algorithm-level techniques for addressing data imbalance in this chapter. These algorithm-level techniques won't change the data but accommodate the model instead. This exploration might uncover new insights or methods to better handle imbalanced data.

This chapter will be on the same lines as *Chapter 5, Cost-Sensitive Learning*, extending the ideas to deep learning models. We will look at algorithm-level deep learning techniques to handle the imbalance in data. Generally, these techniques do not modify the training data and often require no pre-processing steps, offering the benefit of no increased training times or additional runtime hardware costs.

In this chapter, we will cover the following topics:

- Motivation for algorithm-level techniques
- Weighting techniques
- Explicit loss function modification
- Discussing other algorithm-based techniques

By the end of this chapter, you'll understand how to manage imbalanced data through model weight adjustments and loss function modifications using PyTorch APIs. We'll also explore other algorithmic strategies, equipping you to make informed decisions in real-world applications.

Technical requirements

We will mostly be using standard functions from PyTorch and `torchvision` throughout this chapter. We will also use the Hugging Face Datasets library for dealing with text data.

The code and notebooks for this chapter are available on GitHub at `https://github.com/PacktPublishing/Machine-Learning-for-Imbalanced-Data/tree/master/chapter08`. As usual, you can open the GitHub notebook using Google Colab by clicking on the **Open in Colab** icon at the top of this chapter's notebook or by launching it from `https://colab.research.google.com` using the GitHub URL of the notebook.

Motivation for algorithm-level techniques

In this chapter, we will concentrate on deep learning techniques that have gained popularity in both the vision and text domains. We will mostly use a long-tailed imbalanced version of the MNIST dataset, similar to what we used in *Chapter 7, Data-Level Deep Learning Methods*. We will also consider CIFAR10-LT, the long-tailed version of CIFAR10, which is quite popular among researchers working with long-tailed datasets.

In this chapter, the ideas will be very similar to what we learned in *Chapter 5, Cost-Sensitive Learning*, where the high-level idea was to increase the weight of the positive (minority) class and decrease the weight of the negative (majority) class in the cost function of the model. To facilitate this adjustment to the loss function, frameworks such as `scikit-learn` and XGBoost offer specific parameters. `scikit-learn` provides options such as `class_weight` and `sample_weight`, while XGBoost offers `scale_pos_weight` as a parameter.

In deep learning, the idea remains the same, and PyTorch provides a `weight` parameter in the `torch.nn.CrossEntropyLoss` class to implement this weighting idea.

However, we will see some advanced techniques that are more relevant and might give better results for the deep learning models.

With imbalanced datasets, the majority class examples contribute much more to the overall loss than the minority class examples. This happens because the majority class examples heavily outnumber the minority class examples. This means that the loss function being used is naturally biased toward the majority classes, and it fails to capture the error from minority classes. Keeping this in mind, can we change the loss function to account for this discrepancy for imbalanced datasets? Let's try to figure this out.

The cross-entropy loss for binary classification is defined as follows:

$$CrossEntropyLoss\left(p\right) = \begin{cases} -log(p) & if\ y = 1\ (minority\ class\ term) \\ -log(1-p) & otherwise\ (majority\ class\ term) \end{cases}$$

Let's say $y = 1$ represents the minority class and it's the class we are trying to predict. So, we can try to increase the minority class term by multiplying it with a higher value of weight to increase its attribution to the overall loss.

Weighting techniques

Let's continue to use the imbalanced MNIST dataset from the previous chapter, which has long-tailed data distribution, as shown in the following bar chart (*Figure 8.1*):

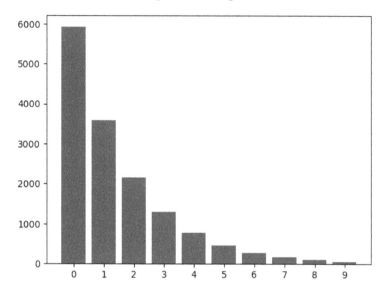

Figure 8.1 – Imbalanced MNIST dataset

Here, the *x* axis is the class label, and the *y* axis is the count of samples of various classes. In the next section, we will see how to use the weight parameter in PyTorch.

We will use the following model code for all the vision-related tasks in this chapter. We have defined a PyTorch neural network class called Net with two convolutional layers, a dropout layer, and two fully connected layers. The forward method applies these layers sequentially along with ReLU activations and max-pooling to process the input, x. Finally, it returns the log_softmax activation of the output:

```
class Net(torch.nn.Module):
    def __init__(self):
        super(Net, self).__init__()
        self.conv1 = torch.nn.Conv2d(1, 10, kernel_size=5)
        self.conv2 = torch.nn.Conv2d(10, 20, kernel_size=5)
        self.conv2_drop = torch.nn.Dropout2d()
        self.fc1 = torch.nn.Linear(320, 50)
        self.fc2 = torch.nn.Linear(50, 10)

    def forward(self, x):
        x = F.relu(F.max_pool2d(self.conv1(x), 2))
```

```
x = F.relu(F.max_pool2d(self.conv2_drop(self.conv2(x)),2))
x = x.view(-1, 320)
x = F.relu(self.fc1(x))
x = F.dropout(x, training=self.training)
x = self.fc2(x)
return F.log_softmax(x, dim=1)
```

Since our final layer of the model uses `log_softmax`, we will be using negative log-likelihood loss (`torch.nn.functional.nll_loss` or `torch.nn.NLLLoss`) from PyTorch.

Using PyTorch's weight parameter

In the `torch.nn.CrossEntropyLoss` API, we have a `weight` parameter:

```
torch.nn.CrossEntropyLoss(weight=None, …)
```

Here, `weight` is a one-dimensional tensor that assigns weight to each class.

We can use the `compute_class_weight` function from `scikit-learn` to get the weights of various classes:

```
from sklearn.utils import class_weight

y = imbalanced_train_loader.dataset.targets

class_weights=class_weight.compute_class_weight( \
    'balanced', np.unique(y), y.numpy())
print(class_weights)
```

This outputs the following:

```
array([0.25002533, 0.41181869, 0.68687384, 1.14620743, 1.91330749,
3.19159483, 5.32697842, 8.92108434, 14.809 , 24.68166667])
```

The `compute_class_weight` function computes the weights according to the following formula for each class, as we saw in *Chapter 5, Cost-Sensitive Learning*:

$$weight\_class\_a = \frac{1}{total\_num\_samples\_for\_class\_a} * \frac{total\_number\_of\_samples}{number\_of\_classes}$$

In *Figure 8.2*, these weights have been plotted using a bar chart to help us see how they relate to the class frequency (*y* axis) for each class (*x* axis):

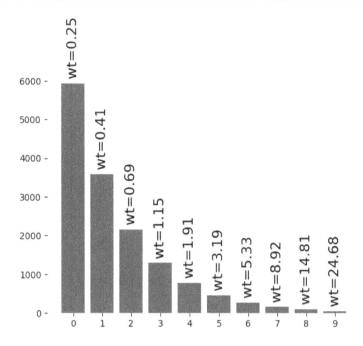

Figure 8.2 – Bar chart showing weights corresponding to each class

As this figure shows, the fewer the number of samples a class has, the higher its weight.

> **Tip**
>
> The key takeaway here is that the weight of a class is inversely proportional to the number of samples of that class, also called inverse class frequency weighting.
>
> Another point to remember is that the class weights should always be computed from the training data. Using validation data or test data to compute the class weights might lead to the infamous data leakage or label leakage problem in ML. Formally, data leakage can happen when some information from outside of the training data is fed to the model. In this case, if we use test data to compute the class weights, then our evaluation of the model's performance is going to be biased and invalid.

The comic in *Figure 8.3* shows a juggler managing weights of different sizes, each labeled with a distinct class label, symbolizing the varying weights assigned to different classes to tackle class imbalance during model training:

Figure 8.3 – Comic illustrating the core idea behind class weighting

> **Tip**
> Another way to compute weights is to empirically tune the weights.

Let's write the training loop:

```
def train(train_loader):
    model.train()
    for batch_idx, (data, target) in enumerate(train_loader):
        data, target = data.to(device), target.to(device)
        optimizer.zero_grad()
        output = model(data)
        loss = torch.nn.functional.nll_loss(output, target weight)
        loss.backward()
        optimizer.step()
```

A lot of other loss functions in PyTorch, including NLLLoss, MultiLabelSoftMarginLoss, MultiMarginLoss, and BCELoss, accept weight as a parameter as well.

Figure 8.4 compares the accuracy of various classes when using class weights versus when not using class weights:

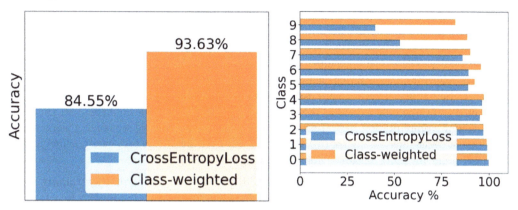

Figure 8.4 – Performance comparison of a model trained using cross-entropy loss with no class weights and with class weights

As we can see, although the accuracy dropped for classes 0-4, it improved dramatically for the most imbalanced classes of 5-9. The overall accuracy of the model went up as well.

> **Warning**
>
> Please note that some loss functions, such as `BCEWithLogitsLoss`, provide two weighting parameters (`BCEWithLogitsLoss` can be used for binary classification or multi-label classification):
>
> • The `weight` parameter is the manual rescaling weight parameter for each example of the batch. This is more like the `sample_weight` parameter of the `sklearn` library.
>
> • The `pos_weight` parameter is used to specify a weight for the positive class. It is similar to the `class_weight` parameter in the `sklearn` library.

> 🚀 **Class reweighting in production at OpenAI**
>
> OpenAI was trying to solve the problem of bias in training data using the image generation model DALL-E 2 [1]. DALL-E 2 is trained on a massive dataset of images from the internet, which can contain biases. For example, the dataset may contain more images of men than women or more images of people from certain racial or ethnic groups than others.
>
> To limit undesirable model capabilities (such as generating violent images), they first filtered out such images from the training dataset. However, filtering training data can amplify biases. Why? In their blog [1], they explain using an example that when generating images for the prompt "a CEO," their filtered model showed a stronger male bias than the unfiltered one. They suspected this amplification arose from two sources: dataset bias toward sexualizing women and potential classifier bias, despite their efforts to mitigate them. This may have resulted in the filter removing more images of women, skewing the training data.
>
> To fix this bias, OpenAI applied reweighting to the DALL-E 2 training data by training a classifier to predict whether an image was from the unfiltered dataset. The weights for each image were then computed based on the classifier's prediction. This scheme was shown to reduce the frequency change induced by filtering, which means that it was effective at counteracting the biases in the training data.

Next, to show its extensive applicability, we will apply the class weighting technique to textual data.

Handling textual data

Let's work with some text data. We will use the `datasets` and `transformers` libraries from Hugging Face. Let's import the `trec` dataset (the **Text Retrieval Conference** (**TREC**), a question classification dataset containing 5,500 labeled questions in the training set and 500 in the test set):

```
from datasets import load_dataset
dataset = load_dataset("trec")
```

This dataset is balanced, so we randomly remove examples from classes ABBR and DESC, making those classes the most imbalanced. Here is how the distribution of various classes looks like in this dataset, confirming the imbalance in data:

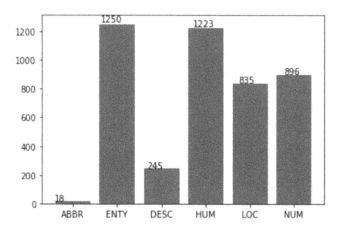

Figure 8.5 – Frequency of various classes in the trec dataset from the Hugging Face Datasets library

Let's create a tokenizer (that splits text into words or sub-words) for the pre-trained DistilBERT language model vocabulary with a maximum input token length of 512:

```
from transformers import AutoTokenizer

model_name = 'distilbert-base-uncased'
tokenizer = AutoTokenizer.from_pretrained(model_name)
tokenizer.model_max_length = 512
```

Next, we will create tokenized train and test sets from the dataset we just imported by invoking the tokenizer:

```
def tokenize_function(examples):
    return tokenizer(examples["text"], padding=False, truncation=True)
tokenized_train_dataset = dataset["train"].shuffle(seed=42).\
    map(tokenize_function, batched=True)
tokenized_test_dataset = dataset["test"].shuffle(seed=42).\
    map(tokenize_function, batched=True)
```

Next, let's instantiate the model:

```
from transformers import \
    AutoModelForSequenceClassification, TrainingArguments

model = AutoModelForSequenceClassification.from_pretrained(\
    model_name, num_labels=6)
```

Now, let's define and invoke a function to get training arguments:

```
def get_training_args(runname):
    training_args = TrainingArguments(
        run_name=runname, output_dir="./results", \
        num_train_epochs=5, evaluation_strategy="epoch",\
        save_strategy="epoch", warmup_ratio=0.1, \
        lr_scheduler_type='cosine', \
        auto_find_batch_size=True, \
        gradient_accumulation_steps=4, fp16=True, \
        log_level="error"
    )
    return training_args
training_args = get_training_args(model_name)
```

The following custom_compute_metrics() function returns a dictionary containing the precision, recall, and F1 score:

```
from transformers import EvalPrediction
from typing import Dict
from sklearn.metrics import precision_score, recall_score, f1_score
def custom_compute_metrics(res: EvalPrediction) -> Dict:
    pred = res.predictions.argmax(axis=1)
    target = res.label_ids
    precision = precision_score(target, pred, average='macro')
    recall = recall_score(target, pred, average='macro')
    f1 = f1_score(target, pred, average='macro')
    return {'precision': precision, 'recall': recall, 'f1': f1}
```

Now, let's implement the class containing the loss function that uses class weights:

```
from transformers import Trainer
class CustomTrainerWeighted(Trainer):

    def compute_loss(self, model, inputs, return_outputs):
        labels = inputs.get("labels")
        outputs = model(**inputs)
        logits = outputs.get('logits')
        loss_fct = nn.CrossEntropyLoss( \
            weight=torch.from_numpy(class_weights).cuda(0).float()
        )
        loss = loss_fct(logits.view(-1,self.model.config.num_labels),\
            labels.view(-1))
        return (loss, outputs) if return_outputs else loss
```

We can initialize the weights similar to how we did previously using the `compute_class_weight` function in `sklearn`, and then feed it to the `CrossEntropyLoss` function in our `CustomTrainerWeighted` class:

```
modelWeighted = AutoModelForSequenceClassification \
    .from_pretrained(model_name, num_labels=4)
trainerWeighted = CustomTrainerWeighted(\
    model=modelWeighted, \
    args=training_args, \
    train_dataset=tokenized_train_dataset, \
    eval_dataset=tokenized_test_dataset, \
    tokenizer=tokenizer, \
    data_collator=data_collator, \
    compute_metrics=custom_compute_metrics)
trainerWeighted.train()
```

As shown in *Figure 8.6*, we can see improvements in performance for the most imbalanced classes. However, a slight reduction was observed for the majority class (trade-off!):

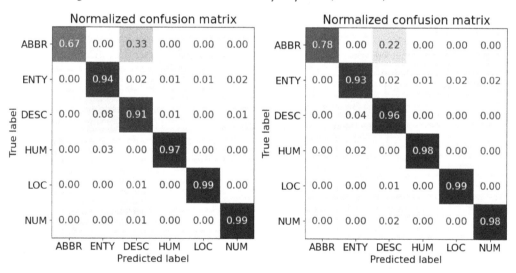

Figure 8.6 – Confusion matrix using no class weighting (left) and with class weights (right)

As we can see, the minority classes, **ABBR** and **DESC**, have improved performance after class weighting at the cost of reduced performance for the **ENTY** class. Also, looking at some of the off-diagonal entries, we can see that the confusion between the **ABBR** and **DESC** classes (0.33 in *Figure 8.6* (left)) and between the **DESC** and **ENTY** classes (0.08 in *Figure 8.6* (left)) significantly dropped when using class weights (0.22 and 0.04, respectively).

Some variants that deal with NLP tasks in particular suggest weighting the samples as the inverse of the square root of class frequency for their corresponding class instead of using the previously used inverse class frequency weighting technique.

In essence, class weighting can usually help with any kind of deep learning model, including textual data, when working with imbalanced data. Since data augmentation techniques are not as straightforward for text as they are for images, class weighting can be a useful technique for NLP problems.

🚀 **Class reweighting in production at Wayfair**

Wayfair used the BERT language model to improve the accuracy of its product search and recommendation system [2]. This was a challenging problem because the number of products that Wayfair sells is very large, and the number of products that a customer is likely to be interested in is much smaller.

There was an imbalance in data because the number of products that a customer had interacted with (for example, viewed, added to cart, or purchased) was much smaller than the number of products that the customer hadn't interacted with. This made it difficult for BERT to learn to accurately predict which products a customer was likely to be interested in.

Wayfair used class weighting to address the data imbalance problem. They assigned a higher weight to positive examples (that is, products that a customer had interacted with) than to negative examples (that is, products that a customer had not interacted with). This helped ensure that BERT learned to accurately classify both positive and negative examples, even when the data was imbalanced.

The model was deployed to production. Wayfair is using the model to improve the accuracy of its product search and recommendation system and to provide a better experience for customers.

In the next section, we will discuss a minor variant of class weighting that can sometimes be more helpful than just the weighting technique.

Deferred re-weighting – a minor variant of the class weighting technique

There is a deferred re-weighting technique (mentioned by Cao et al. [3]) similar to the two-phase sampling approach we discussed in *Chapter 7, Data-Level Deep Learning Methods*. Here, we defer the re-weighting to later, wherein in the first phase of training, we train the model on the full imbalanced dataset without any weighting or sampling. In the second phase, we re-train the same model from the first phase with class weights (that are inversely proportional to the class frequencies) that have been applied to the loss function and, optionally, use a smaller learning rate. The first phase of training serves as a good form of initialization for the model for the second phase of training with reweighted losses. Since we use a smaller learning rate in the second phase of training, the weights of the model do not move very far from what they were in the first phase of training:

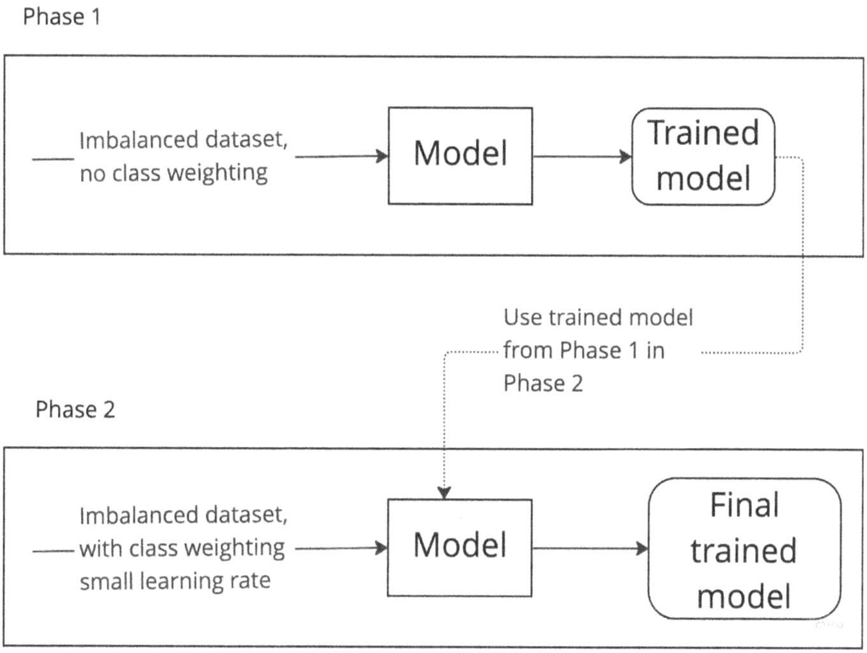

Figure 8.7 – The deferred re-weighting technique

The comic in *Figure 8.8* shows a magician who pulls out a large rabbit from a hat, followed by a smaller one, illustrating the two-phase process of initially training on the imbalanced dataset and subsequently applying re-weighting for more balanced training in the second phase:

Figure 8.8 – A comic illustrating the core idea of deferred re-weighting

Please refer to the notebook titled `Deferred_reweighting_DRW.ipynb` in this book's GitHub repository for more details. After applying the two-phase training part of the deferred re-weighting technique, we can see that the accuracy of our most imbalanced classes improves compared to training with cross-entropy loss:

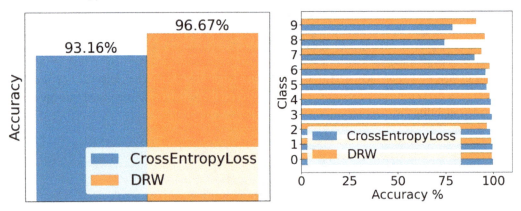

Figure 8.9 – Performance comparison of deferred re-weighting with cross-entropy loss

Next, we will look at defining custom loss functions when the PyTorch standard loss functions don't do everything that we want them to do.

Explicit loss function modification

In PyTorch, we can formulate custom loss functions by deriving a subclass from the `nn.Module` class and overriding the `forward()` method. The `forward()` method for a loss function accepts the predicted and actual outputs as inputs, subsequently returning the computed loss value.

Even though class weighting does assign different weights to balance the majority and minority class examples, this alone is often insufficient, especially in cases of extreme class imbalance. What we would like is to reduce the loss from easily classified examples as well. The reason is that such easily classified examples usually belong to the majority class, and since they are higher in number, they dominate our training loss. This is the main idea of focal loss and allows for a more nuanced handling of examples, irrespective of the class they belong to. We'll look at this in this section.

Understanding the forward() method in PyTorch

In PyTorch, you'll encounter the `forward()` method in both neural network layers and loss functions. That's because both a neural network layer and a loss function are derived from `nn.Module`. While it might seem confusing at first, understanding the context can help clarify its role:

In neural network layers:

The `forward()` method defines the transformation that input data undergoes as it passes through the layer. This could involve operations such as linear transformations, activation functions, and more.

In loss functions:

The `forward()` method computes the loss between the predicted output and the actual target values. This loss serves as a measure of how well the model is performing.

Key takeaway:

In PyTorch, both neural network layers and loss functions inherit from `nn.Module`, providing a unified interface. The `forward()` method is central to both, serving as the computational engine for data transformation in layers and loss computation in loss functions. Think of `forward()` as the "engine" for either process.

Focal loss

The techniques we've studied so far presume that minority classes need higher weights due to weak representation. However, some minority classes may be adequately represented, and over-weighting their samples could degrade the overall model performance. Hence, Tsung-Yi et al. [4] from Facebook (now Meta) introduced **focal loss**, a sample-based weighting technique where each example's weight is determined by its difficulty and measured by the loss the model incurs on it.

The focal loss technique has roots in dense object detection tasks, where there are significantly more observations in one class than the other:

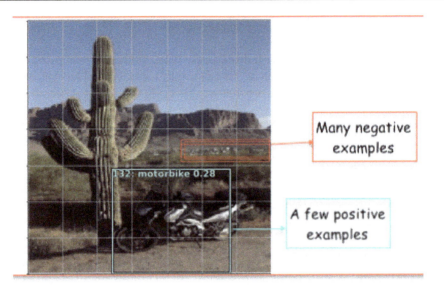

Figure 8.10 – Class imbalance in object detection – majority as background, few as foreground

Focal loss downweighs easy-to-classify examples and focuses on hard-to-classify examples. What this means is that it would reduce the model's overconfidence; this overconfidence usually prevents the model from generalizing well.

Focal loss is an extension of cross-entropy loss. It is especially good for multi-class classification, where some classes are easy and others are difficult to classify.

Let's start with our well-known cross-entropy loss for binary classification. If we let p be the predicted probability that $y = 1$, then the cross-entropy loss can be defined as follows:

$$CrossEntropyLoss\left(p\right) = \begin{cases} -\log(p) & if\, y = 1 \\ -\log(1-p) & otherwise \end{cases}$$

This can be rewritten as $CrossEntropyLoss(p) = -\log(p_t)$, where p_t, the probability of the true class, can be defined as follows:

$$p_t = \begin{cases} p & if\, y = 1 \\ 1-p & otherwise \end{cases}$$

Here, p is the predicted probability that $y = 1$ from the model.

The problem with this loss function is that in the case of imbalanced datasets, this loss function is dominated by the loss contribution from majority classes, and the loss contribution from the minority class is very small. This can be fixed via focal loss.

So, what is focal loss?

$$FocalLoss\left(p_t\right) = -\alpha\left(1-p_t\right)^\gamma \log\left(p_t\right)$$

This formula looks slightly different from cross-entropy loss. There are two extra terms – α and $(1 - p_t)^\gamma$. Let's try to understand the significance of each of these terms:

- α: This value can be set to be inversely proportional to the number of examples of positive (minority) classes and is used to weigh the minority class examples more than the majority class. It can also be treated as a hyperparameter that can be tuned.

- $(1 - p_t)^\gamma$: This term is called the **modulating factor**. If an example is too easy for the model to classify, that would mean that p_t is very high and the whole modulating factor value will be close to zero (assuming $\gamma > 1$), and the model won't focus on this example much. On the other hand, if an example is hard – that is, p_t is low – then the modulating factor value will be high, and the model will focus on this example more.

Implementation

Here's the implementation of focal loss from scratch:

```
class FocalLoss(torch.nn.Module):
    def __init__(self, gamma: float = 2, alpha =.98) -> None:
        super().__init__()
        self.gamma = gamma
        self.alpha = alpha


    def forward(self, pred: torch.Tensor, target: torch.Tensor):
        # pred is tensor with log probabilities
        nll_loss = torch.nn.NLLLoss(pred, target)
        p_t = torch.exp(-nll_loss)
        loss = (1 - p_t)**self.gamma * self.alpha * nll_loss
        return loss.mean()
```

Though the focal loss technique has roots in computer vision and object detection, we can potentially reap its benefits while working with tabular data and text data too. Some recent research has ported focal loss to classical ML frameworks such as XGBoost [5] and LightGBM [6], as well as to text data that uses transformer-based models.

The comic in *Figure 8.11* shows an archer aiming at a small distant target, overlooking a large nearby target, symbolizing the focal loss's emphasis on challenging minority class examples:

Figure 8.11 – Illustration of focal loss

PyTorch's `torchvision` library already has this loss implemented for us to use:

```
torchvision.ops.sigmoid_focal_loss(\
    inputs: Tensor, targets: Tensor, alpha: float = 0.25,\
    gamma: float = 2, reduction: str = 'none')
```

The `alpha` and `gamma` values can be challenging to tune for the model and dataset being used. Using an `alpha` value of `0.25` and a `gamma` value of 2 with `reduction= 'mean'` on CIFAR10-LT (the long-tailed version of the CIFAR10 dataset) seems to do better than the regular cross-entropy loss, as shown in the following graph. For more details, please check the `CIFAR10_LT_Focal_Loss.ipynb` notebook in this book's GitHub repository:

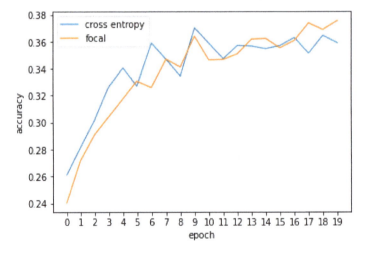

Figure 8.12 – Model accuracy using cross-entropy loss versus focal loss (alpha=0.25, gamma=2) on the CIFAR10-LT dataset as training progresses

In the Pascal VOC dataset for object detection [7], the focal loss helps detect a motorbike in the image, while the cross-entropy loss wasn't able to detect it (*Figure 8.13*):

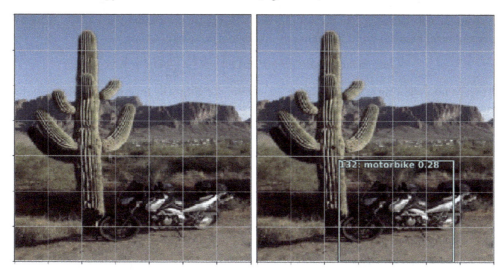

Figure 8.13 – Motorbike not detected by cross-entropy loss (left), while focal loss does detect it (right) on the Pascal VOC dataset. Source: fastai library GitHub repo [8]

Though focal loss was initially designed for dense object detection, it has gained traction in class-imbalanced tasks due to its ability to assign higher weights to challenging examples that are commonly found in minority classes. While the proportion of such samples is higher in minority classes, the absolute count is higher in the majority class due to its larger size. Consequently, assigning high weights to challenging samples across all classes could still cause bias in the neural network's performance. This motivates us to explore other loss functions that can reduce this bias.

🚀 Focal loss in production at Meta

There was a need to detect harmful content, such as hate speech and violence, at Meta (previously Facebook) [9]. ML models were trained on a massive dataset of text and images that included both harmful and non-harmful content. However, the system was struggling to learn from the harmful content examples because they were much fewer in number than the non-harmful examples. This was causing the system to overfit the non-harmful examples, and it was not performing well in terms of detecting harmful content in the real world.

To solve the problem, Meta used focal loss. Focal loss, as we've seen, is a technique that down-weighs the easy-to-classify examples so that the system focuses on learning from the hard-to-classify examples. Meta implemented focal loss in their training pipeline and was able to improve the performance of their AI system when it came to detecting harmful content by up to 10%. This is a significant improvement, and it shows that focal loss is a promising technique for training AI systems to detect rare or difficult-to-classify events. The new system has been deployed into production at Meta, and it has helped to substantially improve the safety of the platform.

Class-balanced loss

The paper by Cui et al. [10] made a minor change to the equation for cross-entropy loss by adding a multiplicative coefficient of $\frac{(1-\beta)}{(1-\beta^n)}$ to the loss function – that is, we use a value of $\alpha = \frac{(1-\beta)}{(1-\beta^n)}$, where β is a hyperparameter between 0 and 1, and n is the number of samples of a class:

$$ClassBalancedCrossEntropyLoss\left(p\right) = -\frac{(1-\beta)}{(1-\beta^n)}log\left(p_t\right)$$

$\beta = 0$ means no weighting at all, while $\beta \to 1$ means re-weighting by inverse class frequency. So, we can consider this method to be a way for the class weight of a particular class to be adjustable between 0 and (1/frequency of a class), depending on the value of the hyperparameter, β, which is a tunable parameter.

This same term can be used in place of the alpha value. It can be used in conjunction with focal loss too:

$$ClassBalancedFocalLoss\left(p_t\right) = -\frac{(1-\beta)}{(1-\beta^n)}\left(1-p_t\right)^\gamma log\left(p_t\right)$$

According to Cui et al., the recommended setting for the beta value is (N-1)/N, where N is the total number of training examples.

The comic in *Figure 8.14* illustrates the core idea of this loss. It shows a tightrope walker who maintains balance using a pole with weights labeled "beta" on both ends, representing the adjustment of class weights to address class imbalance:

Figure 8.14 – Illustration of class-balanced loss

Implementation

Let's take a look at the code for implementing class-balanced loss:

```
class ClassBalancedCrossEntropyLoss(torch.nn.Module):
    def __init__(self, samples_per_cls, no_of_classes, beta=0.9999):
        super().__init__()
```

```
    self.beta = beta
    self.samples_per_cls = samples_per_cls
    self.no_of_classes = no_of_classes

def forward(self, model_log_probs: torch.Tensor, \
            labels: torch.Tensor):
    effective_num = 1.0-np.power(self.beta,self.samples_per_cls)
    weights = (1.0 - beta)/np.array(effective_num)
    weights = weights/np.sum(weights) * self.no_of_classes
    weights = torch.tensor(weights).float()
    loss = torch.nn.NLLLoss(weights)
    cb_loss = loss(model_log_probs, labels)
    return cb_loss
```

In the `forward()` function, `effective_num` effectively computes $(1-\beta^n)$ as a vector, where n is a vector containing the number of samples per class. So, the `weights` vector is $\frac{(1-\beta)}{(1-\beta^n)}$. Using these weights, we compute the loss by using `NLLLoss` between the output of the model and the corresponding labels. *Table 8.1* shows the class-wise accuracy when the model is trained using class-balanced cross-entropy loss for 20 epochs. Here, we can see an accuracy improvement for the most imbalanced classes of 9, 8, 7, 6, and 5:

Class	CrossEntropyLoss	ClassBalancedLoss
0	99.9	99.0
1	99.6	99.0
2	98.1	97.3
3	96.8	94.7
4	97.7	97.5
5	94.2	97.4
6	92.8	98.3
7	81.2	94.3
8	63.6	93.8
9	49.1	91.4

Table 8.1 – Class-wise accuracy using cross-entropy loss (left) and class-balanced cross-entropy loss (right)

Figure 8.15 compares the performance of class-balanced loss and cross-entropy loss:

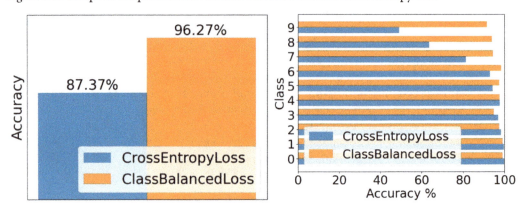

Figure 8.15 – Overall accuracy versus class-wise accuracy using class-balanced loss compared to the baseline model

> 🚀 **Class-balanced loss in production at Apple**
>
> The accessibility team at Apple aimed to ensure usability for all by addressing the lack of proper accessibility information in many apps. They made these apps usable for individuals with disabilities through features such as screen recognition. The researchers aimed to automatically generate accessibility metadata [11] for mobile apps based on their visual interfaces, a problem that had significant class imbalance due to the diverse range of UI elements. UI elements such as text, icons, and sliders were identified from app screenshots. The text elements were highly represented with 741,285 annotations, while sliders were least represented with 1,808 annotations.
>
> The dataset consisted of 77,637 screens from 4,068 iPhone apps, with a wide variety of UI elements, leading to a highly imbalanced dataset, especially considering the hierarchical nature of the UI elements.
>
> A class-balanced loss function and data augmentation were employed to handle the class imbalance effectively. This allowed the model to focus more on underrepresented UI classes, thereby improving the overall performance. The model was designed to be robust and fast, enabling on-device deployment. This ensured that the accessibility features could be generated in real time, enhancing the user experience for screen reader users.

Modern ConvNet classifiers tend to overfit the minority classes in imbalanced datasets. What if we could prevent that from happening? The **Class-Dependent Temperature** (**CDT**) loss function aims to do that.

Class-dependent temperature Loss

In addressing imbalanced datasets, traditional explanations suggest that a model's inferior performance on minority classes, compared to majority classes, stems from its inclination to minimize average per-instance loss. This biases the model toward predicting majority classes. To counteract this, re-sampling and re-weighting strategies have been proposed.

However, Ye et al. [12] introduced the **Class-Dependent Temperature (CDT)** Loss, presenting a novel perspective. Their research indicates that ConvNets tend to overfit minority class examples, as evident from a larger feature deviation between training and test sets for minority classes compared to majority ones. Feature deviation occurs when a model learns the training data distribution of feature values excessively well, subsequently failing to generalize to new data. With CDT loss, the model's decision values for training examples are divided by a "temperature" factor, dependent on each class's frequency. This division makes the training more attuned to feature deviation and aids in effective learning across both prevalent and scarce categories.

Figure 8.16 portrays how CDT loss modifies class weights according to class frequencies, using the visual analogy of a juggler on a unicycle handling items marked with different class names:

Figure 8.16 – A unicyclist juggling items, adjusting class weights based on frequencies

The following class implements this loss function:

```
class CDT(torch.nn.Module):
    def __init__(self, num_class_list, gamma=0.36):
        super(CDT, self).__init__()
        self.gamma = gamma
        self.num_class_list = num_class_list
        self.cdt_weight = torch.FloatTensor(
            [
            (max(self.num_class_list)/i) ** self.gamma\
```

```
            for i in self.num_class_list
            ]
    ).to(device)

def forward(self, inputs, targets):
    inputs = inputs/self.cdt_weight
    loss=torch.nn.functional.nll_loss(inputs,targets)
    return loss
```

Here is an explanation of the CDT class:

- `self.num_class_list` stores the number of examples in each class.
- `self.cdt_weight = torch.FloatTensor([...]).to(device)` computes the class-dependent temperature weights for each class. For each class, the weight is computed as `(max(num_class_list) / num_class_list[i]) ** gamma`.

  The larger the number of examples in a class, the smaller its value in the `self.cdt_weight` list. Majority class examples have lower values, while minority class examples have higher values.

- `inputs = inputs /self.cdt_weight` scales the log probabilities (as inputs) from the model by the class-dependent temperature weights. This increases the absolute values of the negative log probabilities for minority class examples, making them more significant in the loss calculation than those for the majority class. This intends to make the model focus more on the minority class examples.

In *Figure 8.17*, we're plotting the overall accuracy of CDT loss and cross-entropy loss (left) and the accuracies of various classes (right):

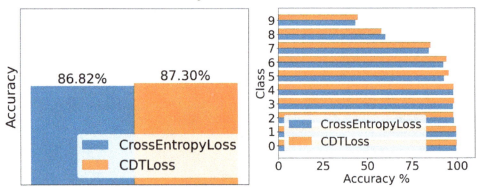

Figure 8.17 – Performance comparison between cross-entropy loss and CDT loss

As we can see, there is an accuracy improvement for some classes, such as 9, 7, 6, 5, and 3, but a decrease in performance for some of the other classes. It seems to give a lukewarm performance on the imbalanced MNIST dataset that we used, but it can potentially be helpful for other datasets.

What if we could dynamically adjust the weights of the classes according to their difficulty for the model during training? We could measure the class difficulty by the accuracy of its predictions for the examples' class and then use this difficulty to compute the weight for that class.

Class-wise difficulty-balanced loss

The paper from Sinha et al. [13] proposed that the weight for a class, c, after training time, t, should be directly proportional to the difficulty of the class. The lower the accuracy of the class, the higher its difficulty.

Mathematically, this can be represented as follows:

$$w_{c,t} = \left(d_{c,t} \right)^{\tau}$$

Here, $w_{c,t}$ is the weight of class c after training time t, and $d_{c,t}$ is the class difficulty, which is defined by the following equation:

$$d_{c,t} = \left(1 - Accuracy_{c,t} \right)$$

Here, $Accuracy_{c,t}$ is the accuracy of class c on the validation dataset after time t, and τ is a hyperparameter.

The point here is that we would want to dynamically increase the weight of the class for which the model's accuracy is lower as training progresses. We could do this every epoch or every few epochs of training and feed the updated weights to the cross-entropy loss. Please look at the corresponding notebook titled `Class_wise_difficulty_balanced_loss.ipynb` in this book's GitHub repository for the full training loop:

```
class ClassDifficultyBalancedLoss(torch.nn.Module):
    def __init__(self, class_difficulty, tau=1.5):
        super().__init__()
        self.class_difficulty = class_difficulty
        self.weights = self.class_difficulty ** float(tau)
        self.weights = self.weights / (
            self.weights.sum() * len(self.weights))
        self.loss = torch.nn.NLLLoss(
            weight= torch.FloatTensor(self.weights))

    def forward(self, input: torch.Tensor, target: torch.Tensor):
        return self.loss(input, target)
```

Figure 8.18 illustrates the concept of difficulty-balanced loss using a comic with an acrobat on a trampoline. Each bounce is labeled with an accuracy score, highlighting how classes with lower accuracy receive increasing weight as the acrobat bounces higher each time:

Figure 8.18 – Illustration of difficulty-balanced loss – the acrobat's
bounces show increasing weight for lower-accuracy classes

Figure 8.19 shows the performance of class-wise difficulty-balanced loss compared to cross-entropy loss as the baseline:

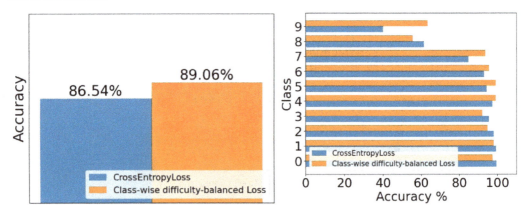

Figure 8.19 – Performance comparison of models trained using class-
wise difficulty-balanced loss and cross-entropy loss

Here, we can see that the performance of several classes improves, including the biggest jump of 40% to 63.5% for the most imbalanced class (9).

Next, we will look at some of the other miscellaneous algorithm-based techniques that can still help us deal with imbalanced datasets.

Discussing other algorithm-based techniques

In this section, we'll explore a diverse set of algorithm-level techniques that we haven't covered so far. Intriguingly, these methods – from regularization techniques that mitigate overfitting to Siamese networks skilled in one-shot and few-shot learning, to deeper neural architectures and threshold adjustments – also have a beneficial side effect: they can occasionally mitigate the impact of class imbalance.

Regularization techniques

The paper from S. Alshammari et al. [14] found that well-known regularization techniques such as L2-regularization and the MaxNorm constraint are quite helpful in long-tailed recognition. The paper proposes to do these only at the last layer of classification (sigmoid or softmax, for example). Here are their findings:

- **L2-regularization** (also called weight decay) generally keeps the weights in check and helps the model generalize better by preventing the model from overfitting.

- The **MaxNorm** constraint is a form of regularization where we clip or limit the weight to not go beyond a maximum limit. Keras has a built-in API called `tf.keras.constraints.MaxNorm`, while PyTorch has `torch.clamp` to help with this.

Siamese networks

On a similar note, previous research has found **Siamese networks** to be very robust to the adverse effects of class imbalance. Siamese networks have been quite useful in the areas of one-shot learning (classifying new data when we have only one example of each class in the training data) and few-shot learning (classifying new data when we have only a few examples of each class in the training data). Siamese networks use a contrastive loss function that takes in pairs of input images and then computes a similarity metric (Euclidean distance, Manhattan distance, or cosine distance) to figure out how similar or dissimilar they are. This can be used to compute the embeddings of each unique class of images in the training data. At inference time or test time, the distance of the new input image from each unique class can be computed to find the appropriate class of the image. The best part of this technique is that it provides a way to learn the feature representation of each class. Siamese networks have found a wide variety of practical applications in the industry regarding vision problems (for example, whether two images are of the same person or not) as well as NLP problems (for example, finding out whether two questions/queries are similar or not on, say, platforms such as Stack Overflow, Quora, Google, and so on).

Figure 8.20 shows a Siamese network where two inputs are fed into the model to get their embeddings, which are then compared for similarity using a distance metric:

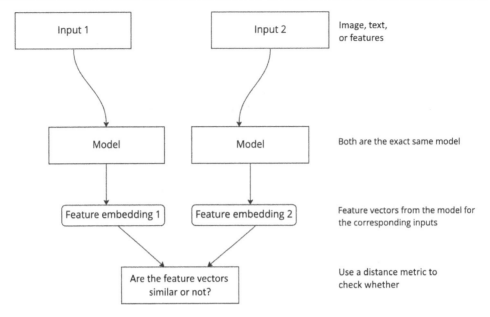

Figure 8.20 – High-level working of the Siamese network model

Deeper neural networks

A study by Ding et al. 2017 [15] discovered that deeper neural networks (more than 10 layers) are more helpful in general with imbalanced datasets for two reasons:

- A faster rate of convergence
- Better overall performance

This is attributed to the fact that deep networks are exponentially more efficient at capturing the complexity of data. Though their experiment was for facial action recognition tasks, this may be useful for trying out deeper networks on other kinds of data and domains.

However, the cons of longer training times, increased hardware cost, and increased complexity may not always be worth the hassle in industry settings.

Threshold adjustment

As we discussed in *Chapter 5, Cost-Sensitive Learning*, threshold adjustment is a cost-sensitive meta-learning technique. Threshold adjustment applies equally well to deep learning models, and it can be critical to make sure that the thresholds for classification are properly tuned and adjusted, especially when the training data distribution has been changed (for example, oversampled or undersampled) or even when class weights or new loss functions are used.

Summary

In this chapter, we explored various loss functions as remedies to class imbalance. We started with the class-weighting technique and deferred re-weighting, both designed to penalize errors on minority class samples. As we progressed, we encountered focal loss, where we shifted from class-centric to sample-centric weighting, focusing on the difficulty of samples. Despite its merits, we learned that focal loss may still be biased toward the majority class when assigning weights to challenging samples across all classes. Subsequent discussions on class-balanced loss, CDT loss, and class-wise difficulty-balanced loss were provided, each introducing unique strategies to dynamically adjust weights or modulate the model's focus between easy and challenging samples, aiming to enhance performance on imbalanced datasets.

To summarize, algorithm-level techniques usually modify the loss functions used by the model in some way to accommodate for imbalances in the dataset. They typically do not increase the training time and cost, unlike data-level techniques. They are well suited for problems or domains with large amounts of data or where gathering more data is hard or expensive.

Even though these techniques improve the performance of minority classes, the majority classes may sometimes suffer as a result. In the next chapter, we will look at some of the hybrid techniques that can combine the data-level and algorithm-level techniques so that we can get the best of both worlds.

Questions

1. Mean false error and mean squared false error:

    Wang et al. [16]proposed that regular loss functions poorly capture the errors from minority classes in the case of high data imbalance due to lots of negative samples that dominate the loss function. Hence, they proposed a new loss function where the main idea was to split the training error into four different kinds of errors:

    - False Positive Error (FPE) = (1/number_of_negative_samples) * (error from negative samples)

    - False Negative Error (FNE) = (1/number_of_positive_samples) * (error from positive samples)

    - Mean False Error (MFE) = FPE+ FNE

    - Mean Squared False Error (MSFE) = FPE^2 + FNE^2

    The error here could be computed using the usual cross-entropy loss or any other loss used for classification. Implement the MFE and MSFE loss functions for both the imbalanced MNIST and CIFAR10-LT datasets, and see whether the model performance improves over the baseline of cross-entropy loss.

2. In this chapter, while implementing the CDT loss function, replace the imbalanced MNIST dataset with CIFAR10-LT (the long-tailed version of CIFAR-10). Check whether you still achieve improved performance over the baseline. You may have to play with the gamma value

or perform any of the other tricks mentioned in the original paper [12] to get an improvement over the baseline.

3. Tversky Loss was introduced in the paper by Salehi et al. [17]. Please read this paper to understand the Tversky loss function and its implementation details. Finally, implement the Tversky loss on an imbalanced MNIST dataset and compare its performance with a baseline model.

4. We used the class-weighting technique and cross-entropy loss with the `trec` dataset in this chapter. Replace cross-entropy loss with focal loss, and see whether model performance improves.

References

1. *DALL·E 2 pre-training mitigations*, 2022, `https://openai.com/research/dall-e-2-pre-training-mitigations`.

2. *BERT Does Business: Implementing the BERT Model for Natural Language Processing at Wayfair*, 2019, `https://www.aboutwayfair.com/tech-innovation/bert-does-business-implementing-the-bert-model-for-natural-language-processing-at-wayfair`.

3. K. Cao, C. Wei, A. Gaidon, N. Arechiga, and T. Ma, *Learning Imbalanced Datasets with Label-Distribution-Aware Margin Loss*, [Online]. Available at `https://proceedings.neurips.cc/paper/2019/file/621461af90cadfdaf0e8d4cc25129f91-Paper.pdf`.

4. T.-Y. Lin, P. Goyal, R. Girshick, K. He, and P. Dollár, *Focal Loss for Dense Object Detection*. arXiv, Feb. 07, 2018, `http://arxiv.org/abs/1708.02002`.

5. Wang et al., *Imbalance-XGBoost: leveraging weighted and focal losses for binary label-imbalanced classification with XGBoost*, `https://arxiv.org/pdf/1908.01672.pdf`.

6. *Focal loss implementation for LightGBM*, `https://maxhalford.github.io/blog/lightgbm-focal-loss`.

7. *The PASCAL VOC project*, `http://host.robots.ox.ac.uk/pascal/VOC/`.

8. *fastai library*, 2018, `https://github.com/fastai/fastai1/blob/master/courses/dl2/pascal-multi.ipynb`.

9. *Community Standards report*, 2019, `https://ai.meta.com/blog/community-standards-report/`.

10. Y. Cui, M. Jia, T.-Y. Lin, Y. Song, and S. Belongie, *Class-Balanced Loss Based on Effective Number of Samples*, p. 10.

11. X. Zhang et al., *Screen Recognition: Creating Accessibility Metadata for Mobile Applications from Pixels*, in Proceedings of the 2021 CHI Conference on Human Factors in Computing Systems, Yokohama Japan: ACM, May 2021, pp. 1–15. doi: `10.1145/3411764.3445186`. Blog: `https://machinelearning.apple.com/research/mobile-applications-accessible`.

12. H.-J. Ye, H.-Y. Chen, D.-C. Zhan, and W.-L. Chao, *Identifying and Compensating for Feature Deviation in Imbalanced Deep Learning.* arXiv, Jul. 10, 2022. Accessed: Dec. 14, 2022. [Online]. Available: `http://arxiv.org/abs/2001.01385`.

13. S. Sinha, H. Ohashi, and K. Nakamura, *Class-Wise Difficulty-Balanced Loss for Solving Class-Imbalance.* arXiv, Oct. 05, 2020. Accessed: Dec. 17, 2022. [Online]. Available at `http://arxiv.org/abs/2010.01824`.

14. S. Alshammari, Y.-X. Wang, D. Ramanan, and S. Kong, *Long-Tailed Recognition via Weight Balancing,* in 2022 IEEE/CVF Conference on Computer Vision and Pattern Recognition (CVPR), New Orleans, LA, USA, Jun. 2022, pp. 6887–6897. Doi: `10.1109/CVPR52688.2022.00677`.

15. W. Ding, D.-Y. Huang, Z. Chen, X. Yu, and W. Lin, *Facial action recognition using very deep networks for highly imbalanced class distribution,* in 2017 Asia-Pacific Signal and Information Processing Association Annual Summit and Conference (APSIPA ASC), Kuala Lumpur, Dec. 2017, pp. 1368–1372. doi: `10.1109/APSIPA.2017.8282246`.

16. S. Wang, W. Liu, J. Wu, L. Cao, Q. Meng, and P. J. Kennedy, *Training deep neural networks on imbalanced datasets,* in 2016 International Joint Conference on Neural Networks (IJCNN), Vancouver, BC, Canada, Jul. 2016, pp. 4368–4374. doi: `10.1109/IJCNN.2016.7727770`.

17. S. S. M. Salehi, D. Erdogmus, and A. Gholipour, *Tversky loss function for image segmentation using 3D fully convolutional deep networks.* arXiv, Jun. 18, 2017. Accessed: Dec. 23, 2022. [Online]. Available at `http://arxiv.org/abs/1706.05721`.

9
Hybrid Deep Learning Methods

In this chapter, we will talk about some of the hybrid deep learning techniques that combine the data-level (*Chapter 7, Data-Level Deep Learning Methods*) and algorithm-level (*Chapter 8, Algorithm-Level Deep Learning Techniques*) methods in some ways. This chapter contains some recent and more advanced techniques that can be challenging to implement, so it is recommended to have a good understanding of the previous chapters.

We will begin with an introduction to graph machine learning, clarifying how graph models exploit relationships within data to boost performance, especially for minority classes. Through a side-by-side comparison of a **Graph Convolutional Network** (**GCN**), XGBoost, and MLP models, using an imbalanced social network dataset, we will highlight the superior performance of the GCN.

We will continue to explore strategies to tackle class imbalance in deep learning, examining techniques that manipulate data distribution and prioritize challenging examples. We will also go over techniques called hard example mining and minority class incremental rectification, which focus on improving model performance through prioritization of difficult instances and iterative enhancement of minority class representation, respectively.

While a significant portion of our discussion will revolve around image datasets, notably the imbalanced MNIST, it's crucial to understand the broader applicability of these techniques. For instance, our deep dive into graph machine learning won't rely on MNIST. Instead, we'll switch gears to a more realistic dataset from Facebook, offering a fresh perspective on handling imbalances in real-world scenarios.

In this chapter, we will cover the following topics:

- Graph machine learning for imbalanced data
- Hard example mining
- Minority class incremental rectification

By the end of this chapter, we will become familiar with some hybrid methods, enabling us to understand the core principles behind more complex techniques.

Technical requirements

Similar to prior chapters, we will continue to utilize common libraries such as numpy, pandas, sklearn, and torch. For graph machine learning, we will use the torch_geometric library as well. The code and notebooks for this chapter are available on GitHub at https://github.com/PacktPublishing/Machine-Learning-for-Imbalanced-Data/tree/master/chapter09. You can open the GitHub notebook using Google Colab by clicking on the **Open in Colab** icon at the top of the chapter's notebook or by launching it from https://colab.research.google.com, using the GitHub URL of the notebook.

Using graph machine learning for imbalanced data

In this section, we will see when graphs can be useful tools in machine learning, when to use graph ML models in general, and how they can be helpful on certain kinds of imbalanced datasets. We'll also be exploring how graph ML models can outperform classical models such as XGBoost on certain imbalanced datasets.

Graphs are incredibly versatile data structures that can represent complex relationships and structures, from social networks and web pages (think of links as edges) to molecules in chemistry (consider atoms as nodes and the bonds between them as edges) and various other domains. Graph models allow us to represent the relationships in data, which can be helpful to make predictions and gain insights, even for problems where the relationships are not explicitly defined.

Understanding graphs

Graphs are the foundation of graph ML, so it's important to understand them first. In the context of computer science, a graph is a collection of nodes (or vertices) and edges. Nodes represent entities, and edges represent relationships or interactions between these entities. For example, in a social network, each person can be a node, and the friendship between two people can be an edge.

Graphs can be either directed (edges have a direction) or undirected (edges do not have a direction). They can also be weighted (edges have a value) or unweighted (edges do not have a value).

Figure 9.1 shows a sample tabular dataset on the left and its corresponding graph representation on the right:

Device Name	IP Address	Connection (Bandwidth, Mbps)
Server	192.168.1.1	Workstation1 (100), Printer (50)
Workstation1	192.168.1.2	Server (100), Workstation2 (200)
Workstation2	192.168.1.3	Workstation1 (200), Printer (150)
Printer	192.168.1.4	Server (50), Workstation2 (150)
Router	192.168.1.254	Server (1000)

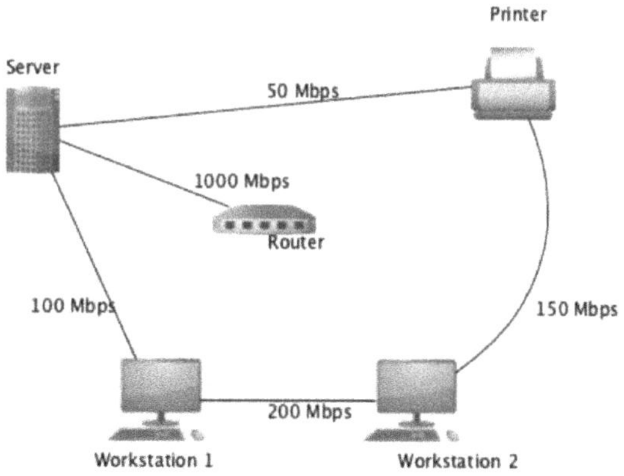

Figure 9.1 – Tabular data (left) contrasted with its visual graph representation (right)

The graph representation on the right emphasizes the relationships between various entities. In the tabular representation on the left, devices and their IP addresses are listed with connection details along with network bandwidth. The graphical representation on the right visually represents these connections, allowing easier comprehension of the network topology. Devices are nodes, connections are edges with bandwidth are the weights. Graphs provide a clearer view of interrelationships than tables, emphasizing network design insights.

In the following section, we will get an overview of how ML can be applied to graphs.

Graph machine learning

Graph Machine Learning (**GML**) is a set of techniques that use the structure of a graph to extract features and make predictions. GML algorithms can leverage the rich information contained in the graph structure, such as the connections between nodes and the patterns of these connections, to improve model performance, especially on imbalanced data.

Two popular neural network GML algorithms are GCNs and **Graph Attention Networks** (**GATs**). Both algorithms use the graph structure to aggregate information from a node's neighborhood. However, they differ in how they weigh the importance of a node's neighbors. GCN gives equal weight to all neighbors, while GAT uses attention mechanisms to assign different weights to different neighbors. We will limit our discussion to GCNs only in this chapter.

Dealing with imbalanced data

In ML, when one class significantly outnumbers the others, the model may become biased toward the majority class, leading to poor performance on the minority class. This is problematic because, often, the minority class is the one of interest. For example, in fraud detection, the number of non-fraud cases significantly outnumbers the fraud cases, but it's the fraud cases that we're interested in detecting.

In the context of GML, the structure of the graph can provide additional information that can help mitigate the effects of data imbalance. For example, minority class nodes might be more closely connected to each other than to majority class nodes. GML algorithms can leverage this structure to improve the performance of the minority class.

GCNs

We will briefly discuss the key ideas behind what GCNs are and how they work.

GCNs offer a unique method of processing structured data. Unlike standard neural networks that assume independent and identically distributed data, GCNs can operate over graph data, capturing dependencies and connections between nodes.

The essence of GCNs is message passing, which can be broken down as follows:

- **Node messaging**: Each node in the graph sends out and receives messages through its edges to and from its neighbors
- **Aggregation**: Nodes aggregate these messages to gain a broader understanding of these local neighborhoods

In GCNs, full feature vectors are passed around instead of just the labels of the nodes.

Think of a GCN layer as a transformation step. The primary operations can be viewed as follows:

- **Aggregate neighbors**: Nodes pull features from their neighbors, leading to an aggregation
- **Neural network transformation**: The aggregated feature set from the previous step then undergoes transformation via the neural network layer

Let's explore GCNs using the example of photos on Facebook. Users upload photos, and our objective is to categorize these images as either spam or non-spam. This categorization is based on the image content as well as the IP address or user ID.

Let's imagine we have a graph where each node is a Facebook photo, and two photos are connected if they were uploaded using either the same IP address or the same account.

Let's say we want to use the actual content of the photo (possibly a feature vector from a pre-trained CNN or some metadata) as a node attribute. Let's assume that we have a 5-dimensional vector representing each photo's features.

Figure 9.2 – An image with a 5-dimensional feature embedding

Step 1 – graph creation

We will create a graph where every vertex symbolizes a Facebook image. We will establish a link between two images if they were uploaded via an identical IP address or user ID.

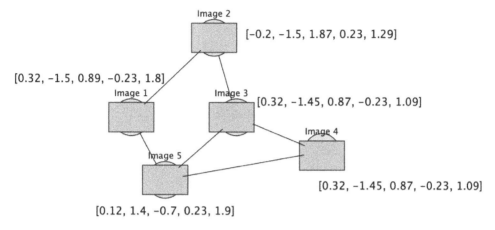

Figure 9.3 – A diagram with images connected to each other if they share the IP or user ID

Step 2 – image representation

Represent each image using a 5-dimensional vector. This can be accomplished by using image metadata, features derived from trained neural networks, or other techniques suitable for image data (*Figure 9.2*).

Step 3 – a singular-layer GCN for image analysis

When a specific image is passed through a single-layer GCN, here is what will happen:

1. We aggregate all the neighboring image's feature vectors. The neighbors are images with matching IP addresses or user IDs.

2. An average function is used to combine vectors. Let's call the combined vector the neighborhood average vector.

3. The neighborhood average vector is multiplied using a weight matrix (of, say, size 5x1, as shown in *Figure 9.4*).

4. Then, an activation function is applied to the outcome to get a single value, which suggests the likelihood of the image being spam.

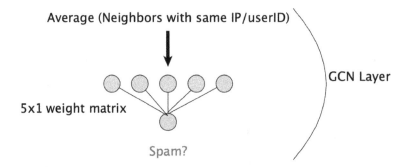

Figure 9.4 – How a single GCN layer works

Step 4 – a dual-layer GCN

Multilayer GCNs, like traditional deep neural networks, can be stacked into multiple layers:

- Raw node features feed into the first layer

- The subsequent layer's input is the previous layer's output

With each added layer, GCNs grasp more extended neighborhood information. For instance, in a two-layer GCN, information can ripple two hops away in the graph.

With a foundational understanding of graph ML and GCNs in place, we're set to explore a case study. We'll compare the performance of a graph model to other models, including a classical ML model, on an imbalanced graph dataset. Our aim is to determine whether graph models can outperform other models by leveraging the relationships between graph structures.

Case study – the performance of XGBoost, MLP, and a GCN on an imbalanced dataset

We will use the Facebook Page-Page dataset from the **PyTorch Geometric** (**PyG**) library, designed to create and train deep learning models on graphs and other irregular structures. This dataset comprises a large collection of social networks from Facebook, where nodes represent official Facebook pages and edges signify reciprocal likes between them. Each node is labeled with one of four categories: Politicians, Governmental Organizations, Television Shows, or Companies. The task is to predict these categories based on the node characteristics, which are derived from descriptions provided by the page owners.

The dataset serves as a challenging benchmark for graph neural network models due to its size and complexity. It was collected via the Facebook Graph API in November 2017 and focuses on multi-class node classification within the four aforementioned categories. You can find more about the dataset at https://snap.stanford.edu/data/facebook-large-page-page-network.html.

We start by importing some of the common libraries and the Facebook dataset:

```
import pandas as pd
from torch_geometric.datasets import FacebookPagePage

dataset = FacebookPagePage(root=".")
data = dataset[0]
```

The data object here is of type `torch_geometric.data`.

Here are some statistics about the graph data:

```
Dataset: FacebookPagePage()
----------------------
Number of graphs: 1
Number of features: 128
Number of classes: 4
Number of graphs: 1
Number of nodes: 22,470
Number of edges: 342,004
Average node degree: 15.22
Contains isolated nodes: False
Contains self-loops: True
Is undirected: True
```

Let's print the features and label in a tabular format:

```
dfx = pd.DataFrame(data.x.numpy())
dfx['label'] = pd.DataFrame(data.y)
dfx
```

This prints the features and labels contained in the `dfx` DataFrame:

	1	2	...	127	label
0	-0.262576	-0.276483	...	-0.223836	0
1	-0.262576	-0.276483	...	-0.128634	2
2	-0.262576	-0.265053	...	-0.223836	1
...	...	...	...	...	...
22468	-0.262576	-0.276483	...	-0.218148	1
22469	-0.232275	-0.276483	...	-0.221275	0

Table 9.1 – A dataset with each row showing feature values; the
last column shows the label for each data point

The overall printed result is as follows:

```
22470 rows × 129 columns
```

These 127 features have been generated using the Doc2Vec technique from the page description text. These features act like an embedding vector for each Facebook page.

In *Figure 9.5*, we visualize the dataset using Gephi, which is a graph visualization software:

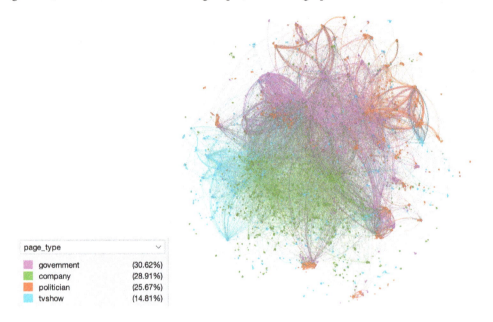

page_type	
government	(30.62%)
company	(28.91%)
politician	(25.67%)
tvshow	(14.81%)

Figure 9.5 – The Facebook Page-Page dataset Gephi visualization

The graph contains both inter-category and intra-category connections, but the latter is more dominant, highlighting the mutual-like affinity within the same category. This leads to distinct clusters, offering a bird's-eye view of the strong intra-category affiliations on Facebook. If we analyze the original dataset for various classes, their proportion is not so imbalanced. So, let's add some imbalance by removing some nodes randomly (as shown in *Figure 9.6*):

Class	Number of nodes in the original dataset	Number of nodes after removing some nodes
0	3,327	3,327
1	6,495	1,410
2	6,880	460
3	5,768	256

Table 9.2 – The distribution of various classes in the dataset

Here is what the distribution of data looks like after adding imbalance:

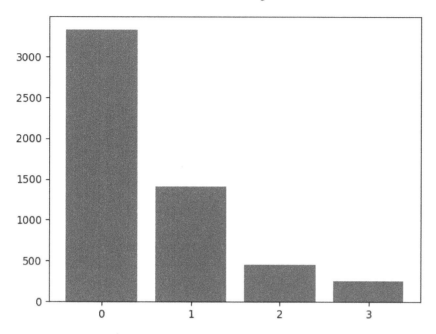

Figure 9.6 – The distribution of various classes after adding imbalance

Let's split the data into training and test sets by specifying their ranges of indices. In the Data object, we can specify this range to denote training and test sets, using masks:

```
# Create masks
data.train_mask = range(4368)
data.val_mask = range(4368, 4611)
data.test_mask = range(4611, 4853)
```

Training an XGBoost model

Let's set up a simple baseline using an XGBoost model on this dataset.

First, let's create our train/test dataset using the masks we created earlier:

```
X_train, X_test, y_train, y_test = \
    data1.x[data1.train_mask].cpu().numpy(), \
    data1.x[data1.test_mask].cpu().numpy(), \
    data1.y[data1.train_mask].cpu().numpy(), \
    data1.y[data1.test_mask].cpu().numpy()
```

Then, we train and evaluate on the data:

```
xgb_clf = XGBClassifier(eval_metric='logloss')
xgb_clf.fit(X_train, y_train)
y_pred = xgb_clf.predict_proba(X_test)
test_acc = accuracy_score(y_test, np.argmax(y_pred,axis=1))
test_acc.round(3)
```

This prints the following accuracy value on the test set:

```
0.793
```

Let's plot the PR curve:

```
y1_test_one_hot = F.one_hot(data1.y[data1.test_mask], \
    num_classes=4)
display_precision_recall_curve(y1_test_one_hot, y_pred)
```

This prints the PR curve (*Figure 9.7*) and area for various classes, using the XGBoost model. The area for the most imbalanced class, 3, is the lowest, as expected.

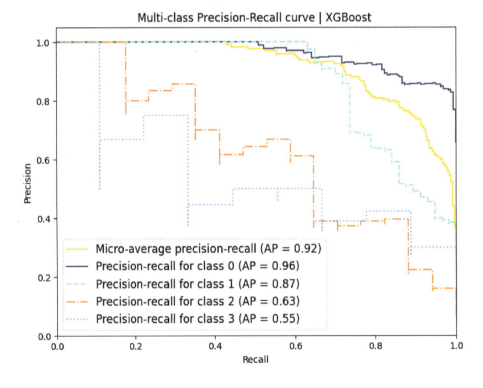

Figure 9.7 – The PR curve using XGBoost

Training a MultiLayer Perceptron model

We can set up another baseline using the simplest of deep learning models, the **MultiLayer Perceptron (MLP)**. *Figure 9.8* shows the PR curve for each class. Overall, the MLP did worse than XGBoost, but its performance on the most imbalanced class, 3, is better than that of XGBoost.

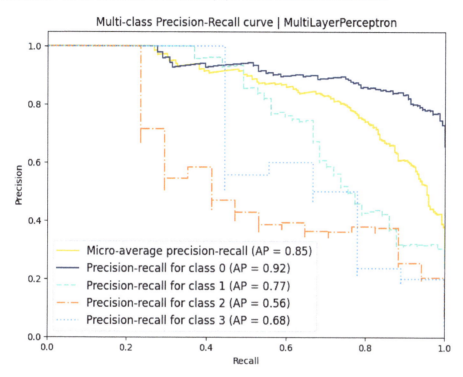

Figure 9.8 – The PR curve using the MLP model

Training a GCN model

Finally, we switch to using a graph convolutional network, which is a generalization of the convolution layers in CNNs. A GCN, as we discussed previously, uses the structure of the graph to update the features of each node, based on its neighbors' features. In other words, each node gets to learn from its friends!

The first step involves importing the required libraries. Here, we import PyTorch, the GCNConv module from PyG, and the functional module from PyTorch:

```
import torch
from torch_geometric.nn import GCNConv
import torch.nn.functional as F
```

The `GraphConvolutionalNetwork` class is a representation of our model. The class inherits from PyTorch's `nn.Module`. It contains an initializer, a forward function for forward propagation, a function to train the model, and a function to evaluate the model:

```
class GraphConvolutionalNetwork(torch.nn.Module):
    def __init__(self, input_dim, hidden_dim, output_dim):
        super().__init__()
        self.convolution_layer1 = GCNConv(input_dim, hidden_dim)
        self.convolution_layer2 = GCNConv(hidden_dim, output_dim)
```

In the `__init__()` function, we initialize the layers of the model. Our model contains two **Graph Convolutional Network layers (GCNConv layers)**. The dimensions of the input, hidden, and output layers are required as arguments.

Then, we define a `forward()` function to perform forward propagation through the network. It takes the node features and edge index as input, applies the first GCN layer followed by a ReLU activation function, and then applies the second GCN layer. The function then applies a `log_softmax` activation function and returns the result:

```
def forward(self, node_features, edge_index):
    hidden_representation = self.convolution_layer1( \
        node_features,edge_index)
    hidden_representation = torch.relu(hidden_representation)

    output_representation = self.convolution_layer2 \
        (hidden_representation, edge_index)

    return F.log_softmax(output_representation, dim=1)
```

The `train_model()` function trains the model. It takes in the data and the number of epochs as input. It sets the model to training mode and initializes the **negative log-likelihood loss (NLLLoss)** as the loss function, and Adam as the optimizer. It then runs a loop for the specified number of epochs to train the model. Within each epoch, it computes the output of the model, calculates the loss and accuracy, performs backpropagation, and updates the model parameters. It also calculates and prints the training and validation losses and accuracies every 20 epochs:

```
def train_model(self, data, num_epochs):
    loss_function = torch.nn.NLLLoss()
    optimizer = torch.optim.Adam(self.parameters(),\
        lr=0.01, weight_decay=5e-4)
    self.train()
    for epoch in range(num_epochs + 1):
        optimizer.zero_grad()
        network_output = self(data.x, data.edge_index)
        true_train_labels = data.y[data.train_mask]
```

```
        loss = loss_function(network_output[data.train_mask], \
            true_train_labels)
        accuracy = compute_accuracy(\
            network_output[data.train_mask].argmax(\
                dim=1), true_train_labels)

        loss.backward()
        optimizer.step()

        if(epoch % 20 == 0):
            true_val_labels = data.y[data.val_mask]
            val_loss = loss_function(\
                network_output[data.val_mask], true_val_labels)
            val_accuracy = compute_accuracy(\
                network_output[data.val_mask].argmax(\
                dim=1), true_val_labels)

            print(f'Epoch: {epoch}\n'\
                f'Train Loss: {loss:.3f}, Accuracy:\
                {accuracy*100:.0f}%\n'\
                f'Validation Loss: {val_loss:.2f},\
                Accuracy: {val_accuracy*100:.0f}%\n'\
                '--------------------')
```

The `evaluate_model` function is used to evaluate the model. It sets the model to evaluation mode and calculates the output of the model and the test accuracy. It returns the test accuracy and the output for the test data.

```
@torch.no_grad()
def evaluate_model(self, data):
    self.eval()
    network_output = self(data.x, data.edge_index)
    test_accuracy = compute_accuracy(\
        network_output.argmax(dim=1)[data.test_mask],\
        data.y[data.test_mask])
    return test_accuracy,network_output[data.test_mask,:]
```

We start the training process and then evaluate the model:

```
gcn = GraphConvolutionalNetwork(dataset.num_features, 16,\
    dataset.num_classes)
gcn.train_model(data1, num_epochs=100)
acc,_ = gcn.evaluate_model(data1)
print(f'\nGCN test accuracy: {acc*100:.2f}%\n')
```

This produces the following output:

```
Epoch: 0
Train Loss: 1.414, Accuracy: 32%
Validation Loss: 1.38, Accuracy: 29%
-------------------
Epoch: 20
Train Loss: 0.432, Accuracy: 85%
Validation Loss: 0.48, Accuracy: 83%
-------------------
Epoch: 40
Train Loss: 0.304, Accuracy: 89%
Validation Loss: 0.43, Accuracy: 86%
-------------------
Epoch: 60
Train Loss: 0.247, Accuracy: 92%
Validation Loss: 0.43, Accuracy: 86%
-------------------
Epoch: 80
Train Loss: 0.211, Accuracy: 93%
Validation Loss: 0.43, Accuracy: 88%
-------------------
Epoch: 100
Train Loss: 0.184, Accuracy: 94%
Validation Loss: 0.44, Accuracy: 88%
-------------------

GCN test accuracy: 90.91%
```

Let's print the PR curves:

```
_, y1_score = gcn.evaluate_model(data1)
y1_test_one_hot = F.one_hot(data1.y[data1.test_mask], num_classes=4)
display_precision_recall_curve(y1_test_one_hot, y1_score)
```

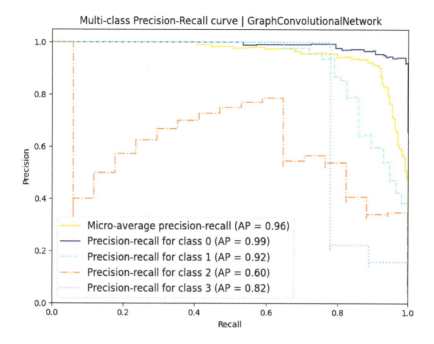

Figure 9.9 – The PR curve using the GCN model

In *Table 9.3*, we compare the overall accuracy values as well as class-wise accuracy values of various models:

Accuracy %	MLP	XGBoost	GCN
Overall	76.5	83.9	**90.9**
Class 0	84.9	95.2	**96.6**
Class 1	72.9	78.0	**88.1**
Class 2	33.3	57.1	**71.4**
Class 3	68.8	37.5	**75.0**

Table 9.3 – Class-wise accuracy values in % on the Facebook Page-Page network dataset

Here are some insights from *Table 9.3*:

- **Overall performance**:
  - GCN outshines both MLP and XGBoost with an overall accuracy of 90.9%. GCN is the best for this network data, excelling in all classes.

- **Class-specific insights**:

  - **Class 0**: GCN and XGBoost do well on class 0.

  - **Classes 1–3**: GCN leads, while MLP and XGBoost struggle, especially in classes 2 and 3. Note in particular that on class 3, which had the fewest number of examples in the training data, GCN performed significantly better than others.

Here, we compared the performance of the traditional ML algorithm of XGBoost and a basic MLP deep learning model with GCN, a graph ML model on an imbalanced dataset. The results showed that graph ML algorithms can outperform traditional algorithms, demonstrating the potential of graph ML to deal with imbalanced data.

The superior performance of graph ML algorithms can be attributed to their ability to leverage the structure of the graph. By aggregating information from a node's neighborhood, graph ML algorithms can capture local and global patterns in data that traditional algorithms might miss.

 Graph ML at Uber and Grab

🎯 **Problem being solved**:

Both Uber and Grab aimed to tackle the complex issue of fraud across their diverse service offerings, ranging from ride-hailing to food delivery and financial services. Uber focused on collusion fraud [1], where groups of users work together to commit fraud. For instance, users can collaborate to take fake trips using stolen credit cards and then request chargebacks from the bank to get refunds for those illegitimate purchases. Grab aimed for a general fraud detection framework that could adapt to new patterns [2].

⚖️ **Data imbalance issue**:

Fraudulent activities were rare but diverse, creating a class imbalance problem. Both companies faced the challenge of adapting to new fraud patterns.

🎨 **Graph modeling strategy**:

- **Graph models**: Both companies employed **Relational Graph Convolutional Networks (RGCNs)** to capture complex relationships indicative of fraud. To determine whether an Uber user is fraudulent, Uber wanted to leverage not just the features of the target user but also the features of users connected to them within a defined network distance.

- **Semi-supervised learning**: Grab's RGCN model was trained on a graph with millions of nodes and edges, where only a small percentage had labels. Tree-based models rely heavily on quality labels and feature engineering, while graph-based models need minimal feature engineering and excel in detecting unknown fraud, using graph structures.

📊 **Real-world impact**:

Graph-based models proved to be effective in detecting both known and unknown fraud risks. They require less feature engineering and are less dependent on labels, making them a sustainable foundation to combat various types of fraud risks. However, Grab does not use RGCN for real-time model prediction due to latency concerns [2].

> 🛠 **Challenges and tips**:
>
> - **Data pipeline and scalability**: Large graph sizes necessitated distributed training and prediction. Future work was needed to enhance real-time capabilities at Uber.
>
> - **Batch real-time prediction**: For Grab, real-time graph updates were computationally intensive, making batch real-time predictions a viable solution.

In conclusion, graph ML offers a promising approach to deal with imbalanced data, when the data either inherently has a graph structure or we think we can exploit the interconnectedness in the data. By leveraging the rich information contained in the graph structure, graph ML algorithms can improve model performance and provide more accurate and reliable predictions. As more data becomes available and graphs become larger and more complex, its potential to deal with imbalanced data will only continue to grow.

In the following section, we will shift our focus to a different strategy called hard example mining, which operates on the principle of prioritizing the most challenging examples in our dataset.

Hard example mining

Hard example mining is a technique in deep learning that forces the model to pay more attention to these difficult examples, and to prevent overfitting to the majority of the samples that are easy to predict. To do this, hard example mining identifies and selects the most challenging samples in the dataset and then backpropagates the loss incurred only by those challenging samples. Hard example mining is often used in computer vision tasks such as object detection. Hard examples can be of two kinds:

- **Hard positive examples** are the correctly labeled examples with low prediction scores

- **Hard negative examples** are incorrectly labeled examples with high prediction scores, which are obvious mistakes made by the model

The term "mining" refers to the process of finding such examples that are "hard." The idea of hard negative mining is not really new and is quite similar to the idea of **boosting**, on which the popular algorithms of boosted decision trees are based. The boosted decision trees essentially figure out the examples on which the model makes mistakes, and then a new model (called a weak learner) is trained on such "hard" examples.

When dealing with large datasets, processing all training data to identify difficult examples can be time-consuming. This motivates our exploration of the online version of hard example mining.

Online Hard Example Mining

In **Online Hard Example Mining (OHEM)** [3], the "hard" examples are figured out for each batch of the training cycle, where we take the k examples, which have the lowest value of the loss. We then backpropagate the loss for only those k examples during the training.

This way, the network focuses on the most difficult samples that have more information than the easy samples, and the model improves faster with less training data.

The OHEM technique, introduced in the paper by Shrivastava et al. [3], has been quite popular. It is a technique primarily used in object detection to improve model performance by focusing on challenging cases. It aims to efficiently select a subset of "hard" negative examples that are most informative to train the model. As an example, imagine we're developing a facial recognition model, and our dataset consists of images with faces (positive examples) and images without faces (negative examples). In practice, we often encounter a large number of negative examples compared to a smaller set of positive ones. To make our training more efficient, it's wise to select a subset of the most challenging negative examples that will be most informative for our model.

In our experiment, we found that online hard example mining did help the imbalanced MNIST dataset and improved our model's performance on the most imbalanced classes.

Here is the core implementation of the OHEM function:

```python
class NLL_OHEM(torch.nn.NLLLoss):
    def __init__(self):
        super(NLL_OHEM, self).__init__()
    def forward(self, cls_pred, cls_target, rate=0.95):
        batch_size = cls_pred.size(0)
        ohem_cls_loss = F.cross_entropy(cls_pred,\
            cls_target, ignore_index=-1)
        keep_num = int(batch_size*rate)
        ohem_cls_loss = ohem_cls_loss.topk(keep_num)[0]
        cls_loss = ohem_cls_loss.sum() / keep_num # mean
        return cls_loss
```

In the NLL_OHEM class, we first computed the regular cross-entropy loss, and then we figured out the k smallest loss values. These k values denote the hardest k examples that the model had trouble with. We then only propagate those k loss values during the backpropagation.

As we did earlier in *Chapter 8, Algorithm-Level Deep Learning Techniques*, we will continue using the long-tailed version of the MNIST dataset (*Figure 9.10*).

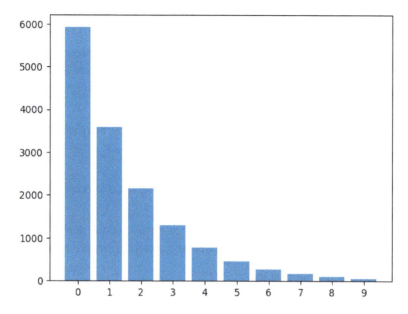

Figure 9.10 – An imbalanced MNIST dataset showing the counts of each class

In *Figure 9.11*, we show the performance of OHEM loss when compared with cross-entropy loss after 20 epochs.

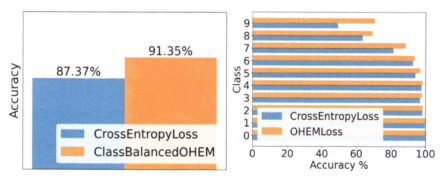

Figure 9.11 – A performance comparison of online hard example
mining when compared with cross-entropy loss

It's evident that the most significant improvements are observed for the classes with the highest level of imbalance. Though some research works [4] have tried to apply OHEM to general problems without much success, we think this is a good technique to be aware of in general.

In the following section, we will introduce our final topic of minority class incremental rectification.

Minority class incremental rectification

Minority class incremental rectification is a deep learning technique that boosts the representation of minority classes in imbalanced datasets using a **Class Rectification Loss** (**CRL**). This strategy dynamically adjusts to class imbalance, enhancing model performance by incorporating hard example mining and other methods.

This technique is based on the paper by Dong et al. [5][6]. Here are the main steps of the technique:

1. **Class identification in each batch**:

   - **Binary classification**: We consider a class as a minority if it makes up less than 50% of the batch. The rest is the majority class.

   - **Multi-class classification**: We define all minority classes as those that collectively account for no more than 50% of the batch. The remaining classes are treated as majority classes.

2. **Compute the class rectification loss**:

   - **Locate challenging samples**:

     - **Find hard positives**: We identify samples from the minority class that our model incorrectly assesses with low prediction scores.

     - **Find hard negatives**: We locate samples from other (majority) classes that our model mistakenly assigns high prediction scores for the minority class.

   - **Construct triplets**:

     - **Use minority samples as anchors**: We use each sample from the minority class as an anchor for triplet formation.

     - **Create triplets**: We form triplets using an anchor sample, a hard positive, and a hard negative.

   - **Calculate distances within triplets**: We define the distance (d) between matched (anchor and hard positive) and unmatched (anchor and hard negative) pairs as follows:

     $d(anchor, hard\ positive)\ =\ |\ Prediction\ score\ of\ anchor - Prediction\ score\ of\ hard\ positive\ |$

     $d(anchor, hard\ negative)\ =\ Prediction\ score\ of\ anchor - Prediction\ score\ of\ hard\ negative$

   - **Impose margin ranking**: We ensure the distance from the anchor to the hard negative is greater than the distance from the anchor to the hard positive, increased by a margin.

3. **Formulate final loss function**:

   - **Class imbalance rectification**: We modify the standard cross-entropy loss to address the class imbalance by introducing a **CRL** term.

- **Custom loss calculation**: We use the formed triplets to compute an average sum of the defined distances.

- **Loss equation**:

$$L_{final} = \alpha \times L_{CRL} + \left(1 - \alpha\right) \times L_{CE}$$

Here, L_{CRL} is the CRL loss, L_{CE} is the cross-entropy loss, and α is a hyperparameter dependent upon the amount of class imbalance in the dataset.

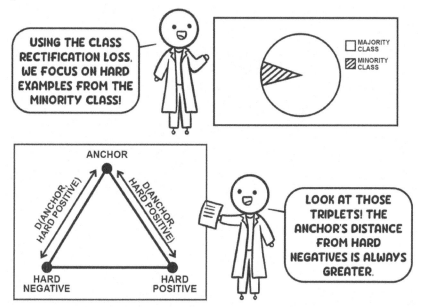

Figure 9.12 – A comic illustrating the usage of triplet loss in class rectification loss

Utilizing the hard sample mining technique in minority class incremental rectification

The minority class incremental rectification technique uses the hard negative technique but with two customizations:

- It uses only minority classes for hard mining

- It uses both hard positives and hard negatives for loss computation (triplet margin loss)

The key highlight of the minority class incremental rectification technique in handling highly imbalanced datasets is that it uses the triplet margin loss on the minority class of the batch that it operates upon. This makes sure that the model incrementally optimizes the triplet loss for the minority class in every batch.

Our results on imbalanced MNIST data by using `ClassRectificationLoss` were relatively mediocre compared to the baseline model that employed cross-entropy loss. This performance difference could be due to the technique's suitability for very large-scale training data, as opposed to a much smaller dataset such as MNIST, which we used here. Please find the complete notebook in the GitHub repo.

It's worth noting that the original authors of the paper applied this method to the CelebA face attribute dataset, which is extensive and multi-label as well as multi-class. *Table 9.4* presents the results from the paper, where they used a five-layer CNN as a baseline and compared CRL with oversampling, undersampling, and cost-sensitive techniques.

Attributes (imbalance ratio)	Baseline (five-layer CNN)	Over-sampling	Under-sampling	Cost-sensitive	CRL
Bald (1:43)	93	92	79	93	99
Mustache (1:24)	88	90	60	88	93
Gray hair (1:23)	90	90	88	90	96
Pale skin (1:22)	81	82	78	80	92
Double chin (1:20)	83	84	80	84	89

Table 9.4 – A performance comparison of CRL on facial attribute recognition on the CelebA benchmark, using class-balanced accuracy (in %) (adapted from Dong et al. [6])

As is evident from the table, the CRL technique consistently outperforms other methods across various facial attributes, even in high imbalance scenarios. Specifically, for the **Bald** attribute, with a 1:43 imbalance ratio, CRL achieved a remarkable 99% accuracy. Its effectiveness is also evident in attributes such as **Mustache** and **Gray hair**, where it surpassed the baseline by 5% and 6%, respectively. This demonstrates CRL's superior ability to address class imbalances.

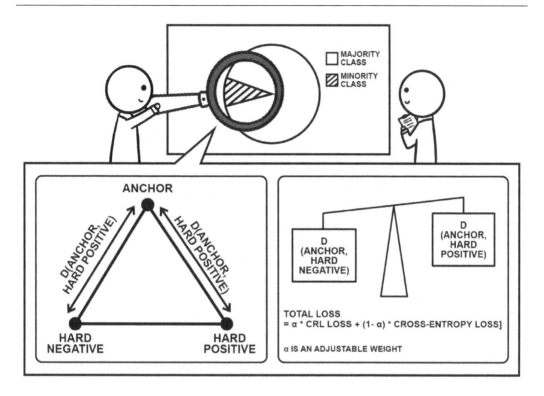

Figure 9.13 – A visual representation of CRL regularization in rectifying
model biases from class-imbalanced training data

Overall, the `ClassRectificationLoss` class provides a custom loss function that combines triplet loss and negative log-likelihood loss while also considering class imbalance in the dataset. This can be a useful tool to train models on imbalanced datasets where the minority class samples are of particular interest.

This chapter explored a few modern deep learning strategies to handle imbalanced data, including graph ML, hard example mining, and minority class incremental rectification. By blending data-level and algorithm-level techniques, and sometimes even transitioning a problem paradigm from tabular to graph-based data representation, we can effectively leverage challenging examples, improve the representation of less common classes, and advance our ability to manage data imbalance.

Summary

In this chapter, we were introduced to graph ML and saw how it can be useful for certain imbalanced datasets. We trained and compared the performance of the GCN model with baselines of XGBoost and MLP on the Facebook page-page dataset. For certain datasets (including tabular ones), where we are able to leverage the rich and interconnected structure of the graph data, the graph ML models can beat even XGBoost models. As we continue to encounter increasingly complex and interconnected data, the importance and relevance of graph ML models will only continue to grow. Understanding and utilizing these algorithms can be invaluable in your arsenal.

We then went over a hard mining technique, where the "hard" examples with the lowest loss values are first identified. Then, the loss for only k such examples is backpropagated in order to force a model to focus on the minority class examples, which the model has the most trouble learning about. Finally, we deep-dived into another hybrid deep learning technique called minority class incremental rectification. This method employs triplet loss on examples that are mined using the online hard example mining technique. Because the minority class incremental rectification method combines hard sample mining from minority groups with a regularized objective function, known as CRL, it is considered a hybrid approach that combines both data-level and algorithm-level deep learning techniques.

We hope this chapter equipped you with the confidence to extract key insights from new techniques and understand their main ideas, taken directly from research papers.

In the following chapter, we will talk about model calibration, its importance, and some of the popular techniques to calibrate ML models.

Questions

1. Apply triplet loss to the imbalanced MNIST dataset, and see whether the model's performance is better than using the cross-entropy loss function.

2. Apply minority class incremental rectification technique to the imbalanced datasets – CIFAR10-LT and CIFAR100-LT. For a reference implementation of this technique on the MNIST-LT dataset, you can refer to the accompanying GitHub notebook.

References

1. *Fraud Detection: Using Relational Graph Learning to Detect Collusion (2021)*: `https://www.uber.com/blog/fraud-detection/`.

2. *Graph for fraud detection (2022)*: `https://engineering.grab.com/graph-for-fraud-detection`.

3. A. Shrivastava, A. Gupta, and R. Girshick, *"Training Region-Based Object Detectors with Online Hard Example Mining,"* in 2016 IEEE Conference on Computer Vision and Pattern Recognition (CVPR), Las Vegas, NV, USA, Jun. 2016, pp. 761–769: `doi: 10.1109/CVPR.2016.89`.

4.   Marius Schmidt-Mengin, Théodore Soulier, Mariem Hamzaoui, Arya Yazdan-Panah, Benedetta Bod-ini, et al. *"Online hard example mining vs. fixed oversampling strategy for segmentation of new multiple sclerosis lesions from longitudinal FLAIR MRI"*. Frontiers in Neuroscience, 2022, 16, pp.100405. 10.3389/fnins.2022.1004050. hal-03836922.

5.   Q. Dong, S. Gong, and X. Zhu, *"Class Rectification Hard Mining for Imbalanced Deep Learning,"* in 2017 IEEE International Conference on Computer Vision (ICCV), Venice, Oct. 2017, pp. 1869–1878. doi: `10.1109/ICCV.2017.205`.

6.   Q. Dong, S. Gong, and X. Zhu, *"Imbalanced Deep Learning by Minority Class Incremental Rectification."* arXiv, Apr. 28, 2018. Accessed: Jul. 26, 2022. [Online]. Available: http://arxiv.org/abs/1804.10851.

10

Model Calibration

So far, we have explored various ways to handle the data imbalance. In this chapter, we will see the need to do some post-processing of the prediction scores that we get from the trained models. This can be helpful either during the real-time prediction from the model or during the offline training time evaluation of the model. We will also understand some ways of measuring how calibrated the model is and how imbalanced datasets make the model calibration inevitable.

The following topics will be covered in the chapter:

- Introduction to model calibration
- The influence of data balancing techniques on model calibration
- Plotting calibration curves for a model trained on a real-world dataset
- Model calibration techniques
- The impact of calibration on a model's performance

By the end of this chapter, you will have a clear understanding of what model calibration means, how to measure it, and when and how to apply it.

Technical requirements

Similar to prior chapters, we will continue to utilize common libraries such as `matplotlib`, `numpy`, `scikit-learn`, `xgboost`, and `imbalanced-learn`. The code and notebooks for this chapter are available on GitHub at `https://github.com/PacktPublishing/Machine-Learning-for-Imbalanced-Data/tree/master/chapter10`. You can open the GitHub notebook using Google Colab by clicking on the **Open in Colab** icon on the top of the chapter's notebook or by launching it from `https://colab.research.google.com` using the GitHub URL of the notebook.

Introduction to model calibration

What is the difference between stating "*The model predicted the transaction as fraudulent*" and "*The model estimated a 60% probability of the transaction being fraudulent*"? When would one statement be more useful than the other?

The difference between the two is that the second statement represents likelihood. This likelihood can be useful in understanding the model's confidence, which is needed in many applications, such as in medical diagnosis. For example, the prediction that a patient is 80% likely or 80% probable to have cancer is more useful to the doctor than just predicting whether the patient has cancer or not.

A model is considered calibrated if there is a match between the number of positive classes and predicted probability. Let's try to understand this further. Let's say we have 10 observations, and for each of them, the model predicts a probability of 0.7 to be of the positive class. If the model is calibrated, then we expect 7 out of those 10 observations to belong to the positive class.

However, surprisingly, most machine learning models are not calibrated, and their prediction values tend to be overconfident or underconfident. What does that mean? An overconfident model would predict the probability to be 0.9 (for example), while the actual probability might have been only 0.6. Similarly, an underconfident model would predict the probability to be 0.6 (for example) while the actual probability might have been 0.9.

Do we always need to calibrate model probabilities?

Actually, it depends upon the problem at hand. If the problem inherently involves the ordering of certain items, say in search ranking, then all we need is relative scores and real probabilities don't matter.

Here is an example of an overconfident model where we can see that most of the time, the predicted probabilities from the model are much higher than the fraction of actual positive examples:

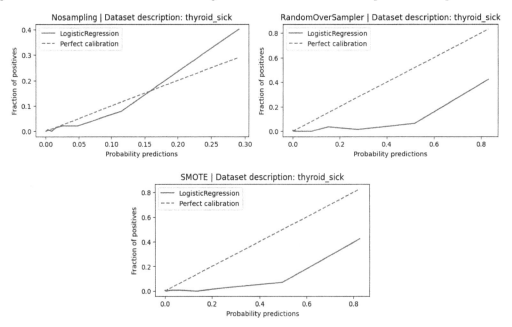

Figure 10.1 – The calibration curve of an overconfident model for
which predicted probabilities are overestimated

Why bother with model calibration

As we've discussed, model calibration may not be necessary if the primary goal is to obtain a relative ranking of items. However, there are several other scenarios where model calibration becomes crucial:

- **Interpreting model predictions as confidence**: Calibrated models allow the scores to be interpreted as the model's confidence in its predictions. For example, in a spam detection system, a calibrated score of 0.9 could mean the model is 90% confident that an email is spam.

- **Interpreting model predictions as probabilities**: These scores can also be viewed as probabilities, making them directly interpretable. In a weather prediction model, a calibrated score of 0.8 could be interpreted as an 80% chance of rain.

- **High-stake applications**: Such calibrated probabilities are particularly useful in high-stake applications such as healthcare for disease prediction or in fraud detection. For instance, in predicting the likelihood of a patient having a certain disease, a calibrated score of 0.7 could mean there's a 70% chance the patient has the disease, guiding further medical tests or treatments.

- **Enhancing human interpretability and trust**: Human interpretability and trust in model predictions are enhanced when the model is calibrated. For example, in a loan approval system, a calibrated score could help loan officers understand the risk associated with a loan application, thereby aiding in the decision-making process.

It is particularly important to be aware of model calibration when working with deep learning models, as several common neural network hyperparameters can affect model calibration:

- **Model capacity**: More layers (depth) and more neurons (width) usually reduce the classification error but have been found to lower the calibration of the model [1].

- **Batch norm**: Although batch norm typically improves training time, has a mild regularizing effect, and might even improve the accuracy of the model, it can also make the model more miscalibrated [1].

- **Weight decay**: Weight decay is a regularization technique, and more weight decay typically helps calibrate the model. So, instead, if we have less weight decay, then we would expect the model to be more miscalibrated [1].

Let's see what kind of model scores typically need to be calibrated.

Models with and without well-calibrated probabilities

The logistic regression model is often assumed to output calibrated probabilities, particularly when it is an appropriate fit for the data [2]. This assumption is based on the model's optimization of the cross-entropy loss or log loss function. However, it's worth noting that logistic regression can produce overconfident predictions, and regularization techniques such as L1/L2 can help the model be more conservative and thus improve calibration.

Naïve Bayes models often push probabilities close to zero or one due to their assumption about feature independence, which can result in poor calibration [2]. On the other hand, bagging models (such as random forests) and boosting models generally produce probabilities that are away from the extremes of zero and one. This is due to the score-averaging nature of the individual decision trees or stumps they use, which often leads to better calibration.

For neural networks, some research studies show that simple networks tend to give calibrated scores [2]. Still, since neural network models are getting more complex day by day, modern neural networks tend to be fairly uncalibrated [1] [3]. As *Figure 10.2* shows, a five-layer LeNet is well calibrated since its confidence levels closely mirror the expected accuracy, evident by the bars roughly aligning along the diagonal. In contrast, while a 110-layer ResNet boasts higher accuracy (lower error), its confidence scores don't align as closely with this accuracy [1].

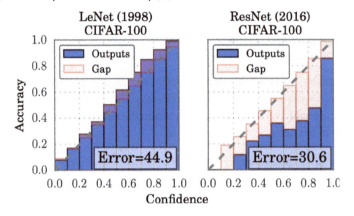

Figure 10.2 – Reliability diagrams for a five-layer LeNet (left) and a 110-layer ResNet (right) on CIFAR-100 (adapted from Guo et al. [1])

Next, we will learn how to measure whether a model is calibrated or not.

Calibration curves or reliability plot

Let's see how we can understand if the model's scores are calibrated or not. Let's assume we have a model that predicts if an image is of a cat or not.

A **calibration curve** is basically obtained by plotting the fraction of actual positive values (*y* axis) against predicted probability scores (*x* axis).

Let's see how to plot the calibration curve, also known as a **reliability plot**:

1.   Create a dataset with two columns: one with actual labels and another with predicted probability.

2.   Sort the data into ascending order using predicted probability.

3. Divide the predicted probability dataset into fixed-size bins ranging from 0 to 1. For example, if we create 10 bins, we get 0.1, 0.2, 0.3, …, 0.9, 1.0. If there are too many examples in the dataset, we can use smaller-size bins and vice versa.

4. Now compute the fraction of actual positives in each bin. These fraction values will be our y axis values. On the x axis, we plot the fixed bin value, i.e., 0.1, 0.2, 0.3, etc.

We get a plot like the one in the following diagram:

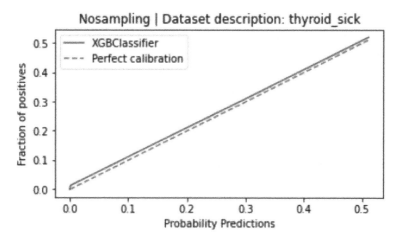

Figure 10.3 – Plotting the probability predictions of an XGBoost classifier against the fraction of positives

We need to be careful with the number of bins chosen because of the following reasons:

- If we choose too few bins, the plot may look linear and well-fitted, giving the impression that the model is calibrated. More importantly, the real danger of using too few bins is that the curve won't have enough detail; it will essentially be just a few points connected together.

- Similarly, if we choose too many bins, then the plot may look noisy, and we may wrongly conclude the model to be uncalibrated.

- It might become particularly difficult to identify whether a model is calibrated or not if we are dealing with imbalanced datasets. If our dataset is not balanced and has a much smaller number of examples of positive classes to plot, then the calibration plot may look noisy or show that the model is underconfident or overconfident.

However, it's worth noting that many models are not perfectly calibrated and their calibration curves may deviate from the perfect calibration line:

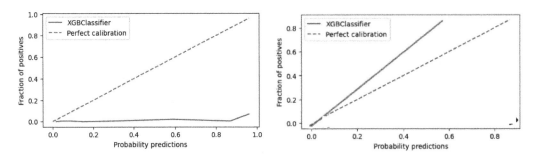

Figure 10.4 – A calibration curve plot when fitted via an XGBoost model; on the left is an overconfident model and on the right is an underconfident model

`scikit-learn` provides a function called `calibration_curve` to easily plot this curve:

```
fraction_of_positives, mean_pred_bin = calibration_curve( \
    y_true,probs, n_bins=8)
```

However, visually judging and comparing various calibration plots can be error-prone, and we might want to use a metric that can make some kind of numerical comparison of the calibrations of two different models.

Brier score

There is a commonly used measure called the **Brier score**, which is basically the mean squared error of the predicted probability obtained from the model as follows:

$$Brier\ score = \frac{1}{N}\Sigma(predicted\_probability - actual\_label)^2$$

where N is the number of examples.

This score varies between 0 (best possible score) and 1 (worst possible score). This metric is very similar to the **Mean Square Error** (**MSE**) or **Root Mean Square Error** (**RMSE**) of linear regression. A lower Brier score is better. Again, `scikit-learn` makes our job a bit easier:

```
import numpy as np
from sklearn.metrics import brier_score_loss
y_pred = np.array([0.1, 0.2,0.8,0.9])
y_actual = np.array([1,0,0,1])
brier_score_loss(y_actual, y_pred)
# order of parameters here is important!
```

This outputs the following Brier score loss value:

```
0.37500000000000006
```

The paper *Class Probability Estimates are Unreliable for Imbalanced Data (and How to Fix Them)* by Wallace and Dahabreh [4] argues that a lower Brier score for an imbalanced dataset might just mean that the calibration is good overall but not necessarily for minority or rare classes. In order to track the calibration of individual classes, they proposed a stratified Brier score:

$$BS^+ = \frac{\sum_{y_i=1}(y_i - \hat{P}\{y_i|x_i\})^2}{N_{pos}}$$

$$BS^- = \frac{\sum_{y_i=0}(y_i - \hat{P}\{y_i|x_i\})^2}{N_{neg}}$$

Figure 10.5 – Stratified Brier scores for positive and negative classes [4]

where N_{pos} denotes the number of positive class examples, N_{neg} denotes the number of negative class examples, y_i is the label, and $\hat{P}$ is the model prediction score.

Let's look at an alternative metric to measure calibration that is more popular among deep learning models.

Expected Calibration Error

Expected Calibration Error (ECE) [5] is another metric for measuring how calibrated a model is. Predicted probabilities from the model are grouped into M bins of equal size. Let's assume B_m is the set of examples whose prediction scores fall into the mth bin.

Then for each bin (B_m), we calculate the difference between the average predicted probability (that is, $conf(B_m)$) and accuracy (that is, the proportion of examples correctly classified). This difference is $|acc(B_m) - conf(B_m)|$.

We also weigh these differences by the number of examples in each bin and finally sum them up to get the overall ECE value. This is equivalent to multiplying the difference by B_m/n, where n is the total number of examples. Finally, we sum this over all the bins to get the final formula:

$$ECE = \sum_{m=1}^{M}|B_m|/n * |acc(B_m) - conf(B_m)|$$

Accuracy and confidence can be defined as follows:

- Accuracy $acc(B_m)$ is the proportion of examples in bin B_m correctly classified by the model:

$$acc(B_m) = (1/|B_m|) * \sum_{i=1}^{|B_m|}I(y_i = \hat{y}_i)$$

- Confidence is the average predicted probability of the examples in bin B_m:

$$conf(B_m) = (1/|B_m|) * \sum_{i=1}^{|B_m|}p_i$$

There is an extension of the previous metric called **Maximum Calibration Error** (MCE) that measures the largest difference between the accuracy and confidence *across all the bins*:

$$MCE = max_{m=1}^{M}|acc(B_m) - conf(B_m)|$$

This can be useful in applications where it is important that the model be well calibrated in all bins, and MCE can then be minimized.

Figure 10.6 shows a reliability diagram with the ECE and MCE values on the MNIST dataset:

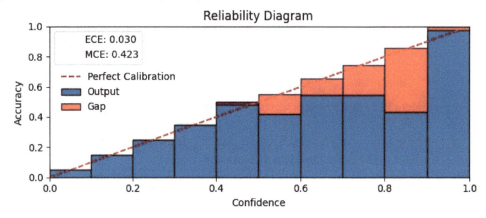

Figure 10.6 – Reliability diagram with ECE and MCE values for the MNIST dataset

---

🚀 **Model calibration in production at Netflix**

🎯 **Problem being solved:**

Netflix aimed to provide recommendations [6] that were closely aligned with a user's varied interests rather than focusing solely on their main preferences.

⚖️ **Data imbalance:**

Traditional recommendation systems can amplify a user's primary interests, thereby overshadowing their secondary or tertiary preferences. This can be considered a form of interest imbalance.

🎨 **Model calibration strategy:**

Netflix employed a greedy re-ranking approach to calibration. The initial model ranked movies based on the predicted likelihood of a user watching them. This ranking is then adjusted using a greedy algorithm to ensure that the top 10 recommended movies match the genre distribution in the user's watch history.

Example: If a user's watch history comprises 50% action, 30% comedy, and 20% drama, the re-ranking algorithm reshuffles the top recommendations to reflect this distribution.

📊 **Additional points:**

The greedy re-ranking algorithm was straightforward to implement. It was empirically shown to improve recommendation performance across various datasets.

This approach ensured that Netflix's recommendations cater to the full spectrum of a user's interests, preventing any single interest from dominating the suggestions.

In the next section, let's try to understand how data balancing techniques can affect the calibration of models.

The influence of data balancing techniques on model calibration

The usual impact of applying data-level techniques, such as oversampling and undersampling, is that they change the distribution of the training data for the model. This means that the model sees an almost equal number of all the classes, which doesn't reflect the actual data distribution. Because of this, the model becomes less calibrated against the true imbalanced distribution of data. Similarly, algorithm-level cost-sensitive techniques that use `class_weight` to account for the data imbalance have a similar degraded impact on degrading the calibration of the model against the true data distribution. *Figure 10.7* (log scale) from a recent study [7] shows the degrading calibration of a CNN-based model for pneumonia detection task, as `class_weight` increases from 0.5 to 0.9 to 0.99. The model becomes over-confident and hence less calibrated with the increase in `class_weight`.

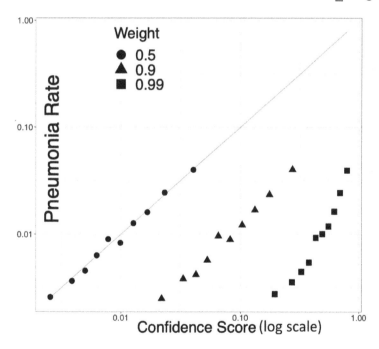

Figure 10.7 – Degrading calibration of a CNN model as class_weight changes
from 0.5 to 0.9 to 0.99 (log scale) (image adapted from Caplin, et al. [7])

Similarly, in *Figure 10.8*, we show the calibration curve for the logistic regression model on the `thyroid_sick` UCI dataset. The corresponding notebook can be found in the GitHub repo of this book.

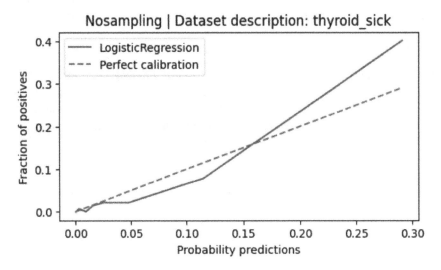

Figure 10.8 – A calibration curve using logistic regression with no sampling

Figure 10.9 and *Figure 10.10* demonstrate how oversampling techniques can worsen a model's calibration:

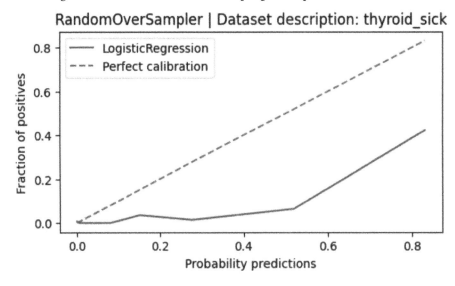

Figure 10.9 – A calibration curve using logistic regression with random oversampling

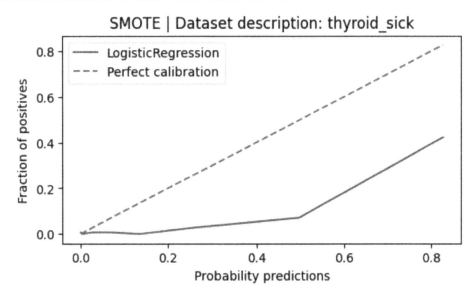

Figure 10.10 – A calibration curve using logistic regression with SMOTE

Similarly, *Figure 10.11* shows a similar effect for undersampling techniques:

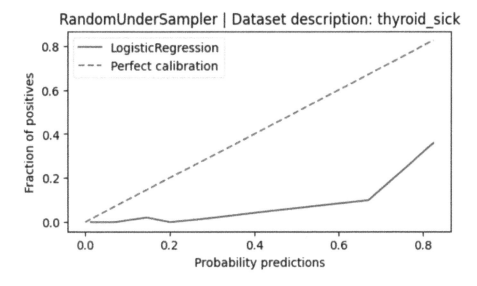

Figure 10.11 – A calibration curve using logistic regression with random undersampling

Figure 10.12 shows how class weighting can negatively affect the model calibration:

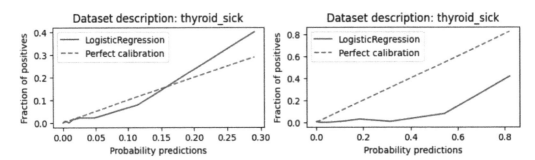

Figure 10.12 – A calibration curve with no sampling technique (left)
and class weighting (right) using logistic regression

In the plots that we just saw, both undersampling and oversampling made the model over-confident. Undersampling can make the model optimistic about its ability to classify the minority class while oversampling can lead the model to overestimate the likelihood of encountering minority instances. This overconfidence arises because the model assumes the altered training data represents the real-world distribution. To elaborate, when we undersample or oversample, we're essentially telling the model that the minority class is more common (or less rare) than it actually is. The model can then generalize this skewed view to new, unseen data. As a result, it can become overconfident in its predictions for the minority class, thinking these outcomes are more likely than they actually are. This overconfidence doesn't extend to the majority class because the model still sees plenty of those examples during training. Therefore, the model ends up being miscalibrated and tends to be overly sure of its predictions for the minority class.

In the following section, we will utilize a real-world dataset, train a model using this dataset, and then determine the calibration of the model by plotting calibration curves.

Plotting calibration curves for a model trained on a real-world dataset

Model calibration should ideally be done on a dataset that is separate from the training and test set. Why? It's to avoid overfitting because the model can become too tailored to the training/test set's unique characteristics.

We can have a hold-out dataset that has been specifically set aside for model calibration. In some cases, we may have too little data to justify splitting it further into a separate hold-out dataset for calibration. In such cases, a practical compromise might be to use the test set for calibration, assuming that the test set has the same distribution as the dataset on which the model will be used to make final predictions. However, we should keep in mind that after calibrating on the test set, we no longer have an unbiased estimate of the final performance of the model, and we need to be cautious about interpreting the model's performance metrics.

We use the `HR Data for Analytics` dataset from Kaggle (`https://www.kaggle.com/datasets/jacksonchou/hr-data-for-analytics`). This dataset contains employee profiles of a large company, where each record is an employee.

The downloaded dataset `HR_comma_sep.csv` has been added to the GitHub repo of the book. Let's load the dataset into a `pandas` DataFrame:

```
df = pd.read_csv('HR_comma_sep.csv')
df
```

This shows some sample rows from the dataset:

	last_evaluation	left	...	sales	salary
0	0.53	1	...	sales	low
1	0.86	1	...	sales	medium
2	0.88	1	...	sales	medium
3	0.87	1	...	sales	low
4	0.52	1	...	sales	low
...	...	...	...	...	...
14994	0.57	1	...	support	low
14995	0.48	1	...	support	low
14996	0.53	1	...	support	low
14997	0.96	1	...	support	low
14998	0.52	1	...	support	low

Table 10.1 – Sample rows from the HR Data for Analytics dataset from Kaggle

It's clear that some of the columns, such as `sales` and `salary`, are categorical. The `left` column is our labels column. Let's get the imbalance in the dataset:

```
import seaborn as sns
print(df['left'].value_counts())
df['left'].value_counts().plot(kind='bar')
```

This gives us the count of the labels:

```
0       11428
1        3571
```

We need to convert the categorical columns into ID labels using `LabelEncoder` and then standardize these columns using `StandardScaler` from `sklearn`. After preprocessing, we split the dataset into three subsets: 80% for the training set and 10% each for the validation and test sets. We'll skip the code for these steps and jump straight into training the model. For the complete code, please refer to the accompanying GitHub notebook.

As usual, we will train a random forest model on the training set and use the test set for evaluating the model. We will use a validation set for calibrating the model.

```
model = RandomForestClassifier(n_estimators=100, random_state=49)
model.fit(X_train, y_train)
```

Let's figure out how calibrated the model is. We print the Brier's score and plot the calibration curve:

```
# Get model probabilities on test set(uncalibrated model)
probs_uncalibrated = model.predict_proba(X_test)[:, 1]

# Calculate Brier score for the uncalibrated model
brier_uncalibrated = brier_score_loss(y_test, probs_uncalibrated)

print(f"Brier Score for Uncalibrated Model: \
    {round(brier_uncalibrated, 4)}")

# Compute the calibration curve for the uncalibrated model
fraction_of_positives_uncalibrated,mean_predicted_value_uncalibrated=\
    calibration_curve(y_test, probs_uncalibrated, n_bins=10)
```

This gives the following output:

```
Brier Score for Uncalibrated Model: 0.0447
```

Let's plot the calibration curve:

```
plt.figure(figsize=(6, 4))
plt.plot([0, 1], [0, 1], "k:", label="Perfectly calibrated")
plt.plot(mean_predicted_value_uncalibrated, \
    fraction_of_positives_uncalibrated, label="Uncalibrated")
plt.xlabel('Mean Predicted Value')
plt.ylabel('Fraction of Positives')
plt.title('Calibration Curve (Test Set)')
plt.legend()
plt.show()
```

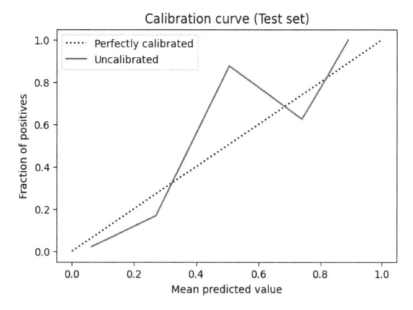

Figure 10.13 – A calibration curve of an uncalibrated random forest model

Figure 10.13 shows that the model is overconfident in the initial range of predictions (0 to ~0.4) and is then underconfident afterward.

In the next section, we will look at some techniques to improve the calibration of the models.

Model calibration techniques

There are several ways to calibrate a model. There are two broad categorizations of the calibration techniques based on the nature of the method used to adjust the predicted probabilities to better align with the true probabilities: parametric and non-parametric:

- **Parametric methods**: These methods assume a specific functional form for the relationship between the predicted probabilities and the true probabilities. They have a set number of parameters that need to be estimated from the data. Once these parameters are estimated, the calibration function is fully specified. Examples include Platt scaling, which assumes a logistic function, and beta calibration, which assumes a beta distribution. We will also discuss temperature scaling and label smoothing.

- **Non-parametric methods**: These methods do not assume a specific functional form for the calibration function. They are more flexible and can adapt to more complex relationships between the predicted and true probabilities. However, they often require more data to produce a reliable calibration. Examples include isotonic regression, which fits a piece-wise constant function, and spline calibration, which uses spline (piecewise-defined polynomial) functions to fit the predicted probabilities.

First, we will explore a theoretical, formula-based method for calibrating scores for models trained on sampled data, specifically in the context of imbalanced data. Next, we'll examine popular methods such as Platt's scaling and isotonic regression, which are commonly used with classical machine learning models. Finally, we'll introduce supporting techniques such as temperature scaling and label smoothing, which are more prevalent among deep learning models.

The calibration of model scores to account for sampling

If we used oversampling or undersampling to balance a dataset, we can derive a theoretical calibration formula. As we saw in *Chapter 2, Oversampling Methods, Chapter 3, Undersampling Methods* (both based on sampling), and *Chapter 7, Data-Level Deep Learning Methods*, we can apply some (over/under) sampling techniques or data augmentation techniques to bump up the relative number of samples of the minority classes(s) in order to account for a data imbalance. As a result, we change the distribution of training data. Although downsampling enhances the model's ability to distinguish between classes, it also leads to an overestimation of the predicted probabilities. Because of this, the model scores during inference (real-world prediction) time are still in the downsampled space, and we should bring the scores back to the real distribution.

Typically, the goal of downsampling is to balance the dataset in terms of the number of instances of positive and negative classes.

As an example, if there are 100 positive class instances and 200 negative class instances after downsampling, the ratio is $w = 100/200 = 0.5$.

Assuming the number of negative class examples is more than the number of positive class examples, we define w as the ratio:

$$w = \frac{Number\ of\ positive\ class\ instances\ in\ downsampled\ dataset}{Number\ of\ negative\ class\ instances\ in\ downsampled\ dataset}$$

Now, let's assume p is the probability of selecting a positive class example from the original dataset (without any kind of downsampling used).

If p is the probability of selecting a positive class in the original dataset, then the probability p_d of selecting a positive class from the downsampled dataset can be computed using the following formula [8]:

$$p_d = \frac{p}{p + w(1-p)}$$

Note that if $w=1$, that is, when no downsampling is done, $p_d = p$. You can refer to the paper by Moscatelli et al. [9] for a proof of this relationship between the original and downsampled dataset probabilities.

Explaining the denominator

The following are the various terms in the denominator of the previous formula:

- p is the probability of selecting a positive class instance in the original dataset
- $(1 - p)$ is the probability of selecting a negative class instance in the original dataset

- $w(1 - p)$ is the probability of selecting a negative class instance when downsampling is used
- The summation $p + w(1 - p)$ is the total sum of probabilities for both the positive and downsampled negative classes in the dataset after downsampling the negative class by a factor of w

Now that we understand the previous formula, we can flip it to find out the probability p of selecting a positive class in the original dataset [10]:

$$p = \frac{p_d}{p_d + \frac{1-p_d}{w}}$$

where:

- w is the ratio of positive class to negative class (called the negative downsampling ratio)
- p_d is the probability of selecting a positive class from the downsampled dataset

Let's understand this with some numbers:

- We have a total of 100,000 examples with 10,000 from the positive class and 90,000 from the negative class.
- Let's say we use a downsampling rate $w = 0.5$, which means that after downsampling, we have 10,000 positives and 20,000 negatives. This also implies that during downsampling, for every positive class example, we selected only two negative class examples.
- Let's assume our prediction score from a model when trained on the downsampled dataset, p_d, is 0.9.
- Let's compute the prediction score in the original dataset. From the previous defined formula, $p = \frac{p_d}{p_d + \frac{1-p_d}{w}} = \frac{0.9}{0.9 + \frac{1-0.9}{0.5}} = \frac{0.9}{0.9 + 0.2} = 0.82$.
- So, a model prediction score of 0.9 in downsampled example changed to 0.82 in the original dataset. Notice how the probability got lowered.

A more generic and simpler formula [11] is the relationship between odds before and after sampling:

$$odds\_after = odds\_before * \frac{proportion\_of\_1\_before\_sampling * (1 - proportion\_of\_1\_after\_sampling)}{(1 - proportion\_of\_1\_before\_sampling) * (proportion\_of\_1\_after\_sampling)}$$

where *odds* are a way to express the probability of an event as follows:

$$odds = \frac{probability}{1 - probability}$$

Figure 10.14 and *Figure 10.15* show the model calibration plots before and after applying the previous calibration formula, respectively, when using random undersampling on the `thyroid_sick` UCI dataset available from the `imblearn.datasets` package. You can find the complete notebook on GitHub.

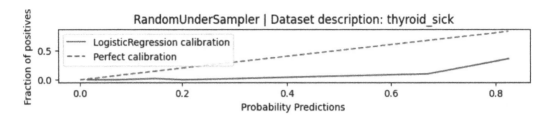

Figure 10.14 – A model calibration plot before calibration when using undersampling

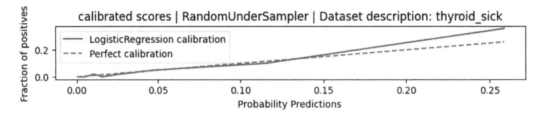

Figure 10.15 – A model calibration plots after calibration when using undersampling

🚀 Model calibration in production at Meta

🎯 **Problem being solved:**

Meta aimed to accurately predict **Click-Through Rates (CTR)** for ads to optimize online bidding and auctions in Meta's advertising system [10]. Accurate click prediction is crucial for optimizing online bidding and auctions.

⚖️ **Data imbalance issue:**

Meta dealt with massive volumes of data, which inherently contained imbalances. A full day of Facebook ad impression data contained a huge number of instances. Meta used negative downsampling to speed up training and improve model performance.

🫣 **Model calibration strategy:**

Since Meta used downsampling, they used the formula from the previous section,

$p = \frac{P_d}{P_d + \frac{1 - P_d}{w}}$, to re-calibrate the model prediction score.

📊 **Additional important points:**

They explored the impact of data freshness and online learning on prediction accuracy. The efficiency of an ads auction depended on the accuracy and calibration of click prediction. They also used normalized cross-entropy loss and calibration as their major evaluation metrics.

Platt's scaling

With this technique, we try to map the classifier's probabilities to the perfect calibration line. More precisely, we just fit a logistic regression model, with the input being the original model's probability scores and the labels being the actual labels. The `CalibratedClassifierCV` API in `sklearn` already facilitates the implementation of this technique:

```
# Calibrate the model on the validation data using Platt's scaling
platt_scaling = CalibratedClassifierCV(model, \
    method='sigmoid', cv='prefit')
platt_scaling.fit(X_val, y_val)

# Get model probabilities on test set (calibrated model)
probs_ps = platt_scaling.predict_proba(X_test)[:, 1]

# Compute Brier score for Platt's scaling calibrated model
brier_platt = brier_score_loss(y_test, probs_ps)
print(f"Brier Score for Platt's Scaled Model: \
    {round(brier_platt, 4)}")

# Compute the calibration curve for Platt's scaling
fraction_of_positives_ps, mean_predicted_value_ps = \
    calibration_curve(y_test, probs_ps, n_bins=10)
```

Here is the Brier score output:

```
Brier Score for Platt's Scaled Model: 0.032
```

The Brier score for Platt's scaled model is smaller than that of the uncalibrated model, which was 0.0447, meaning that the Platt's scaled model is calibrated better.

Isotonic regression

Isotonic regression is particularly useful when we expect a monotonic relationship between the input variables and the output. In this context, a monotonic function is one that is either entirely non-decreasing or entirely non-increasing. The monotonicity here refers to the relationship between the model's raw output and the true probabilities, not the arrangement of the data points.

If the model's output does not follow this expected monotonic behavior, isotonic regression can be applied to enforce it. Isotonic regression can be used in cases such as credit scoring or medical diagnosis, where a higher score should consistently indicate a higher likelihood of a particular outcome.

```
isotonic_regression = CalibratedClassifierCV(model, \
    method='isotonic', cv='prefit')
isotonic_regression.fit(X_val, y_val)
probs_ir = isotonic_regression.predict_proba(X_test)[:, 1]
brier_isotonic = brier_score_loss(y_test, probs_ir)
print(f"Brier Score for Isotonic Regression Calibrated \
    Model: {round(brier_isotonic, 4)}")
```

```
fraction_of_positives_ir, mean_predicted_value_ir = \
    calibration_curve(y_test, probs_ir, n_bins=10)
```

Here is the output:

```
Brier Score for Isotonic Regression Calibrated Model: 0.0317
```

This Brier score value is a further improvement over Platt's scaling method.

Let's plot the calibration curves for both the techniques:

```
plt.figure(figsize=(6, 4))
plt.plot([0, 1], [0, 1], "k:", label="Perfectly calibrated")
plt.plot(mean_predicted_value_uncalibrated, \
    fraction_of_positives_uncalibrated, label="Uncalibrated")
plt.plot(mean_predicted_value_ps, fraction_of_positives_ps, \
    label="Platt's scaling", linestyle='-.')
plt.plot(mean_predicted_value_ir, fraction_of_positives_ir, \
    label="Isotonic regression", linestyle='--')
plt.xlabel('Mean predicted value')
plt.ylabel('Fraction of positives')
plt.title('Calibration curves (Test Set)')
plt.legend()
plt.show()
```

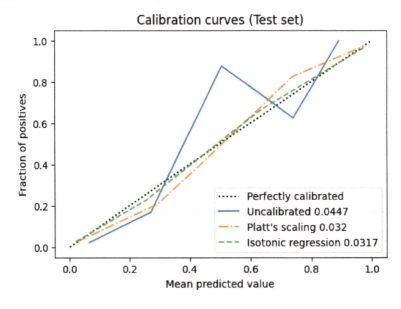

Figure 10.16 – Calibration curves for a random forest model

As *Figure 10.16* shows, the isotonic regression is the closest to the perfectly calibrated curve; hence, it performed the best for our model and data. Platt's scaling did pretty well at calibrating the model, too.

Choosing between Platt's scaling and Isotonic regression

Platt's scaling is considered more apt for problems where the model predictions follow the sigmoid curve. This makes sense because logistic regression (which is used by Platt's scaling) uses a sigmoid to fit the data points. Isotonic regression has a much broader coverage of distortions that it can cover for the predicted probabilities. However, some research studies [2] show that isotonic regression is more prone to overfitting the predicted probabilities. Hence, its performance can be worse than Platt's scaling when we only have a limited dataset since it doesn't generalize well with the limited dataset.

> **A general rule to follow**
>
> When the dataset at hand is very small or limited, choose Platt's scaling. However, when data is sufficient enough not to have an overfitted model, isotonic regression usually does better than Platt's scaling.

For the calibration of a multi-class classifier, we can use the **one-vs-rest** approach with individual calibration plots per class. We can apply techniques such as Platt's scaling or Isotonic regression for enhanced predictability, just like binary classification.

Temperature scaling

Temperature scaling is a post-processing technique used to improve the calibration of neural networks. It works by scaling the logits (the output of the final layer of the network before applying the softmax function) using a temperature parameter. This has the effect of sharpening or softening the probabilities assigned to each class depending on the temperature value. By adjusting the temperature parameter, it is possible to achieve better calibration of the model's confidence estimates, which can be useful in applications such as classification or ranking.

Temperature scaling can be considered a multi-class extension of Platt's scaling with only one hyper-parameter of temperature $T > 0$ for all classes.

Label smoothing

Label smoothing [12] is a regularization technique that's known to improve model calibration. It modifies the training data that is used to train the model and is usually handled as a part of the model training. It is not a post-processing technique like temperature scaling and previous techniques.

When neural networks are trained, they often develop excessive confidence in their predictions, which can hinder their ability to generalize and perform well on new, unseen data. Therefore, it is beneficial to introduce a form of **regularization** that reduces the network's level of certainty and improves its performance on new data.

Let's say we have a binary classification problem where the true labels can be either 0 or 1. Without label smoothing, the training labels would be one-hot encoded, meaning the true label would be 1 for positive examples and 0 for negative examples.

With label smoothing, we add a small amount of **noise** to the true labels. For example, we can set a smoothing factor of 0.1.

Here is an example of the original and smoothed labels for a positive example in binary classification:

```
Original one-hot encoded label: [1, 0]
Smoothed one-hot encoded label: [0.9, 0.1]
```

By adding this noise to the labels, the model is encouraged to be less confident in its predictions and to be more robust to small changes in the input data. This can lead to improved performance on unseen data.

In large datasets, mislabeled data can be a concern. Neural networks should be designed to approach the correct answer cautiously to mitigate the impact of incorrect labels. Label smoothing helps in this regard by slightly adjusting the target labels, making the model less confident about its predictions. This can prevent the model from overfitting to noisy or incorrect labels.

According to the paper by Müller [13], label smoothing can improve model calibration by automatically adjusting the network's output probabilities. This eliminates the need for manual temperature scaling.

Label smoothing can help improve accuracy in various domains, such as image classification, text, and speech recognition problems. Most of the modern machine learning frameworks, including TensorFlow, PyTorch, and Transformers (from Hugging Face), provide built-in implementations for label smoothing in some form in their APIs.

In PyTorch, it's implemented in the cross-entropy loss function:

```
torch.nn.CrossEntropyLoss(label_smoothing=0.1, …)
```

Here we can specify the amount of smoothing (as a floating-point value between 0 and 1) when computing the loss and where a value of 0.0 (default) means no smoothing.

In general, it can be helpful to add label smoothing to the loss functions if you are looking to add some regularization to your network.

Arguments against label smoothing

There are some arguments against label smoothing. It's just another hyperparameter to tune, and when there are few better regularization techniques such as weight decay and L1 regularization, it may be overkill to make your network more complex and implicitly modify the labels of your training data. Another point to consider is that since it adds random noise to the labels, it's possible that the network might underfit in certain cases.

There are some further improved variants of label smoothing, such as **label-aware smoothing**, as mentioned in Zhong et al.'s *Improving Calibration for Long-Tailed Recognition* [14].

The following table shows a comparison of the four techniques we just discussed for model calibration:

Theme	Temperature scaling	Label smoothing	Platt's scaling	Isotonic Regression
Change in label values	No change in label values of training data	Change in label values of training data	No change in the label values of the training data	No change in the label values of the training data
Timing	After training has been completed, the value of the hyperparameter T is computed on a validation dataset	Done during the actual training of the model	Applied after training	Applied after training
Prediction value adjustment	Prediction values from the model are manually adjusted	Predicted values are changed by applying label smoothing	Prediction values from the model are manually adjusted	Prediction values from the model are manually adjusted
Role	Acts as a regularizer	Acts as a regularizer	Acts as a model calibrator or prediction score transformer	Acts as a model calibrator or prediction score transformer

Table 10.2 – Comparing temperature scaling, label smoothing, Platt's scaling, and isotonic regression

There are other model calibration techniques that we didn't get a chance to explore. For instance, **spline calibration** [15][16] is a non-parametric method that employs a spline function, a piece-wise polynomial function that is smooth and continuous. This technique is somewhat similar to isotonic regression in its non-parametric nature.

On the other hand, **beta calibration** [17] is a parametric method that fits a beta distribution to the model's predictions. This technique is conceptually similar to Platt's scaling, as both are parametric methods. Beta calibration is particularly useful for modeling probabilities, such as click-through rates or customer conversion rates.

Focal loss, discussed in *Chapter 8, Algorithm-Level Deep Learning Techniques*, is another method commonly used in deep learning models. As demonstrated in the paper by Mukhoti et al. [3], focal loss produces well-calibrated models and is often combined with temperature scaling for optimal results. Given that neural networks with multiple layers tend to be overconfident in their predictions, focal loss serves as a regularizing effect. It forces the model to focus on harder examples, thereby reducing overconfidence and improving calibration [3].

> 🚀 **Model calibration with focal loss at Amazon**
>
> 🎯 **Problem being solved:**
>
> When Amazon deployed conversational bots [18] to handle customer requests, the calibration of the underlying ML models proved to be of importance. In one instance, Amazon's chatbot was tasked with automatically classifying return reason codes. These return reason codes exhibited class imbalance. When a customer wanted to return an item, determining the appropriate reason became pivotal for efficient return processing. For instance, if a customer expressed dissatisfaction with an item's size or color, it was classified under "Customer Preference." In such cases, Amazon understood that offering a replacement wasn't the optimal solution; rather, a refund was more appropriate.
>
> 🎨 **Model calibration strategy:**
>
> Through rigorous testing, they uncovered the robustness of focal loss in addressing model miscalibration in such real-world tasks. Focal loss was used as a calibration method. Moreover, it wasn't merely about adopting focal loss; the value of γ within the loss function played a crucial role in enhancing model calibration.
>
> 📊 **Additional points:**
>
> Focal loss outperformed traditional cross-entropy loss in achieving better-calibrated models. The technique was tested in an internal A/B experiment at Amazon. The results showed improvements in automation rate and customer experience, meaning the bot could resolve more queries without human intervention and receive more positive responses from customers.

Next, let's see in what ways calibration might impact the performance of a model.

The impact of calibration on a model's performance

Accuracy, log-loss, and Brier scores usually improve because of calibration. However, since the model calibration still involves approximately fitting a model to the calibration curve plotted on the held-out calibration dataset, it may sometimes worsen the accuracy or other performance metrics by small amounts. Nevertheless, the benefits of having calibrated probabilities in terms of giving us actual interpretable probability values that represent likelihood far outweigh the slight performance impact.

As discussed in *Chapter 1, Introduction to Data Imbalance in Machine Learning*, ROC-AUC is a rank-based metric, meaning it evaluates the model's ability to distinguish between classes based on the ranking of predicted scores rather than their absolute values. ROC-AUC doesn't make any claim about accurate probability estimates. Strictly monotonic calibration functions, which continuously increase or decrease without any flat regions, preserve this ranking; they adjust the scale of the probabilities without altering their relative order. For instance, if one score is higher than another before calibration, it remains higher afterward. Because ROC-AUC is concerned with the ranking of predictions rather than the actual probability values, it remains unaffected by such monotonic calibration functions.

However, in rare cases, closely ranked predictions might become tied due to calibration, especially if the calibration function is loosely monotonic and has flat stretches. This could slightly affect the ROC-AUC.

Summary

In this chapter, we went through the basic concepts of model calibration, why we should care about it, how to measure whether a model is calibrated, how data imbalance affects the model calibration, and, finally, how to calibrate an uncalibrated model. Some of the calibration techniques we talked about include Platt's scaling, isotonic regression, temperature scaling, and label smoothing.

With this, we come to the end of this book. Thank you for dedicating your time to reading the book. We trust that it has broadened your knowledge of handling imbalanced datasets and their practical applications in machine learning. As we draw this book to a close, we'd like to offer some concluding advice on how to effectively utilize the techniques discussed.

Like other machine learning techniques, the methods discussed in this book can be highly useful under the right conditions, but they also come with their own set of challenges. Recognizing when and where to apply these techniques is essential, as overly complex solutions can lead to less-than-optimal performance.

Establishing a sound baseline solution is crucial. Implementing various methods, such as those in cost-sensitive learning and algorithm-level deep learning techniques, can offer insights into handling imbalanced datasets effectively. Each method has its pros and cons.

For specialized problems, the book provides targeted solutions. For small datasets, the oversampling methods can help manage computational resources. For large datasets, the chapter on undersampling methods offers suitable techniques.

Occasionally, more modern approaches such as graph machine learning algorithms can be applied to the problem at hand. The model calibration and threshold tuning techniques are useful for decision-making based on model predictions.

Sometimes, data imbalance may not be a problem at all, and we highly encourage you to establish the baseline performance with the imbalanced data without applying any of the techniques discussed in this book. A lot of the real-world data also tends to be tabular, where tree-based models such as XGBoost can be robust to certain kinds of data imbalance.

We encourage you to apply this knowledge, experiment with new approaches, and continue to expand your expertise as you progress in this field. The landscape of machine learning is constantly changing, and your skills will only increase in value as you keep up with its evolution. We hope that the knowledge you've gained will empower you to pick up any research paper that you feel interested in and be able to reproduce its results. We appreciate your commitment to reading this book, and we wish you success in all your future endeavors.

Questions

1. Can a well-calibrated model have low accuracy? What about the reverse: can a model with high accuracy be poorly calibrated?

2. Take a limited classification dataset with, say, only 100 data points. Train a decision tree model using this dataset and then assess its calibration.

   A. Calibrate the model using Platt's scaling. Measure the Brier score after calibration.

   B. Calibrate the model using isotonic regression. Measure the Brier score after calibration

   C. How do the Brier scores differ in (A) and (B)?

   D. Measure the AUC, accuracy, precision, recall, and F1 score of the model before and after calibration.

3. Take a balanced dataset, say with 10,000 points. Train a decision tree model using it. Then check how calibrated it is.

   A. Calibrate the model using Platt's scaling. Measure the Brier score after calibration.

   B. Calibrate the model using isotonic regression. Measure the Brier score after calibration.

   C. How do the Brier scores differ in (a) and (b)?

   D. Measure the AUC, accuracy, precision, recall, and F1 score of the model before and after calibration and compare their values.

4. Given a classification dataset, compare how calibrated the following models are by default without applying any calibration techniques by comparing their Brier scores:

   A. Logistic regression

   B. Decision tree

   C. XGBoost

   D. Random forest

   E. AdaBoost

   F. Neural network

5. Take an imbalanced dataset and train three models with logistic regression, a random forest model, and an XGBoost model, respectively. Measure the calibration of these models using the calibration curve and Brier scores. Finally, apply these techniques to handle data imbalance and measure the calibration again:

   A. Undersampling

   B. Oversampling

C. Cost-sensitive learning: increase the `class_weight` by doubling the previous value. Did the model get less calibrated because of doubling the `class_weight`?

References

1. C. Guo, G. Pleiss, Y. Sun, and K. Q. Weinberger, *"On Calibration of Modern Neural Networks."* arXiv, Aug. 03, 2017. Accessed: Nov. 21, 2022, `http://arxiv.org/abs/1706.04599`

2. A. Niculescu-Mizil and R. Caruana, *"Predicting good probabilities with supervised learning,"* in Proceedings of the 22nd International Conference on Machine Learning - ICML '05, Bonn, Germany, 2005, pp. 625–632. doi: 10.1145/1102351.1102430.

3. J. Mukhoti, V. Kulharia, A. Sanyal, S. Golodetz, P. H. S. Torr, and P. K. Dokania, *"Calibrating Deep Neural Networks using Focal Loss"*. Feb 2020, `https://doi.org/10.48550/arXiv.2002.09437`

4. B. C. Wallace and I. J. Dahabreh, *"Class Probability Estimates are Unreliable for Imbalanced Data (and How to Fix Them),"* in 2012 IEEE 12th International Conference on Data Mining, Brussels, Belgium, Dec. 2012, pp. 695–704. doi: 10.1109/ICDM.2012.115.

5. M. Pakdaman Naeini, G. Cooper, and M. Hauskrecht, *"Obtaining Well Calibrated Probabilities Using Bayesian Binning,"* AAAI, vol. 29, no. 1, Feb. 2015, doi: 10.1609/aaai.v29i1.9602.

6. H. Steck, *"Calibrated recommendations,"* in Proceedings of the 12th ACM Conference on Recommender Systems, Vancouver British Columbia Canada: ACM, Sep. 2018, pp. 154–162. doi: `10.1145/3240323.3240372`.

7. A. Caplin, D. Martin, and P. Marx, *"Calibrating for Class Weights by Modeling Machine Learning."* arXiv, Jul. 31, 2022. Accessed: Dec. 09, 2022. [Online]. Available at `http://arxiv.org/abs/2205.04613`

8. A. D. Pozzolo, O. Caelen, R. A. Johnson, and G. Bontempi, *"Calibrating Probability with Undersampling for Unbalanced Classification,"* in 2015 IEEE Symposium Series on Computational Intelligence, Cape Town, South Africa, Dec. 2015, pp. 159–166. doi: 10.1109/SSCI.2015.33, `https://dalpozz.github.io/static/pdf/SSCI_calib_final_noCC.pdf`

9. M. Moscatelli, S. Narizzano, F. Parlapiano, and G. Viggiano, *Corporate default forecasting with machine learning.* IT: Banca d'Italia, 2019. Accessed: Oct. 14, 2023. [Online]. Available at `https://doi.org/10.32057/0.TD.2019.1256`

10. X. He et al., *"Practical Lessons from Predicting Clicks on Ads at Facebook,"* in Proceedings of the Eighth International Workshop on Data Mining for Online Advertising, New York NY USA, Aug. 2014, pp. 1–9. doi: 10.1145/2648584.2648589.

11. G. King and L. Zeng, *"Logistic Regression in Rare Events Data,"* 2001.

12. Szegedy, V. Vanhoucke, S. Ioffe, J. Shlens, and Z. Wojna, *"Rethinking the Inception Architecture for Computer Vision."* arXiv, Dec. 11, 2015. Accessed: Dec. 17, 2022. [Online]. Available at `http://arxiv.org/abs/1512.00567`

13. R. Müller, S. Kornblith, and G. Hinton, *"When Does Label Smoothing Help?"* arXiv, Jun. 10, 2020. Accessed: Dec. 11, 2022. [Online]. Available at `http://arxiv.org/abs/1906.02629`

14. Zhong et al., Improving Calibration for Long-Tailed Recognition. CVPR 2021. `https://arxiv.org/abs/2104.00466`

15. B. Lucena, *"Spline-Based Probability Calibration."* arXiv, Sep. 20, 2018. Accessed: Jul. 22, 2023. [Online]. Available at `http://arxiv.org/abs/1809.07751`

16. K. Gupta, A. Rahimi, T. Ajanthan, T. Mensink, C. Sminchisescu, and R. Hartley, *"Calibration of Neural Networks using Splines."* arXiv, Dec. 29, 2021. Accessed: Jul. 22, 2023. [Online]. Available at `http://arxiv.org/abs/2006.12800`

17. M. Kull and P. Flach, *"Beta calibration: a well-founded and easily implemented improvement on logistic calibration for binary classifiers,"* in Proceedings of the twentieth International Conference on Artificial Intelligence and Statistics (pp. 623–631).

18. C. Wang, J. Balazs, G. Szarvas, P. Ernst, L. Poddar, and P. Danchenko, "Calibrating Imbalanced Classifiers with Focal Loss: An Empirical Study," in Proceedings of the 2022 Conference on Empirical Methods in Natural Language Processing: Industry Track, Abu Dhabi, UAE: Association for Computational Linguistics, 2022, pp. 145–153. doi: `10.18653/v1/2022.emnlp-industry.14`.

Appendix
Machine Learning Pipeline in Production

In this appendix, we will look at when and at which step we incorporate the data imbalance-handling techniques within a production machine learning pipeline. This mainly applies to supervised classification problems.

Machine learning training pipeline

A machine learning pipeline is the end-to-end process of training one or more machine learning models and then deploying them to a live environment. It may involve stages such as data collection, model training, validation, deployment, monitoring, and iterative improvement, with a focus on scalability, efficiency, and robustness.

Various steps during the offline training are shown in *Figure A.1*. Please note that some of the steps may not be necessary depending on the problem at hand.

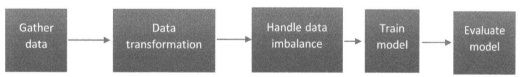

Figure A.1 – High-level steps in a machine learning training pipeline

The following is the sequence of steps involved in building a model that can handle data imbalance:

1. **Gather data**: The first step involves gathering the necessary data for training the machine learning model. This data can be sourced from various places such as databases, files, APIs, or through web scraping. Immediately after gathering, it's often beneficial to perform **data validation**. During this phase, the data schema and data range can be verified, along with any custom data validation checks. Subsequently, the data is partitioned into a training set, a validation

set, and a test set. Many production systems often do not prioritize producing validation sets. The primary function of producing these validation sets is to aid in model-tuning activities, such as hyperparameter adjustment, early stopping, model calibration, threshold tuning, and so on. Such tuning often takes place during the model development phase, outside of the main production pipeline. **It's crucial to split the data prior to executing any data transformations or imbalance handling techniques**. This precaution ensures data leakage is avoided, which could otherwise lead to a biased model performance.

2. **Data transformation**: The next step is to transform the data into a format that can be easily fed into the machine learning model. This may involve tasks such as data cleaning, feature selection, normalization, and scaling. These transformation steps may need to be stored in order to apply them during model prediction time. It can be helpful to store these transformations somewhere (for example, a file or database) so that they can be retrieved later during inferencing.

3. **Handle data imbalance (if needed)**: The machine learning model might underperform on a minority class(es) due to a bias toward the majority class. Throughout this book, we've delved into both data-level and algorithm-level techniques. To summarize, data-level techniques focus on resampling the dataset to achieve balanced samples across each class, whereas algorithm-level techniques modify the learning algorithm to address imbalanced data. For a deeper understanding, please refer to the relevant chapters in the book.

4. **Train model**: After the data has been preprocessed, it's time to train the machine learning model. This step involves the following:

   I.   Selecting an appropriate algorithm

   II.   Setting its hyperparameters

   III. Feeding the preprocessed data into the algorithm

   The training process may require several iterations to fine-tune the model until it produces satisfactory results. The trained model binary should be versioned and stored for future use, including deploying to a production environment for online inferencing.

   If any data imbalance handling technique was applied, it could miscalibrate the model. If calibrated prediction scores are expected from the model, it's crucial to recalibrate the prediction scores. For more information on various model calibration techniques, please refer to *Chapter 10, Model Calibration*.

5. **Evaluate model**: This step involves assessing the performance of the trained model on the test set produced in *step 1*. For classification problems, metrics such as accuracy, precision, and recall are typically used, while for other types of problems, appropriate metrics should be chosen. If the model's performance doesn't meet the desired benchmarks, you may need to not only revisit the data transformations (as outlined in *step 2*) but also consider adjusting the model's architecture, hyperparameters, or even the problem formulation. For binary classification models specifically, you'll want to determine an appropriate threshold for classifying predictions. For more in-depth information on threshold tuning techniques, please refer to *Chapter 5, Cost-Sensitive Learning*.

After successfully evaluating the model, its fitness for deployment as a service is assessed, enabling it to handle live traffic or make batch predictions. We will delve deeper into inferencing in the following section.

Inferencing (online or batch)

Inferencing is a process of using a trained machine learning model to make predictions on new unseen data. **Online inferencing** refers to making predictions in real time on live data as it arrives. Latency is of utmost importance during online inferencing in order to prevent any lags to the end user.

There is another type called **batch inferencing**, where predictions are made on a large set of already collected data in an offline fashion.

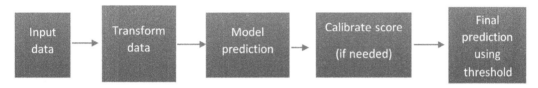

Figure A.2 – Process flow when live data comes to the model for scoring (inferencing)

Inferencing is a process of using a trained machine learning model to make predictions on new input (unseen) data in real time. The following are the steps involved in the inferencing process:

1. **Input data**: The first step is to receive new input data that needs to be classified or predicted. This data could be in the form of text, images, audio, or any other data format.

2. **Transform data**: Before predicting, the input data needs to undergo transformations (such as normalization and scaling) to make it compatible with the trained model. It's crucial to apply the same transformations that were used during training.

3. **Model prediction**: Once the input data has been transformed, it is fed into the trained model to generate a predicted score. The predicted score represents the likelihood of the input belonging to a particular class or category.

4. **Calibrate score (if needed)**: Model calibration can be essential when model predictions are not reliable. Notably, when any data imbalance handling techniques are used, the risk of model miscalibration increases. For a comprehensive understanding of this topic, please refer to *Chapter 10, Model Calibration*.

5. **Final prediction using threshold**: The calibrated score is then used to make the final prediction using an appropriate threshold and take any action—for example, notification to the customer, human reviews, and so on.

> ✲ **Monitoring data as well as model in production**
>
> Monitoring data and its distribution is crucial as it can change over time, potentially impacting the effectiveness of any initially applied imbalance-handling techniques. Such shifts can affect model performance and evaluation metrics, necessitating a re-evaluation and potential recalibration of strategies. Beyond just data imbalance, phenomena such as model drift and data drift—where there is a change in the model's performance or the nature of incoming data—pose significant concerns. Implementing automated mechanisms to track these variations is essential for ensuring optimal model performance and consistent predictions.

In conclusion, inferencing entails transforming new input data, producing a predicted score using a trained machine learning model, calibrating that score, and determining a final prediction using a threshold. This procedure is reiterated for every incoming data point requiring a prediction.

Assessments

Chapter 1 – Introduction to Data Imbalance in Machine Learning

1. The choice of loss function when training a model can greatly affect the performance of the model on imbalanced datasets. Some loss functions may be more sensitive to class imbalance than others. For instance, a model trained with a loss function such as cross-entropy might be heavily influenced by the majority class and perform poorly on the minority class.

2. The PR curve is more informative than the ROC curve when dealing with highly skewed datasets because it focuses on the performance of the classifier on the positive (minority) class, which is often the class of interest in imbalanced datasets. The ROC curve, on the other hand, considers both the TPR and the FPR and thus might give an overly optimistic view of the model's performance when the negative class dominates the dataset.

3. Accuracy can be a misleading metric for model performance on imbalanced datasets because it does not take into account the distribution of classes. A model that always predicts the majority class will have high accuracy, but it is not useful if our goal is to correctly classify instances of the minority class.

4. In the context of imbalanced datasets, feature engineering poses a unique challenge due to the limited number of instances in the minority class. With so few examples, it becomes difficult even for human experts to identify features that are truly indicative of the minority class. Poorly chosen features can worsen the problem: if the features capture noise rather than the underlying pattern, the model is likely to overfit. Conversely, if the features are too generic and fail to capture the nuances of the minority class, the model may underfit, leading to poor performance on new, unseen data.

5. The choice of "k" in k-fold cross-validation can impact the model's performance on imbalanced datasets. With imbalanced datasets, some folds may contain very few or even no examples from the minority classes, potentially leading to misleading evaluations of the model. A solution to this issue is to use stratified k-fold cross-validation, available through the `sklearn.model_selection.StratifiedKFold` API, which ensures that each fold maintains a similar distribution of the various classes.

6. Usually, the greater the imbalance in the test set, the more negatively the PR curve is affected. In contrast, the ROC curve is not affected by the class distribution in the test set.

    In *Figures 1.13* and *1.14*, we presented three test sets with imbalance ratios of 1:9, 1:3, and 1:1. The ROC-AUC for all these cases is 0.96, as shown in *Figure 1.13*. On the other hand, the average precision value is inversely proportional to the level of imbalance in the test set, as illustrated in *Figure 1.14* (that is, greater imbalance results in lower average precision):

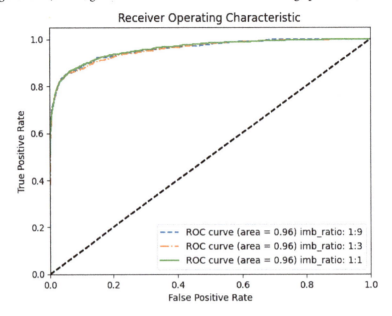

Figure B.1 – ROC curves remain the same when the imbalance ratio changes in the test set

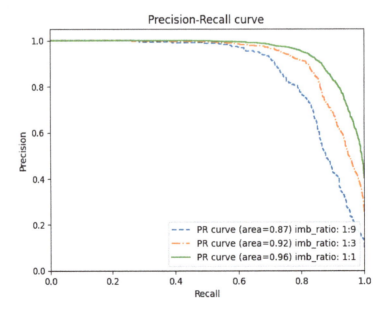

Figure B.2 – The PR curve changes considerably when the imbalance ratio changes in the test set

7. Having a high AUC-ROC but a low AUC-PR in the context of an imbalanced dataset could indicate that the model is performing well in distinguishing between the classes overall (as indicated by the high AUC-ROC), but it is not doing a good job at identifying the positive (minority) class (as indicated by the low AUC-PR).

8. Sampling bias can contribute to the challenge of imbalanced datasets in machine learning because it can lead to an overrepresentation of one class and an underrepresentation of another. This can skew the model's learning and result in poor performance in the underrepresented class.

9. Labeling errors can contribute to the challenge of imbalanced datasets in machine learning because they can lead to an incorrect representation of the classes in the data. If instances of the minority class are mistakenly labeled as the majority class, the model might learn incorrect patterns and perform poorly on the minority class.

10. There are many real-world scenarios where dealing with imbalanced datasets is inherently part of the problem. Some examples include fraud detection (where fraudulent transactions are rare compared to legitimate ones), medical diagnosis (where diseases are often rare compared to healthy cases), and spam detection (where spam emails are typically fewer than non-spam emails). Can you think of any others?

11. Here are the answers:

    A. Its value ranges from -1 (worst value) to +1 (best value).

    B. The dummy model always predicts class 1, so here are our various confusion matrix values:

    TP = 90, TN = 0, FP=10, FN = 0

    $$MCC = \frac{TP \cdot TN - FP \cdot FN}{\sqrt{(TP + FP) \cdot (TP + FN) \cdot (TN + FP) \cdot (TN + FN)}}$$

    The confusion matrix values are as follows:

    • TP = 90

    • TN = 0

    • FP = 10

    • FN = 0

    By plugging these values into the formula, we get the following:

    $$MCC = \frac{(90 \times 0) - (10 \times 0)}{\sqrt{(90 + 10) \times (90 + 0) \times (0 + 10) \times (0 + 0)}}$$
    $$= \frac{0 - 0}{\sqrt{100 \times 90 \times 10 \times 0}}$$

    Since the denominator becomes zero (because of the term $(TN + FN = 0 + 0)$), the MCC is undefined.

We can compute the other metrics as follows:

- Accuracy = TP+TN/ (TP+TN+FP+FN) = 0.90

- Precision = TP/(TP+FP) = 90/(90+10) = 0.90

- Recall = TP/(TP+FN) = 90/(90+0) = 1

- F1 score = 2*Precision*Recall/(Precision+Recall) = 2*0.90*1/(0.90+1) = 0.95

Let's compute MCC for the previous values. It's undefined (0/0), which would mean something is wrong with the model, and we should go back and fix any issues with the data or the model.

C.   In summary, MCC is a metric that generates a high score only if the model does well on both positive and negative class examples from the test set. Also, MCC can help inform the user about ongoing prediction issues.

D.   This is left as an exercise for you.

Chapter 2 – Oversampling Methods

1.   This is left as an exercise for you.

2.   One approach is to oversample the minority class by 20x to balance both classes. It's important to note that achieving the perfect balance between the classes is not always necessary; a slight imbalance may be acceptable, depending on the specific requirements and constraints. This technique is not applied at test time as the test data should remain representative of what we would encounter in the real world.

3.   The primary concern with oversampling before splitting the data into training, test, and validation sets is data leakage. This occurs when duplicate samples end up in both the training and test/ validation sets, leading to overly optimistic performance metrics. The model may perform well during evaluation because it has already seen the same examples during training, but this can result in poor generalization to new, unseen data. To mitigate this risk, it's crucial to first split the data into training, test, and validation sets and then apply balancing techniques such as oversampling exclusively to the training set.

4.   Data normalization can help indirectly in dealing with data imbalance by ensuring that all features have the same scale, which can lead to better model performance. However, normalization may not directly address the imbalance between the classes in the dataset. To tackle data imbalance, other techniques can be employed, such as various sampling techniques, cost-sensitive approaches, or threshold adjustment techniques.

5.   This has been left as an exercise for you.

Chapter 3 – Undersampling Methods

1. This has been left as an exercise for you.

2. This has been left as an exercise for you.

3. This has been left as an exercise for you.

4. `TomekLinksNCR` is a custom undersampling method that combines Tomek links and NCR. It removes Tomek links and then applies NCR to remove more noisy and borderline samples from the majority class. This aims to create a more balanced dataset while retaining the underlying structure of the data.

Chapter 4 – Ensemble Methods

1. This has been left as an exercise for you.

2. The main difference between `BalancedRandomForestClassifier` and `BalancedBaggingClassifier` is the base classifier and the ensemble learning method they employ. `BalancedRandomForestClassifier` uses decision trees as base classifiers and follows a random forest as the estimator, while `BalancedBaggingClassifier` can use any base classifier that supports sample weighting and follows a bagging approach.

    Random forest can be considered an extension of bagging that incorporates an additional layer of randomness by also randomly selecting a subset of features at each split in the decision tree. This helps create more diverse trees and generally results in better performance of random forest models.

Chapter 5 – Cost-Sensitive Learning

This chapter's questions have been left as exercises for you.

Chapter 6 – Data Imbalance in Deep Learning

1. The main challenge stems from the different types of data these models handle. Classical machine learning models typically work with structured, tabular data, while deep learning models handle unstructured data such as images, text, audio, and video.

2. An imbalanced version of the MNIST dataset can be created by randomly selecting a certain percentage of examples for each class. This process involves choosing indices of the samples to remove and then actually removing these samples from the training set.

3. This has been left as an exercise for you.

4. Random oversampling is used to address imbalance in the dataset. It works by duplicating samples from the minority classes until each class has an equal number of samples. This technique is usually considered to perform better than no sampling.

5. Data augmentation techniques can include rotating, scaling, cropping, blurring, adding noise to the image, and much more. However, ensuring these augmentations preserve the original labels and avoiding inadvertently removing important details from the data is crucial. Please refer to *Chapter 7, Data-Level Deep Learning Methods*, for a detailed discussion of the various data augmentation techniques.

6. Undersampling reduces the instances of the majority class to balance the dataset. However, this method has a significant limitation: important information might be lost if instances from the majority class are randomly removed, especially when the majority class has a lot of variation.

7. The data augmentation techniques must preserve the original labels because the model learns to associate the features of the data with these labels. If the labels change due to augmentation, the model might learn incorrect associations, which would degrade its performance when making predictions.

Chapter 7 – Data-Level Deep Learning Methods

This chapter's questions have been left as exercises for you.

Chapter 8 – Algorithm-Level Deep Learning Techniques

1. This has been left as an exercise for you.

2. This has been left as an exercise for you.

3. Tversky loss is based on the Tversky index, which is defined by the following formula:

$$TverskyIndex = \frac{TruePositive}{TruePositive + \alpha * FalsePositive + (1 - \alpha) * FalseNegative}$$

A smoothing factor is added to both the numerator and denominator to avoid division by zero. `alpha` is a hyperparameter that can be tuned:

```python
import torch
import torch.nn.functional as F

def Tversky(y_true, y_pred, smooth=1, alpha=0.8):
    y_true_pos = y_true.view(-1)
    y_pred_pos = y_pred.view(-1)
    true_pos = torch.sum(y_true_pos * y_pred_pos)
    false_neg = torch.sum(y_true_pos * (1 - y_pred_pos))
    false_pos = torch.sum((1 - y_true_pos) * y_pred_pos)
    return (true_pos + smooth) / (true_pos + alpha * false_pos \
        + (1 - alpha) * false_neg + smooth)
```

4. This has been left as an exercise for you.

Chapter 9 – Hybrid Deep Learning Methods

1. We don't provide a full answer here, but only some functions that will help you with the main task.

We could use `torch.nn.functional.triplet_margin_loss()`, or we could implement it from scratch:

```
import torch
import torch.nn as nn
from torch.nn import functional as F
class TripletLoss(nn.Module):
    def __init__(self, margin=1.0):
        super(TripletLoss, self).__init__()
        self.margin = margin

    def forward(self, anchor, pos, neg):
        pos_dist = F.pairwise_distance(anchor, pos)
        neg_dist = F.pairwise_distance(anchor, neg)
        loss = torch.relu(pos_dist - neg_dist + self.margin)
        return loss.mean()
```

You would want to generate triplets for the imbalanced MNIST dataset. The following function generates a list of triplets (anchor, positive, and negative) for a batch of images. It generates one triplet per class present in the batch. We assume that there are at least two examples for each class in the batch:

```
def generate_triplets(images, labels):
    triplets = []
    classes_present = labels.unique()
    for c in classes_present:
        # Find indices of anchor and positive examples
        pos_indices = (labels == c).nonzero(as_tuple=True)[0]
        anchor_idx, positive_idx = \
            torch.choice(pos_indices, 2, replace=False)
        anchor, positive = images[anchor_idx], \
            images[positive_idx]

        # Find index of negative example
        neg_indices = (labels != c).nonzero(as_tuple=True)[0]
        negative_idx = torch.choice(neg_indices)
        negative = images[negative_idx]

        # Add the triplet to the list
        triplets.append((anchor, positive, negative))

    return triplets
```

2. This has been left as an exercise for you.

Chapter 10 – Model Calibration

1. Yes, a well-calibrated model can have low accuracy and vice-versa. Let's take a dumb model that always outputs 0.1 probability for any input example. This model is perfectly calibrated, but its accuracy is only 90%, which is quite low for an imbalanced dataset with a 1:9 imbalance ratio. Here is the implementation of such a model:

```
from sklearn.datasets import make_classification
from sklearn.calibration import calibration_curve
import matplotlib.pyplot as plt
import numpy as np

# Make an imbalanced binary classification dataset
y = np.array([0, 0, 0, 0, 0, 0, 0, 0, 0, 0, 1, 0, 0, \
    1, 0, 0, 0, 0, 0, 0])

# Dummy model always predicts not-1 (i.e., 0) with full
confidence
y_pred = np.array([0.1, 0.1, 0.1, 0.1, 0.1, 0.1, 0.1,\
    0.1, 0.1, 0.1, 0.1, 0.1, 0.1, 0.1,\
    0.1, 0.1, 0.1, 0.1, 0.1, 0.1])

y_pred_labels = np.array([0, 0, 0, 0, 0, 0, 0, 0, 0, \
    0, 0, 0, 0, 0, 0, 0, 0, 0, 0, 0])

# Calculate the calibration curve
fraction_of_positives, mean_predicted_value = \
    calibration_curve(y, y_pred)

# Calculate accuracy
accuracy = (y == y_pred_labels).mean()
print('accuracy: ', accuracy)

# Plot calibration curves
plt.plot([0, 1], [0, 1], "k:", label="Perfectly calibrated")
plt.plot(mean_predicted_value, fraction_of_positives,\
    "s-", label="Model A")
plt.legend()
plt.show()
```

This produces the accuracy value and calibration plot:

```
accuracy:   0.9
```

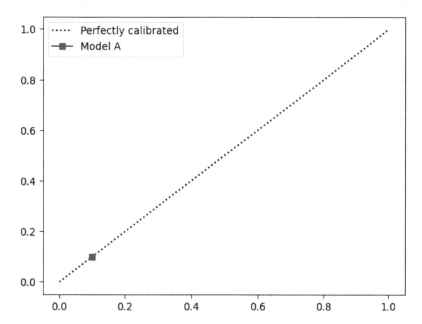

Figure B.3 – A dummy model with perfect calibration but a low accuracy score

2. This has been left as an exercise for you.
3. This has been left as an exercise for you.
4. This has been left as an exercise for you.
5. This has been left as an exercise for you.

Index

www.packtpub.com

Subscribe to our online digital library for full access to over 7,000 books and videos, as well as industry leading tools to help you plan your personal development and advance your career. For more information, please visit our website.

Why subscribe?

- Spend less time learning and more time coding with practical eBooks and Videos from over 4,000 industry professionals

- Improve your learning with Skill Plans built especially for you

- Get a free eBook or video every month

- Fully searchable for easy access to vital information

- Copy and paste, print, and bookmark content

Did you know that Packt offers eBook versions of every book published, with PDF and ePub files available? You can upgrade to the eBook version at packtpub.com and as a print book customer, you are entitled to a discount on the eBook copy. Get in touch with us at customercare@packtpub.com for more details.

At www.packtpub.com, you can also read a collection of free technical articles, sign up for a range of free newsletters, and receive exclusive discounts and offers on Packt books and eBooks.

Other Books You May Enjoy

If you enjoyed this book, you may be interested in these other books by Packt:

Machine Learning with PyTorch and Scikit-Learn

Sebastian Raschka, Yuxi (Hayden) Liu, Vahid Mirjalili

ISBN: 978-1-80181-931-2

- Explore frameworks, models, and techniques for machines to 'learn' from data
- Use scikit-learn for machine learning and PyTorch for deep learning
- Train machine learning classifiers on images, text, and more
- Build and train neural networks, transformers, and boosting algorithms
- Discover best practices for evaluating and tuning models
- Predict continuous target outcomes using regression analysis
- Dig deeper into textual and social media data using sentiment analysis

Graph Machine Learning

Claudio Stamile, Aldo Marzullo, Enrico Deusebio

ISBN: 978-1-80020-449-2

- Write Python scripts to extract features from graphs
- Distinguish between the main graph representation learning techniques
- Learn how to extract data from social networks, financial transaction systems, for text analysis, and more
- Implement the main unsupervised and supervised graph embedding techniques
- Get to grips with shallow embedding methods, graph neural networks, graph regularization methods, and more
- Deploy and scale out your application seamlessly

Packt is searching for authors like you

If you're interested in becoming an author for Packt, please visit `authors.packtpub.com` and apply today. We have worked with thousands of developers and tech professionals, just like you, to help them share their insight with the global tech community. You can make a general application, apply for a specific hot topic that we are recruiting an author for, or submit your own idea.

Share Your Thoughts

Now you've finished *Machine Learning for Imbalanced Data*, we'd love to hear your thoughts! Scan the QR code below to go straight to the Amazon review page for this book and share your feedback or leave a review on the site that you purchased it from.

`https://packt.link/r/1-801-07083-0`

Your review is important to us and the tech community and will help us make sure we're delivering excellent quality content.

Download a free PDF copy of this book

Thanks for purchasing this book!

Do you like to read on the go but are unable to carry your print books everywhere?

Is your eBook purchase not compatible with the device of your choice?

Don't worry, now with every Packt book you get a DRM-free PDF version of that book at no cost.

Read anywhere, any place, on any device. Search, copy, and paste code from your favorite technical books directly into your application.

The perks don't stop there, you can get exclusive access to discounts, newsletters, and great free content in your inbox daily

Follow these simple steps to get the benefits:

1. Scan the QR code or visit the link below

https://packt.link/free-ebook/9781801070836

2. Submit your proof of purchase
3. That's it! We'll send your free PDF and other benefits to your email directly

www.ingramcontent.com/pod-product-compliance
Lightning Source LLC
Chambersburg PA
CBHW080620060326
40690CB00021B/4756